Implementing Educational Language Policy in Arizona

BILINGUAL EDUCATION & BILINGUALISM

Series Editors: Nancy H. Hornberger, *University of Pennsylvania, USA* and Colin Baker, *Bangor University, Wales, UK*

Bilingual Education and Bilingualism is an international, multidisciplinary series publishing research on the philosophy, politics, policy, provision and practice of language planning, global English, indigenous and minority language education, multilingualism, multiculturalism, biliteracy, bilingualism and bilingual education. The series aims to mirror current debates and discussions.

Full details of all the books in this series and of all our other publications can be found on http://www.multilingual-matters.com, or by writing to Multilingual Matters, St Nicholas House, 31–34 High Street, Bristol BS1 2AW, UK.

BILINGUAL EDUCATION & BILINGUALISM
Series Editors: Nancy H. Hornberger, *University of Pennsylvania, USA* and Colin Baker, *Bangor University, Wales, UK*

Implementing Educational Language Policy in Arizona

Legal, Historical and Current Practices in SEI

Edited by
M. Beatriz Arias and Christian Faltis

MULTILINGUAL MATTERS
Bristol • Buffalo • Toronto

Library of Congress Cataloging in Publication Data
Implementing Educational Language Policy in Arizona: Legal, Historical and Current
Practices in SEI / Edited by M. Beatriz Arias and Christian Faltis.
Bilingual Education & Bilingualism: 86
Includes bibliographical references
1. Language policy--Arizona. 2. Education, Bilingual--Arizona. 3. English language--
Study and teaching--Immersion method. 4. English language--Study and teaching--
Arizona--Foreign speakers. I. Arias, M. Beatriz. II. Faltis, Christian, 1950-
P119.32.A75I47 2012
306.44'9791—dc23   2012009134

British Library Cataloguing in Publication Data
A catalogue entry for this book is available from the British Library.

ISBN-13: 978-1-84769-745-5 (hbk)
ISBN-13: 978-1-84769-744-8 (pbk)

Multilingual Matters
UK: St Nicholas House, 31–34 High Street, Bristol BS1 2AW, UK.
USA: UTP, 2250 Military Road, Tonawanda, NY 14150, USA.
Canada: UTP, 5201 Dufferin Street, North York, Ontario M3H 5T8, Canada.

The policy of Multilingual Matters/Channel View Publications is to use papers that are
natural, renewable and recyclable products, made from wood grown in sustainable for-
ests. In the manufacturing process of our books, and to further support our policy, preference is given to printers that have FSC and PEFC Chain of Custody certification. The FSC
and/or PEFC logos will appear on those books where full certification has been granted
to the printer concerned.

Typeset by Techset Composition Ltd., Salisbury, UK.
Printed and bound in Great Britain by Short Run Press Ltd.

Contents

Contributors

H.D. Adamson is Professor of English at the University of Arizona, where he has served as Director of the Interdisciplinary PhD Program in Second Language Acquisition and Teaching and Director of the English Language/Linguistics Program. He has conducted ethnographic classroom research involving English learners in Tucson, Arizona, which was reported in *Language Minority Students in American Schools: An Education in English* (2005). His research interests also include studying the sociolinguistic competence of English learners within a Labovian variationist framework, as reported in *Interlanguage Variation in Theoretical and Pedagogical Perspective* (2009).

M. Beatriz Arias (PhD Stanford University, 1976) is an Associate Professor in the Department of English Education at Arizona State University. She is the author and editor of several books and more than 30 scholarly articles and chapters on issues of language policy, bilingual education, school desegregation and equity for Latino students. She is a recognized national expert in the area of school desegregation, having served as a court-appointed expert in the Los Angeles, San Jose, Denver and Chicago desegregation cases. Currently, Dr Arias is a principal investigator on a 1.4 million dollar grant to prepare secondary teachers to earn an ESL endorsement.

Mary Carol Combs is a Professor in the Department of Teaching, Language and Sociocultural Studies, University of Arizona, where she teaches courses in bilingual and multicultural education, language policy and English as second language (ESL) methods. Her current research focuses on the English language acquisition and literacy development of young English language learners in Structured English Immersion classes. She is a former Director of the Washington, DC-based English Plus Information Clearinghouse, a national clearinghouse on language rights and public policy. She remains active in national networks concerned with policy developments in the education of English language learners.

Alexandria Estrella-Silva is a PhD student in her final year at Arizona State University, pursuing a degree in Curriculum and Instruction with a concentration in Language and Literacy. Her experience involves teaching middle school level Language Arts for several years, preparing undergraduate pre-service teachers for students from linguistically and culturally diverse backgrounds, and graduate courses that address bi-literacy and parent involvement in secondary schools. Upon completing her doctorate degree. She hopes to pursue research that address issues of equity for adolescent English language learners, as well as critically examine and explore topics related to adolescent literacy in home and school.

Christian Faltis (PhD Stanford University, 1983) is the Dolly and David Fiddyment Chair in Teacher Education and Professor of Language, Literacy and Culture in the School of Education at University of California (UC), Davis. He is author and editor of 16 books, and more than 60 scholarly journal articles and book chapters on bilingual education and Latino students. In 2001, he was recognized by American Educational Research Association (AERA) as a Distinguished Scholar of the Role and Status of Minorities in Education. Prior to coming to UC Davis in 2008, he taught at Arizona State University since 1991.

Nancy Harris-Murri taught elementary school for 12 years prior to working on her PhD at Arizona State University. There she worked with pre-service and practicing teachers learning to teach diverse populations. Her research interests pertain to teacher learning through inquiry and reflective practices in politically contested school environments. Murri has presented her work at the local, state and national levels. Following her work at the University, she served as a teacher leader and Gifted Education Coordinator in a rural school district. Currently, she chooses to continue to teach elementary students full-time in Colorado.

Stephen Krashen is Professor Emeritus at the Rossier School of Education, University of Southern California, Los Angeles. He has published hundreds of papers and books, and introduced several influential concepts to the fields of second language acquisition, bilingual education and reading.

Mike Long is a Professor of Second Language Acquisition at the University of Maryland. He is currently working with Gisela Granena on a study of maturational constraints on the acquisition of Spanish by native speakers of English and Chinese; on a study of content teaching through the medium of a foreign language when neither teacher nor students are native speakers of the language; and on a TBLT project for a large ESL program for Latino migrant workers and their families. Recent publications include the *Handbook of SLA* (Blackwell, 2003), *Second Language Needs Analysis* (Cambridge, 2005), *Problems in SLA* (Lawrence Erlbaum, 2007) and the *Handbook of Language Teaching* (Wiley-Blackwell, 2009).

Jeff MacSwan is Professor of Education and Applied Linguistics at the University of Maryland-College Park. His research focuses on the linguistic study of bilingualism (codeswitching and language contact, in particular), on the role of language in theories of academic achievement differences among language minority students and education policy related to English language learners in US schools. MacSwan serves on a number of prominent editorial boards and is a current editor of the *International Multilingual Research Journal*. MacSwan is a National Academy of Education/Spencer Postdoctoral Fellow, and has given numerous invited talks in the United States and abroad. He has served as a visiting scholar in the Massachusetts Institute of Technology Linguistics Department, the Hamburg University Centre for the Study of Multilingualism and the Bangor University ESRC Centre for Research on Bilingualism in Wales.

Amy Markos is a Teacher Educator, preparing teachers for linguistically and culturally diverse learners. Her research interests include understanding teachers' dispositions and beliefs about English Learners (ELs) and the use of critical reflection in teacher learning. She values participatory action research that explores policies and pedagogical practices related to ELs' access to quality education. Her recent publications include *Mandated to Learn, Guided to Reflect: Preservice Teachers' Evolving Understandings of English Language Learners* (Markos, in press), and *Issues in Teacher Education and Policy in Practice: The Implementation of Structured English Immersion in Arizona* (Lillie *et al.*, 2010) published through The Civil Rights Project at University of California, Los Angeles (UCLA).

Sarah Catherine K. Moore has researched the role and impact of language politics, planning and policy on the education of language minority students at local, state and national levels. Moore's areas of expertise include program models and methods for the instruction of language learners, approaches to language educator professional development and the process through which language policies are implemented. She has been an Educator and Teacher Educator in K-12, community college and university settings. Moore's PhD is from Arizona State University in Education Policy with an emphasis on Language Policy.

Kate Olson, PhD, is an Adjunct Assistant Professor and independent scholar in the Department of Education at Vassar College. She has a breadth of experience both teaching and conducting research at the K-12 and university levels in education. Her professional interests include research on teaching, teacher education and the influence of educational policies and programs on teaching and learning for English learners.

Kellie Rolstad is an Associate Professor of Education and Applied Linguistics at the University of Maryland-College Park. Her research interests include language education, language diversity and multilingualism, in addition to more recent work on unschooling and democratic education. Rolstad has served as a visiting scholar in the Graduate School of Education at both Harvard University and UCLA, and has worked as a Spanish–English bilingual kindergarten teacher in the Los Angeles Unified School District. She has published numerous articles and book chapters, appearing in prestigious journals such as *Educational Policy, Teachers College Record, Bilingual Research Journal, Bilingual Review* and *Hispanic Journal of Behavioral Sciences.* Her work also appeared in a 2003 anthology of readings in sociolinguistics called *Sociolinguistics: The Essential Readings* (Blackwell).

Ko-Yin Sung is Assistant Professor of Chinese in the Department of Languages, Philosophy and Speech Communication in the College of Humanities, Arts and Social Sciences at Utah State University. Her research interests include Chinese language teaching and learning, language-learning strategies and technology-assisted language learning.

Terrence G. Wiley is President of the Center for Applied Linguistics in Washington, DC. He is also Professor Emeritus at Arizona State University. He received his PhD from the University of Southern California in Education with an emphasis in Linguistics. He is founding co-editor of the *Journal of Language, Identity and Education* (Routledge). He has published widely on language policy, literacy/biliteracy and language minority education. His recent work includes: *Handbook on Heritage and Community Languages in the United States* (co-editor, forthcoming), *The Education of Language Minority Immigrants in the United States* (Multilingual Matters, co-editor, 2009), *Literacy and Language Diversity in the United States* (Center for Applied Linguistics, 2005) and *Ebonics in the Urban Education Debate* (Multilingual

Matters, co-editor, 2005). He is founding co-editor of the *Journal of Language, Identity, and Education* (Routledge).

Wayne E. Wright, PhD, is an Associate Professor and Chair of the Master's Degree program in Teaching English as a Second Language at the University of Texas at San Antonio. He is author of *Foundations for Teaching English Language Learners: Theory, Research, Policy, Practice* (Caslon, 2010), editor of the *Journal of Southeast Asian American Education and Advancement*, and book review editor for *the International Multilingual Research Journal*. Wright's research has been published widely in books and leading academic journals. He has many years of K-12 bilingual and ESL teaching experience and was a Fulbright Scholar in Cambodia in 2009.

Foreword: From Restrictive SEI to Imagining Better

Terrence Wiley

This collection provides an important case study of the implementation and impact of state-prescribed educational policies and their impact on language minority students in Arizona. It is rare that a single volume can provide such a sweeping multidimensional analysis assessing the evolution and conse-quences of a single state's educational policy. The case of Arizona is particu-larly significant because the state, with the sanction of its voters in 2000, opted to implement a restrictive educational language policy that has all but eliminated bilingual education in public schools. Following the passage of Proposition 203 in 2000, the state then initiated a course of action that dic-tates instructional policy by prescribing structured English immersion (SEI) as the only model for the instruction of language minorities. By so doing, it has limited the professional choices that may be made by educational admin-istrators and teachers, as well as those of parents in determining the educa-tional opportunities available for their children.

Why do states have such authority? Arizona provides an important case study because under the United States Constitution states are allowed to play a significant role in formulating and implementing educational policies. The degree to which states, rather than the federal government have this authority is largely an artifact of historical timing, since the Constitution was written and ratified a half century before the public school movement gained prominence. Thus, at its inception in the late 18th century, the fed-eral government did not assume responsibility for education. At that time, support for education was largely a matter local governments or commu-nity-based efforts. Beginning in the late 1830s, Massachusetts became one of the first states to promote public education under the leadership of Horace Mann (1796–1859). It was not until the American Civil War (1861–1865) that the federal government began to assert a role in stimulating states to promote institutions of higher education. With the conclusion of the Civil War, previously enslaved African Americans were able to attend school during the period of Reconstruction (1865–1877). From the end of Reconstruction until the 1950s, racial segregation by the states was upheld by the federal courts.

The educational authority of states related to educational language policies remained largely unchallenged by the federal government until shortly after World War I (1914–1917). By 1919, some 34 states had passed laws restricting instruction in foreign languages and mandating instruction in English only. During the 1920s, the constitutionality of restrictive state educational language policies was contested in several US Supreme Court cases. Of these, *Meyer v. Nebraska*, 262 US 390 (1923), was the most notable. The *Meyer* ruling held that states could not constitutionally restrict the teaching of foreign languages. *Meyer*, however, also affirmed the primacy of English as the language of instruction, so it did not imply any right to bilingual education (Wiley, 1998, 2007, 2010a).

When we attempt to classify language policies or practices that have the affect of *managing* (Spolsky, 2009) or *controlling* (Leibowitz, 1974) instruction, they can be categorized as being: (1) promotion-oriented; (2) accommodation/expediency-oriented; (3) tolerance-oriented; (4) restriction-oriented; and (5) repression-oriented policies (Kloss, 1998; Wiley, 2004, 2007, 2010a,b). Beatriz Arias (Chapter 1) applies this framework to her critical analysis of Arizona educational language policies.

Much of the controversy regarding the use of transitional bilingual education has been based on a confusion of accommodation with promotion. Tolerance-oriented policies reflect the absence of governmental interference in the people's linguistic lives. Restrictive language policies are those that constrict or prohibit the use or teaching of certain languages. In many respects, Arizona's policies, since the passage of Proposition 203 and California, represent a return to the restrictive policies of the Americanization Movement (1914–1925), which championed rapid assimilation and a restriction on the teaching and public use of immigrant languages (Wiley, 1998).

As Arias notes (Chapter 1), the line between restrictive and repressive policies and practices is one of degree. Repressive policies aim at coercive linguistic and cultural assimilation through ethnolinguistic deculturation (Spring, 1994). In US history, the most explicit example of deculturation occurred prior to the US Civil War when enslaved Africans were prohibited from using their native languages and were also subjected to compulsory illiteracy laws, which made it illegal for them to be taught to read or write. After the Civil War, Native Americans were subjected to compulsory assimilation in boarding schools where English was mandate and their own languages were disallowed (Weinberg, 1995).

Over the course of US history, educational policies and practices have fluctuated between tolerance, restriction and repression of languages other than English. This assessment is not a radical critique, but one easily supported by the impact of repressive policies of that past on indigenous language minorities. Since the early 1990s, the US government has endorsed the preservation of native languages in an effort to redress its former repressive policies that resulted in the reduction and extinction of many indigenous languages. Given this conflicted history, a number of scholars have advocated close scrutiny of educational policies and practices to ascertain their impact on language minority students (Corson, 1999; Haas, 1992). The various authors in this volume follow in this tradition through their critical analysis of contemporary restrictive policies.

Direct federal involvement and intervention in education did not become prevalent until after World War II. Federal funding was used as an incentive for key initiatives designed to make the United States more internationally competitive, particularly in math and science education. With the rise of national and international concern regarding civil and human rights, however, the federal government also began to promote and expand educational opportunities for poor and minority students in an effort to redress racial discrimination, which had remained legal in many states until the 1950s. Following the *Brown v. Board* of Education of Topeka, 347 U.S. 483 (1954) ruling, the federal government began to intervene directly in state and local educational policy in order to ensure civil rights.

During the 1960s, the role of the federal government also became important in asserting the educational rights of *language minority*[1] students, those who were considered racial minorities and whose native language was not English. During the Johnson Administration (1963–1969), the US Congress debated the efficacy of using bilingual education as an accommodation for addressing the needs of the growing and largely Spanish-speaking immigrant and domestic student population. In 1968, the Bilingual Education Act was implemented and the US Federal government allowed the use of native-language instruction to accommodate the language development needs of language minority students. A few years after the passage of the act, the US Supreme Court ruled in *Lau v. Nichols et al.*, 414 U.S. No. 72-6520 (1974) that schools were obligated to accommodate non-English-speaking students to learn the language of instruction. The court, however, did not mandate any specific instructional model, such as bilingual education. Thus, specific types of accommodation were left to the states and local school districts.

There were some attempts to establish standards for federally funded programs during the 1970s, but there was no follow through or enforcement during the Reagan Administration (1981–1989) (Crawford, 2000). From the late 1970s through the 1990s, progress was made in developing transitional bilingual programs and culturally responsive models for teacher preparation. During the same period, however, advocates of English-only instruction, whose views were reminiscent of the Americanization movement (1914–1925) of the early 20th century, sponsored legislation to promote English-only instruction, and there were efforts in the US Congress and a number of states to promote English as the official policy. Starting in California in the late 1990s, and quickly followed by Arizona and Massachusetts, voter-approved initiatives were passed to restrict bilingual education (Wiley, 2010a,b).

Arizona's current SEI program model claims to be based on 'scientific-based' research. In Chapter 2, Christian Faltis and M. Beatriz Arias explain that the process of determining 'appropriate action' for English learners (ELs) was addressed in *Castañeda v. Pickard*, 648 F.2d 989; 1981 U.S., which has been the most significant language case since *Lau*. *Castañeda* has particular relevance for authors in this collection because it held that an accommodation program must be (1) based on sound educational theory, (2) implemented effectively with adequate resources and (3) must be proven effective over time. As noted by Faltis and Arias, establishing just what appropriate expertise and professional knowledge are has proven challenging in the courts. Thus, they argue for the need to establish a standard of support which distinguishes between speculative or anecdotal claims and evidence-based research. They also critique important court interpretations of *Castañeda* in an effort to understand how judges determine what counts as sound educational theory, and whose expertise counts in making that determination. *Castañeda* also has relevance for Michael Long and Douglas Adamson's (Chapter 3) discussion regarding concerns that Arizona's SEI model is not theoretically sound or evidence based. They conclude that the model conflicts with second language acquisition (SLA) research findings in several areas and note that, by design, Arizona's four-hour SEI block segregates language minority students from native speakers of English, who normally would serve as models for English language acquisition. Beyond that Long and Adamson note, based on a review of the research evidence, that acquiring academic competence in English requires much more developmental time than the one year currently allowed.

The No Child Left Behind Act (NCLB) (Public Law 107-110) made a number of important changes to federal policy for language minority students. Of primary interest to language minority policy, NCLB subsumed the federal Bilingual Education Act of 1968 by dropping any reference to bilingual education. The former Office of Bilingual Education and Language Minority Affairs (OBEMLA) was replaced by the Office of English Language Acquisition (OELA). Similarly, the National Clearinghouse on Bilingual Education (NCBE) became the National Clearinghouse for English Language Acquisition (NCELA). These changes signaled a strategic shift from emphasizing students' language minority status to positing them more amorphously as *English learners* (García, 2005). This shift in federal policy weakened the leadership of the federal role in promoting accommodations for language minority students at the same time that some states such as Arizona and California had become more restrictive in disallowing bilingual education as a program model for these students. Thus, the shift in federal policy under No Child Left behind was significant in setting the stage for a major shift in Arizona's accommodation of language minority students.   •

NCLB also ushered in a series of accountability measures requiring states to demonstrate compliance with the new federal law. With reference to this context, Wayne Wright and Ko-Yin Sung (Chapter 5) detail how Arizona's initial attempts at compliance with NCLB, while simultaneously implementing Proposition 203, were largely superficial. Their findings are based on analyses of results from a statewide survey of experienced third-grade teachers of language minorities, also known as ELLs, and they also present findings from classroom case studies regarding school language policies that resulted from Proposition 203. Wright and Sung conclude that that Arizona's school accountability labeling policies and manipulation of students' proficiency scores masked schools' actual effectiveness educating minority students.

It is clear from this collection that the extent of the imposition instructional models by the Arizona Department of Education (ADE) has been significant. Beyond merely dictating the language of instruction, ADE has dictated a model of instruction, SEI, along with specific instructional practices that are controversial as various authors note. Mary Carroll Combs (Chapter 4), for example, contends that Arizona's prescribed ELL instructional policies have reinvented both theory and practice at both state and classroom levels. The state's model of implementation, the four-hour block, also requires pulling students out of mainstream classes, which runs the risk of segregating students, as previously noted.

How teachers are prepared and how professional knowledge is conceptualized and transmitted is of major importance in teacher preparation (Darling-Hammond, 2001). For more than a century, curriculum theorists have understood that designing appropriate curricula and instructional approaches begins with knowledge of the students to be served. To do so, teachers should have knowledge of a wide range of practices, techniques and skills, from which to draw, in order to meet the variety needs of the diverse students they teach. In other words, they need extensive pre-service and continuing in-service education to be able to develop professional judgment. In top-down, state-mandated models of educational reform, however, teachers often are treated as technicians who lack control and choice regarding which methods or materials may be used. Thus, they 'have little control over most of the mechanisms that determine professional standards' (Darling-Hammond, 2001c: 260). For this reason, teacher preparation as addressed by the authors in this collection is an important area for scrutiny. Thus, their analyses consider the impact of Arizona's restrictive language policy not only on students but also on teacher preparation and certification.

Sarah Moore (Chapter 6) addresses the policy formation, content and implementation of Arizona's SEI training program. She concludes that its goal is to promote an English-only ideology. She also focuses on the importance of trainers' interpretations of SEI prescriptions for practice and explores the role of trainers from different organizations, who have attempted to interpret policy for teachers. Also focusing on teacher preparation, Nancy Murri, Amy Markos and Alexandria Estrella (Chapter 7) present the results of a survey of pre-service, novice and experienced teachers regarding their self-assessed sense of preparedness to teach ELLs. They also probe the relevance of the state-mandated SEI coursework for their teaching. Murri et al. note the impact of restrictive policy particularly as it has affected the acquisition of literacy and English. Along complementary lines, Kate Olsen (Chapter 8) presents findings from another study of pre-service teachers. Like Moore, Olsen contends that it is necessary to analyze the ideological assumptions of pre-service curricula and how they impact the beliefs of those preparing to be teachers. Olsen offers useful suggestions regarding how teachers can be better prepared to understand the needs of their students.

A major question raised in this volume is whether ideology has trumped professional knowledge and research. Stephen Krashen, Jeff MacSwan and Kellie Rolstad (Chapter 9) address this question based on their critical analysis of the ADE's English Language Learners Task Force's report, which purported to present a scholarly and balanced review of current scientific knowledge regarding effective programs for ELLs and SEI. The authors detail significant limitations and incorrect interpretations of the literature in the task forces' finding.

The contributors to this collection have conducted a very thorough analysis of Arizona's language minority educational policies and practices since the implementation of Proposition 203. Prior to Proposition 203, it is important to also note that since 1992, Arizona has been a site of contestation regarding appropriate levels of funding for language minority students in a contestation between the state and federal government. In various iterations of *Flores v. Arizona* that began in 1992, the state has been involved in a suit regarding the underfunding English accommodations for language minority students. Most recently, the state appealed *Flores v. Arizona* 516 F.3d 1140 (9th Cir. 2008) to the Supreme Court, and won a partial victory, but remains in follow-up litigation regarding appropriate funding for language minority students as of this writing.

In analyzing educational policies in Arizona, it is also important to note that the restrictions on the use of native language instruction have recently been followed by a state law supported by the ADE State Superintendent of Education to ban ethnic studies in public schools. Is this a mere coincidence? That is unlikely. Many years ago, Arnold Leibowitz (1969, 1971, 1974), a legal expert in United States territorial law and language policy, noted that language restrictionism is usually symptomatic of a broader field of societal concerns. He suggested language is one instrument of social control, which should be assessed across educational, economic, political and social domains. In other words we should look for broader patterns of social controls on minority groups. This suggests that it is useful to look at language restrictions in Arizona within the broader field of minority politics and ethnic relations. Anyone paying attention to this arena will note that, in the national debate over immigration and minority civil rights, Arizona has become ground zero. Since the passage of Proposition 203, through a combination of state laws and additional propositions, Arizona has made English the official language, while making English instruction for those who are undocumented illegal. It also mandates that students who were brought to the United States as children must be charged nonresident tuition regardless of whether they have lived most of their lives in Arizona. The state has passed employer sanctions that punish US citizens for hiring the undocumented, and it has required stringent proof of citizenship requirements for voters (as of this writing the latter measure has just been overturned by a federal court). Lastly, it has passed a controversial law allowing police to detain those suspected of not being in the country legally. This statute has been partially nullified by a federal court but will probably be considered by the US Supreme Court.

These measures, nevertheless, have not been sufficient to satisfy some who are pushing for even stronger forms of restrictionism and social control. Public references to 'illegal children' are now becoming more prevalent as some politicians and pundits are now calling for a repeal of the Fourteenth Amendment, which granted citizenship to those born in the United States. Had the Fourteenth Amendment in its day been presented as a proposition within the states that had formerly practiced legalized slavery, it is unlikely that it would have ever passed. Thus, one lesson from history broadly and United States history specifically, is that minority rights need to be federally ensured in order to protect the minority from a potentially oppressive majority.

In focusing attention on the broader political arena, it is also necessary to put the association between language restrictionism and other manifestations of social control in perspective. As Spolsky (2009) has recently noted, when analyzing formal or informal attempts to control or 'manage language' behavior, it is important to remember that language is not autonomous but 'reflects the social, political, economic, religious, ideological, emotional context in which human life goes on'. Language discrimination accounts for only '... part of prejudice, injustice, and suffering' (Spolsky, 2009: 9).

Imagining Something Better: Societal Multilingualism as a Basis for Educational Language Policies

Within the domain of educational policies and practice, we should and can imagine better. Restrictive propositions in Arizona and California were often presented to voters as false dichotomies, as if parents and their children faced only the options of learning English or maintaining their native tongues. As we now enter the greatest era of interaction among peoples around the globe, it is useful to consider a wider range of options and opportunities, not only for language minorities but for society at large. It is useful to imagine what a 'comprehensive' national policy that promotes English and other languages could entail. As Rumbaut (2009) has recently noted, the fundamental language problem in the United States is not that minorities are not trying to learn English. Rather, the fundamental language problem is *language loss*, the loss of heritage and ancestral languages by immigrants and native peoples.

In contemplating what an inclusive national language policy might entail, for starters we should recognize that societal multilingualism is both a reality and resource on which we should build. Rather than restricting languages, we should promote policies that (1) ensure there is no linguistic discrimination; (2) provide programs that effectively teach English because English is the dominant language and the primary language of instruction; (3) develop respect for educating those who achieve multilingual ability because their achievement represents a greater resource not only for themselves but society at large; (4) support community-based efforts to maintain and promote heritage and community languages; and (5) develop effective language programs that link K-12 programs with community based and higher education programs (see Spolsky, 2001, 2002; Wiley, 2010a; and Alliance for Heritage Languages in America, 2010 for further discussion). Despite the recent expansion of restrictive and repressive language policies and practices, we can imagine and advance better policies that are more inclusive and mutually rewarding for language minorities and the greater society.

Note

(1) The federal government has used various labels for language minority students since the 1960s, all of which define students based on the relationship to learning English. Currently, English language learners (ELLs) or ELs are in vogue. In my discussion, the phrase language minority is used to draw attention to students' minority status, which provides the primary basis for making any legal claims regarding their educational treatment.

References

Alliance for Heritage Languages in America (2010) Online document, accessed 19 May 2011. http://www.cal.org/heritage/index.html
Brown v. Board of Education of Topeka, 347 U.S. 483 (1954).
Castañeda v. Pickard, 648 F.2d 989; 1981 U.S.
Corson, D. (1999) *Language Polices in Schools. A Resource for Teachers and Administrators.* Mahwah, NJ: Lawrence Erlbaum.
Crawford, J. (2000) *At War with Diversity: U.S. Language Policy in an Age of Anxiety.* Clevedon: Multilingual Matters.
Darling-Hammond, L. (2001) Standard setting in teaching. In V. Richardson (ed.) *Handbook of Research on Teaching* (4th edn, pp. 751–776). Washington, DC: American Educational Research Association (AERA).
Flores v. Arizona 516 F.3d 1140 (9th Cir. 2008).
García, O. (2005) Positioning heritage languages in the United States. *The Modern Language Journal* 89, 601–605.
Haas, M. (1992) *Institutional Racism: The Case of Hawai'i.* Westport, CT: Praeger.
Kloss, H. (1998) *The American Bilingual Tradition.* Washington, DC: Center for Applied Linguistics.
Lau v. Nichols et al., 414 U.S. No. 72–6520 (1974).
Leibowitz, A.H. (1969) English literacy: Legal sanction for discrimination. *Notre Dame Lawyer* 25, 7–66.
Leibowitz, A.H. (1971) Educational policy and political acceptance: The imposition of English as the language of Instruction in American Schools. Eric No. ED 047 321.
Leibowitz, A.H. (1974) Language as a means of social control. Paper presented at the VIII World Congress of Sociology, University of Toronto, Toronto, Canada.
Meyer v. Nebraska, 262 US 390 (1923).

Rumbaut, R. (2009) A linguistic graveyard? The evolution of language competencies, preferences and use among young adult children of immigrants (pp. 35–72). In T.G. Wiley, J.S. Lee and R. Rumberger (eds) *The Education of Language Minorities in the United States*. Bristol: Multilingual Matters.

Spolsky, B. (2001) Heritage languages and national security: An ecological view. In S.J. Baker (ed.) *Language Policy: Lessons from Global Models* (pp. 103–114). Monterey, CA: Monterey Institute of International Studies.

Spolsky, B. (2002) National policy statement on heritage language development: Toward an agenda for action. Heritage languages in America: Building on our national resources. Conference Paper. Tysons Corner, VA.

Spolsky, B. (2009) *Language Management*. Cambridge: Cambridge University Press.

Spring, J. (1994) *Deculturation and the Struggle for Equality: A Brief History of the Education of Dominated Cultures in the United States*. New York: McGraw-Hill.

Weinberg, M. (1995) *A Chance to Learn: A History of Race and Education in the United States* (2nd edn). Long Beach, CA: California State University Press.

Wiley, T.G. (1998) The imposition of World War I era English-only policies and the fate of German in North America. In T. Ricento and B. Burnaby (eds) *Language and Politics in the United States and Canada* (pp. 211–241). Mahwah, NJ: Lawrence Erlbaum.

Wiley, T.G. (2004) Language policy and English-only. In E. Finegan and J.R. Rickford (eds) *Language in the USA: Perspectives for the Twenty-first Century*. Cambridge: Cambridge University Press.

Wiley, T.G. (2007) Accessing language rights in education: A brief history of the U.S. context. In O. Garcia and C. Baker (eds) *Bilingual Education: An Introductory Reader* (pp. 89–109). Clevedon: Multilingual Matters. Reprint: Wiley, T.G. (2002) Accessing language rights in education: A brief history of the U.S. context. In J. Tollefson (ed.) *Language Policies in Education: Critical Readings* (pp. 39–64). Mahwah, NJ: Lawrence Erlbaum.

Wiley, T.G. (2010a) Language policy in the United States. In K. Potowski (ed.) *Exploring Language Diversity in the United States* (pp. 255–271). Cambridge: Cambridge University Press.

Wiley, T.G. (2010b) The United States. In J.A. Fishman and O. García (eds) *Handbook of Language and Ethnic Identity* (pp. 302–322). Oxford: Oxford University Press.

Introduction

Educational language policy is a critical component for addressing equal educational opportunities for language minority students. With the increase in linguistic and cultural diversity in the United States over the last 20 years, we are witnessing the struggle within educational language policy circles for educational language rights against concerted efforts to limit equal educational opportunity by mandating one type of instructional model for English learners. Nowhere is this conflict between dominant and language minority educational policy more evident than in Arizona, where a restrictive educational language policy promoted by dominant English-only proponents has defined both instruction for English language learners (ELs) and professional development for all teachers.

As educators and scholars who have focused for decades on second language acquisition and instruction for English learners, we are concerned that Arizona's model for EL instruction lacks theoretical and empirical support and rigor (Davenport, 2011; Krashen *et al.*, this volume). The inconsistent implementation of unproven instructional methodology bodes poorly for addressing the educational needs of ELs, who lag significantly in achievement as compared with their non-EL peers (Institute of Education Sciences, 2009). We are concerned for students in P-12 classrooms as well as for students in teacher preparation programs who are unknowingly socialized to an English-only policy perspective. Our commitment to students and teachers brought us together to inform educators of how a restrictive language policy can infiltrate university classrooms and set the curriculum for teacher preparation, promoting an English-only ideology.

We believe that Arizona is ground zero for the most restrictive language policies in the country and this policy is having a negative social and educational impact on language minority students and educators (Lillie *et al.*, 2010; Rios-Aguilar *et al.*, 2010). This concern has motivated us to work with our colleagues to devote this volume to study the ramifications of Arizona's educational language policy on teacher preparation and consolidate the research that critiques structured English immersion (SEI), the state-mandated model of teaching English learners in Arizona. The information presented here serves as a case study on the consequences of a restrictive language policy on educational equality for English learners.

Our perspective on language education policy views it as both a mechanism and a process. Shohamy states:

> Language education policy refers to decisions made in schools beyond those made explicitly about language itself. Language is central in school, for it is through language that students learn and come to know. (Shohamy, 2006: 76)

But we also maintain that these policy decisions are acted upon locally and therefore emerge differently in everyday contexts (Tollefson, 1991). McCarty urges us to see the interactive aspect of educational language policy noting that it is a

> Sociocultural process that includes public and official documents but equally important, it constitutes and is constituted by the practices each of us engages in every day. (McCarty, 2004: 72)

Furthermore, in this process, we agree with Menken and Garcia (2010) who emphasize the agency of educators especially teachers. They assert that educators are at the center of language education policy implementation. We proceed on the assumption that educators (teachers and professors) are the implementers of the policy, knowingly or unknowingly. And so,

> Language education policies provide a structure or text, which then engages educators in behaviors situated in their own local contexts. (Garcia & Menken, 2010: 256)

As teacher educators, we turn our attention to official documents mandating the content of teacher preparation for English learners and how language policy shapes the university syllabus. Our review suggests that teacher educators rarely engage teachers' reflection on language policy and what it means for teaching on a daily basis. We are informed by Wiley who notes that:

> Teacher preparation programs must address the responsibility to inform teachers about the ways in which they may become conflicted by or complicit in, promoting policies that disadvantage or discriminate against language minority children. (Wiley, 2008: 233)

The consequences of implementing a restrictive policy in schools and classrooms must be critically examined, especially for teachers working with English learners. As Wiley suggests,

> Given the negative legacy of discriminatory language policies in education for language minorities, some focus on the history of educational language policies to the detriment of language minority students should be a part of teacher preparation. (Wiley, 2008: 238)

We examine teacher preparation practices mandated in Arizona for promotion of restrictive language policies. We focus on educators as language policy-makers, who have agency to modify language policy within their contexts.

This volume provides a case study of the policy and implementation of SEI in teacher preparation and provides a critique of the research that undergirds the SEI classroom model. The chapters in this book are, therefore, divided into three main parts. Part 1 offers reviews of the nexus of language policy and teacher preparation. In the first chapter, Arias applies a language policy framework to teacher preparation and affirms that restrictive language policies contribute to molding teacher beliefs, leading to deficit views of non-English speakers. Next, Faltis and Arias focus on professional and political critiques of SEI, and the legal standards used to support its use for developing English. Faltis and Arias trace the evolution of how the courts have considered who counts as an expert in determining the soundness or unsoundness of a particular educational program for English learners. They stresses that courts have slowly, but surely deferred to school districts as experts in determining appropriate action for English learners. In the next chapter, Long and Adamson base their critique of SEI on second language research to assert that Arizona's new SEI program is fundamentally flawed. They show how Arizona's approach to SEI is inconsistent with what well-designed and peer-reviewed SLA research has shown about how children learn new languages and about how best to teach them. They make the point that the new program, with a single focus on language form will not enable English learners develop the language needed for accessing and promoting academic competence.

Part 2 examines the impact of implementing SEI in Arizona classrooms. Combs explores how Arizona's SEI model promotes three 'folk theories,' or 'cultural models'—simplified versions of complex events or processes of second language acquisition: (a) that young children learn English better than older students; (b) that immersion in an all English setting would help students acquire the language more rapidly; and (c) that such an approach would teach them enough English in one year to be academically successful in the mainstream classroom. In the chapter by Wright and Sung, we learn that many EL teachers throughout Arizona value bilingualism, in society, and want children to learn English well. However, the teachers also opined strongly that the SEI model is insufficient to ensure equal access for ELs to the curriculum. In the final chapter of this section, Krashen, MacSwan and Rolstad present a critique the research literature the Arizona Department of Education (ADE) cited to substantiate the particular approach SEI developed for Arizona. These authors argue that the ADE document neglects to reference significant research bearing on the questions raised, and frequently presents an incomplete view of the research, limiting its citations to studies and non-peer refereed reports that appear to support its position leading to inappropriate conclusions.

Part 3 turns attention to how teachers are prepared to address the needs of English learners in Arizona. Moore's research focuses on the Arizona Department of Education mandated SEI professional development for teachers, with an eye toward how teachers are prepared across the state. Moore points out that state and community college providers tended to privilege English-only methodology and strategies for teaching language forms, while universities and districts emphasized culturally relevant teaching and communicative approaches to language development. The chapter by Murri, Markos and Estrella documents how language policies affect the daily interaction that occurs within teacher education colleges, schools and classrooms. Finally in this part, Olson shows that preservice teachers in Arizona are not required to examine their ideological beliefs and assumptions about ELs. She argues strongly that teacher educators need to examine their ideological beliefs as a way to counter existing deficit perspective on ELs, their home languages, and their cultural backgrounds.

Taken as a whole, these critiques of Arizona's SEI lead to a strong conclusion that SEI instruction as developed and mandated in Arizona is ideologically promoted and does not conform to decades of either established or new (see Tomlinson, 2007; Valdés et al., 2011) research-based second language development practices. In this book, we endeavor to show how the English-only ideology represented through the Arizona version of SEI has been served.

We examine pedagogical choices, content, materials and language use and concur with Auerbach:

> Pedagogical choices about curriculum development, content, materials, classroom processes, and language use, although appearing to be informed by apolitical professional consideration, are, in fact, inherently ideological in nature, with significant implications for learners. (Auerbach, 1995: 9)

We apply the lens of this review to both pedagogical choices in higher education and in the design of the SEI K-12 model. We hope that these chapters will inform our readers and influence the crafting of educational language policies in other contexts. This volume is the result of a joint effort on the part of our authors, readers and editors. We wish to thank our colleagues in the university and in schools across Arizona who have supported our efforts to make explicit the implications of restrictive language policy, on students and teachers. We wish to thank the dedicated efforts of our graduate students: Dr Silvia Noguerón-Liu, Dr Amy Markos, Dr Nancy Murri, Dr Melissa Rivers and Tracy Nguyen who helped with the editing and author contact. We are grateful for the editorial comments provided by our publisher, Tommi Grover, and all those who provided thoughtful recommendations. We are thankful for the patience that our families extended to us as we worked on the manuscript. However, as editors, and authors we take responsibility for the issues and conclusions raised in this volume.

M. Beatriz Arias, Phoenix, AZ
Christian Faltis, Davis, CA

References

Auerbach, E. (1995) The politics of the ESL classroom: Issues of power in pedagogical choices. In J. Tollefson (ed.) *Power and Inequality in Language Education* (pp. 9–33). New York: Cambridge University Press.

Davenport, D.K. (2011) *Arizona English Language Learner Program, Fiscal Year 2010* (Report No. 11-06). State of Arizona Office of the Auditor General. Retrieved from http://www.azauditor.gov/Reports/School_Districts/Statewide/2011/ELL_Report.pdf. Last accessed 30.07.11

Garcia, O. and Menken, K. (2010) Stirring the onion: Educators and the dynamics of language educations policies (looking ahead). In K. Menken and O. Garcia (eds) *Negotiating Language Policies in Schools: Educators as Policymakers* (pp. 249–261). New York: Routledge.

Institute of Education Sciences (2009) *The Nation's Report Card: Science 2009.* Washington, DC: U.S. Department of Education.

Lillie, K.E., Markos, A., Estrella, A., Nguyen, T., Peer, K., Perez, K., Trifiro, A., Arias, M.B. and Wiley, T.G. (2010) *Policy in Practice: The Implementation of Structured English Immersion in Arizona.* Los Angeles, CA: Civil Rights Project: University of California, Los Angeles.

McCarty, T. (2004) Dangerous difference: A critical historical analysis of language education policies in the United States. In J. Tollefson and A. Tsui (eds) *Medium of Instruction Policies: Which Agenda? Whose Agenda?* (pp. 71–96). Mahwah, NJ: Lawrence Erlbaum Associates.

Rios-Aguilar, C., González-Canche, M. and Moll, L. (2010) *A Study of Arizona's Teachers of English Language Learners.* University of California, Los Angeles: Civil Rights Project.

Shohamy, E. (2006) *Language Policy: Hidden Agendas and New Approaches.* London: Routledge.

Tollefson, J. (1991) *Planning Language, Planning Inequality: Language Policy in the Community*. London: Longman.

Tomlinson, B. (ed.) (2007) *Language Acquisition and Development: Studies of First and Other Language*. London: Continuum.

Valdés, G., Capitelli, S. and Alvarez, L. (2011) *Latino Children Learning English*. New York: Teachers College Press.

Wiley, T. (2008) Language policy and teacher education. In S. May and N. Hornberger (eds) *Encyclopedia of Language and Education* (Vol. 1, pp. 229–241). New York: Springer.

Part 1

Language Policy in Arizona

1 Language Policy and Teacher Preparation: The Implications of a Restrictive Language Policy on Teacher Preparation

M. Beatriz Arias

The sanctions against mother-tongue instruction in the English-only states of Arizona, California and Massachusetts, have brought renewed interest to the study of language education policy (LEP). Several authors have looked at how these policies influence students, classrooms and language minority communities (Crawford, 1997; Stritikus & Garcia, 2003; Wiley, 2002; Wright, 2005). Other studies have reported on the impact of restrictive language policies on educational programs (Combs *et al.*, 2005; de Jong *et al.*, 2005; Garcia & Curry-Rodriguez, 2000). According to Christ 'hardly any research has been conducted thus far on language policy in teacher education' (Christ, 1997: 234). This chapter addresses this need by providing an opportunity to examine how a restrictive language policy becomes reified in teacher preparation. In this case study, I suggest that the Structured English Immersion (SEI) curriculum mandated for all teachers in Arizona reflects an English-only orientation, promotes a limited understanding of English learners, second language acquisition and LEP. The context of this study is embedded in teacher preparation as mandated by the State of Arizona (ADE, 2007, 2009). There are two SEI policies in effect in Arizona: (1) there is an instructional SEI model that prescribes the content and time allocated to learning English in the K-12 classroom, and (2) there is the SEI curriculum, which is required for all Arizona colleges of education as part of teacher preparation.

This study is situated within a framework that recognizes that LEP is dynamic, and refers to 'affecting decisions people make about languages and their uses in society in the specific context of education, school and universities' (Shohamy, 2006: 77). These decisions are part of a sociocultural and sociopolitical process. As McCarty has noted, LEP is a sociocultural process: 'Language policies both reflect and reproduce the distribution of power within the larger society' (McCarty, 1972: 72) and Tollefson and Tsui ask us to regard debates around language of instruction policy situated in their sociopolitical contexts, 'which are inseparable from their historical contexts' (Tollefson & Tsui, 2004: 3). This dynamic conception of LEP extends at every level of implementation so that while there may be a clearly articulated policy at one end, 'educators are at the epicenter of this dynamic process, acting on their agency to change the various language education policies they must translate into practice' (Menken & Garcia, 2010). As we review the implementation of the restrictive language policy in Arizona, we hope to attend to the space where educator agency, both at the university and classroom level, mediate policy implementation.

The focus of this study is the content of a state-mandated teacher preparation curriculum for the SEI required of all Arizona educational personnel. I contrast the implementation of restrictive language policies with the need to inform teachers of their role as the primary agents of language policy. This chapter examines how a restrictive language policy becomes enacted and embedded in a state-required teacher endorsement and looks for opportunities for implementation and ideological space as conceptualized by Hornberger (2002).

The growth of language minority communities across the country, coupled with the fact that most teachers will encounter English language learners (ELLs) in their classrooms, makes it imperative that teacher educators develop awareness of issues of LEP. Teachers need to understand how their attitudes, dispositions and knowledge of language policy issues can inform, enrich and enhance their practice. As many have noted, teachers are the primary constructors and implementers of language policy (de Jong, 2008; Ricento & Hornberger, 1996), teachers are on the front line of helping students bridge new languages. Yet in many ways, teachers are viewed as 'instruments of the state' (Wiley, 2008: 232) whose role is to implement policy rather than critique it. As Wiley has noted, with specific reference to language minority populations, teachers are asked to 'implement policies that either promote, accommodate or restrict languages' (Wiley, 2008: 230). Shohamy also refers to teachers as the 'main agents through whom the ideology is spread and turns from political statement about LEP to de facto practices of language learning. Wiley has also noted that teacher education programs need to inform teachers about ways in which they may become conflicted by, and complicit in, promoting policies that disadvantage or discriminate against language minority children' (Shohamy, 2006: 233).

LEP is also a state policy (Corson, 1999). We know that the state policy plays a critical role in the socialization of teachers. State policy sets the tone for acceptance and recognition of minority languages. At issue is how a state's restrictive language policy influences teacher preparation through the articulation and requirement of prescriptive instructional practices.

This chapter begins with a framework for understanding the relationship between types of language policies and teacher preparation. This is followed by a summary of the literature on what teachers of ELLs need to know and how language policy is part of this schema. A content analysis of the SEI curriculum required for all Arizona educators is contrasted with the essential components for ELL teacher preparation cited in the literature. The requirements for the SEI endorsement are critiqued for under preparing teachers in the sociopolitical dimensions of language, and failing to provide 'ideological clarity' regarding issues of power and language. The SEI endorsement promotes linguicism,[1] linguistic assimilation, and a biased and flawed perspective on second language acquisition. The concern raised, is that by law, institutions of higher education are required to reproduce this ideology through implementation of a state-approved syllabus in teacher preparation. Thus, rather than preparing teachers for ELLs, the SEI restricts teacher understanding of second language learners, their communities and instructional alternatives.

State Policy and Teacher Socialization

The research on teacher socialization emphasizes that 'state educational policies frame the socialization of new teachers, especially when these policies prescribe instructional practices and assess outcomes' (Achinstein et al., 2004). State policies that mandate instructional practices can have an especially potent impact on teacher practice (Ogawa et al., 2003; Rowan & Miskel, 1999). This is particularly relevant to Arizona, which as an English-only state, has articulated prescribed instructional practices for ELLs and for teacher preparation, commonly referred to as Structured English Immersion (SEI) and the SEI. Other states that have highly prescriptive instructional policies specifying standards, curricula and pedagogy, claim to provide teachers with clearer guidelines as to what and how to teach (Schmoker & Marzano, 1999). Similarly, the Arizona Department of Education (ADE) claims that the SEI endorsement prepares teachers for the ELL student population (ADE, 2009). Upon close inspection, the SEI promotes English-only instruction, presents immersion as the most efficacious approach to teaching ELLs, and limits recognition of the importance of students' native language in their daily lives and identity development. Furthermore, the English-only policy is reproduced with an ADE-scripted curriculum required in pre-service education which focuses primarily on structured immersion pedagogy, the state's ELL standards, and mandated assessments. I propose that this prescriptive curriculum reflects the states' restrictive language policy and promotes a monolingual ideology which is pedagogically detrimental to ELLs and that the endorsement has become an intrusion into the traditional role of teacher-preparation institutions to design teacher-preparation curriculum.

Language Policy and Teacher Preparation

Research in LEP examines choices about which language(s) will be the medium of instruction in schools and how language is taught (Spolsky, 2004). It is important to recognize that these choices are not conducted in a vacuum but are subject to political pressure, power and attitudes toward ELL assimilation and acculturation. Varghese and Stritikus (2005) have emphasized that teachers of ELLs need knowledge of how their decision-making on language use in classrooms is in fact language policy development. State sanctions against native language use become critical in shaping teachers beliefs regarding the importance and usefulness of students' first language. Teachers need to recognize their role and the role of language in the acculturation process that they are helping ELLs navigate. We know that language plays a critical role in identity and identity formation. Teachers can help students develop positive attitudes toward the benefits of proficiency in two languages. Yet in states with restrictive language policies, teachers may become conflicted over choosing the best instructional approach for ELL students. Consequently, teachers need support and direction to develop an appropriate stance toward minority languages, at the state level, at the district level and school level.

According to Wiley (2007), there are several language policy orientations which influence the selection of languages in schools. By viewing language policies in terms of the desired outcome – promotion, tolerance or repression – we can anticipate the type of support there will be for second language programs, student bilingualism and teacher preparation for ELLs. In Table 1.1, I have displayed how these language policy orientations might impact decisions at the state level on teacher preparation. I have included the five language policy orientations identified by Kloss (1977), as modified by Wiley (2007). There are five language policy orientations, spanning a range from promotion-oriented to repressive-oriented policies.

Table 1.1 Language policy orientations

Language policy orientation	Policy characteristics at state education level	Implications for teacher preparation
Promotion-oriented policies	The state allocates resources to support the official use of minority languages	State offers ESL/BLE licensure Courses are required for ESL/BLE certification
Expediency-oriented policies	State mandates and supports efforts for short-term minority language development	State offers ESL/BLE licensure Courses are required for ESL/BLE certification
Tolerance-oriented policies	State does not legislate in the linguistic life of the language minority community	Preparation in ESL/BLE is optional Courses in BLE/ESL are optional
Restrictive-oriented policies	State prohibits or curtails the use of minority languages in specific settings, i.e. schools	State may/may not offer ESL/BLE licensure State requires SEI endorsement for all Courses are required for ESL/BLE/SEI certification
Repression-oriented policies	State consciously works to eradicate minority languages	No state licensure Courses in BLE/ESL are optional

This chart is modeled after Kloss's (1977) schema and Wiley's (2005) adaptation

Repressive- and restrictive-oriented language policies both perceive minority languages as a problem and thereby seek their elimination and/or repression. Most recently, repressive language policy orientations were exemplified in the Bureau of Indian Affairs (BIA) schools which sanctioned the use of indigenous languages and fostered linguistic assimilation (Wiley, 2007). Restrictive language policies do not seek the elimination of the language, but they set sanctions on the use of minority language. Tolerant language policies are neutral with regard to minority language use, neither restricting nor supporting it. Expediency- and promotion-oriented language policies view language as a resource, and provide financial and legislative support for language development.

Across the United States there is variation in language policy orientation. Some promotion-oriented policy states would describe themselves as 'English Plus' states, stressing the importance of proficiency in more than one language: New Mexico, Oregon, Rhode Island (Menken, 2008). Several states including Illinois and Texas, (see Crawford, 2004) promote the expediency model, allowing short-term transitional and developmental bilingual education, and dual language and English as a second language programs for their ELLs. Other states such as Nebraska demonstrate a tolerance model, not mandating or sanctioning bilingual programs. Finally, there are the English-only states, Arizona, California and Massachusetts, which display a restrictive language policy orientation, prohibiting and proscribing the use of L1 in classrooms. These restrictive language-oriented state policies have emerged in the last decade in the United States as the English-Only Movement has made its way through ballot measures to the classroom (Wright & Choi, 2005). While all three states mandate English as the official language of instruction, Arizona is the most restrictive, sanctioning the use of students native language in classrooms and pre-scribing a teacher preparation endorsement that promotes a restrictive language policy.

Teachers as Agents of LEP

LEP is a sociocultural process which not only derives from public and official acts and documents, but is also framed and enacted by our daily practices (McCarty, 2004). The literature suggests that in their daily activity, teachers may be unconsciously promoting language policies that could be detrimental to their students, or lead to misunderstandings with parents and students. According to Auerbach (1995) teachers implement policies (e.g. using only English in the ESL classroom) that reflect broader social attitudes and not specific school policies, without realizing it. They do so in many ways and on many levels; for example, teachers may internalize normative social attitudes toward speakers of nonofficial languages or nonstandard varieties of official languages, or they may believe that bilingual education programs put language minority students at disadvantage. Further, the ideologies of schools, communities and states helps reinforce unstated beliefs, so that teachers come to believe not only that what they are doing reflects explicit policies, but also that such policies are generally in the best interest of students. Auerbach argues that 'the day-to-day decisions that practitioners make inside the classroom both shape and are shaped by the social order outside the classroom' (Auerbach, 1995: 9).

It is clear that teachers are considered by most policymakers to be the centerpiece of educational change (Datnow *et al.*, 2002). For Hornberger and Evans, teachers are at the core of language policy implementation 'as teachers interpret and modify received policies, they are, in fact, primary language policymakers' (Hornberger & Evans, 2005: 417). They elaborate:

> We place the classroom practitioner at the heart of language policy. Teachers have daily opportunities to make small changes in their practices, from the topics they choose for discussion, to how they structure the classroom, to the interest they demonstrate in students' problems. Teachers send implicit messages in other ways, too. As individuals, members of communities, and citizens of a country, ESL/EFL practitioners serve as role models, informants, and advisors on a daily basis. They may reinforce dominant cultural values (to one degree or another), or they may question and even oppose those values, thereby modeling possible alternative views of social reality often unavailable to students struggling to survive in a new culture or acquiring English for instrumental purposes. (Hornberger & Evans, 2005: 417)

Skilton-Sylvester's 2003 study of ESL teachers finds that the decisions that teachers make with regard to the ELLs in their classroom is the most powerful type of language policy, noting 'much of language teaching can also be seen as language policymaking' (Skilton-Sylvester, 2003: 7). Teachers, then, are seen as active constructors of language policies, as they transform practices within their own classrooms.

Teacher preparation for ELLs must bring explicit attention to the opportunities for access to English provided ELLs, the distribution of language use in the community, formal and informal policies for language use. Varghese and Stritikus state that:

> Given the ambiguous and contentious guidelines and policies relating to the education of ELLs, teacher educators must begin to seriously consider how teachers respond to and create language policy, explicitly preparing teachers to deal with the social and policy contexts in which their work will occur. (Varghese & Stritikus, 2005: 75)

Literature on preparing mainstream teachers to teach ELLs documents the challenges they face in a field fraught with controversy from reform efforts, ranging between multiculturalists and assimilationists, multilingualists and monolinguists (Harper & de Jong, 2004). The prevalence of discussions on the preparation of teachers for ELLs has ranged from a 'methods fetish' (Bartolome, 1998) to an almost exclusive focus on the language components (Wong-Filmore & Snow, 2002).

Varghese and Stritikus (2005) take note of this contentious policy atmosphere that surrounds the discourse on the education of ELLs, and propose that teachers more than ever need to understand how language policy (overt and covert) will become an essential backdrop to their practice. Teacher preparation for all teachers needs to provide a meta-awareness for the ways in which language shapes the politics of language, that decisions on language choice are never neutral, that learning a second language is a crucial part of identity and community. Despite the importance attributed to language policy issues in foundational teacher preparation, a review of several recent surveys of essential knowledge for all teachers working with ELL finds scant reference to preparation regarding language policy and teacher's role in the implementation of language policy.

What Do Teachers of ELLs Need to Know?

There has been general consensus about the competencies and knowledge base that mainstream teachers need in order to be able to work effectively with ELLs for almost 20 years. Two comprehensive reviews of the competencies needed by ELL teachers are of interest here. The first one, conducted by Gándara et al. (2005), builds on the elements of what constitutes a highly qualified teacher for ELLs based on early work by Milk et al. (1992). They reiterated their findings on fundamental skills, attitudes and knowledge and added:

(1) Ability to use the student native language and English for instruction;
(2) Ability to communicate high expectations for student learning;
(3) Ability to use 'active' teaching behaviors;
(4) Constant student monitoring;
(5) Sense of efficacy.

Nevertheless, while noting the importance of these competencies for teachers of ELLs they acknowledge that these competences are 'seldom if ever, taught in standard teacher preparation programs' (Milk et al., 1992: 108).

In a more recent literature review of mainstream teacher preparation, Lucas and Grinberg (2008) assert that the mis-education of ELLs can be avoided through teacher preparation. They focus on the language-related experiences, attitudes and beliefs, knowledge and skills that teachers need for teaching ELLs:

• *Language-related experiences*: including foreign language study and contact with people who speak languages other than English.

- *Language-related attitudes and beliefs*: including affirming views of linguistic diversity and bilingualism, awareness of the sociopolitical dimension of language use and language education, and an inclination to collaborate with colleagues who are language specialists.
- *Language-related knowledge*: including the language backgrounds experiences and proficiency of students', second language development, the connection between language culture and identity, and language forms, mechanics and use.

While there are many similarities between these two summations of teacher competencies, only Lucas and Grinberg (2008) acknowledge the importance of teachers' awareness of the sociopolitical dimension of language use and language education. This competency is most relevant to this discussion of language policy. They argue that foundational knowledge regarding the political and social dimension of language is critical. It is important to dispel the myth that language is politically neutral, acknowledge that structural inequalities exist and show that historically language choice derives its power from the speakers of that language. Sociolinguistic awareness is needed so that teachers can appreciate the implication that many ELLs are considered speakers of subordinated languages and recognize the challenges that members of this marked community confront in language acquisition. We will return to consideration of the knowledge base for teachers of ELL later, as we contrast Arizona's requirements for the SEI endorsement with the literature.

SEI in Arizona

Mandated language policy is one specific variable that influences preparing teachers for ELLs. While many states offer certification for teachers to specifically obtain their English as a second language (ESL) or bilingual education (BLE) certifications, these states implement ESL and BLE programs that require staffing with specially certified teachers. Most states offer ESL certification ($n = 49$) and 26 states offer BLE certification (National Comprehensive Center for Teacher Quality, 2009). Few states, however, have requirements for all teachers in the areas specifically addressing the needs of ELLs. According to a survey of state departments of education conducted by the National Comprehensive Center for Teacher Quality, five states (Alaska, Arizona, California, Florida and New York) require all mainstream teachers to complete coursework in methods of teaching ELLs. Two of these states, Arizona and California are English-only states and require SEI as an instructional strategy. However, only Arizona has mandated an SEI preparing all teachers for ELLs.

This endorsement extends the articulation of a restrictive language policy from the classroom to teacher preparation. In Arizona, SEI is defined as follows:

> SEI means an English language acquisition process for *young children* in which *nearly* all classroom instruction is in English but with the curriculum and presentation *designed* for children who are learning the language. Books and instructional materials are in English and all reading, writing, and subject matter are taught in English. Although teachers may use a *minimal amount* of the child's native language when necessary, *no subject matter* shall be taught in any language other than English, and children in this program learn to read and write solely in English. This educational methodology represents the standard definition of *'sheltered English'* or *'structured English'* found in educational literature. (Arizona Revised Statutes, 2000)

The SEI was developed to make all teachers in the state competent to deliver the SEI instructional model. The components of the SEI endorsement become the framework through which pre-service and in-service teachers come to view second language learners, their communities and strategies for instructing them. In this regard, the knowledge base articulated by the endorsement was widely viewed as inadequate (Wright, 2005).

Despite the fact that the SEI mandate dismantled most bilingual programs, it is noteworthy that the state has not eliminated certification for ESL and BLE. These endorsements require significantly more coursework than the SEI endorsement (18 credit hours compared with six credit hours, respectively). Furthermore, teachers who have the ESL or BLE endorsement are exempt from requirements to obtain the SEI. Nevertheless, the SEI is a mandated requirement for all teachers and it has had significant impact across the state. Since the law went into effect, thousands of pre-service and in-service teachers have obtained the full or partial SEI endorsement. Table 1.2 displays the numbers of

Table 1.2 Arizona teachers by endorsement and employment

Year	Bilingual endorsement (BLE)	English as a second language (ESL)	Structured English immersion (SEI)
2006	2955	7732	16,225
2007	2743	7416	17,505
2008	2606	7532	17,326
2009	2479	7177	17,134

Source: Arizona Department of Teacher Certification (2009)

teachers who have received their full or partial BLE/ESL/SEI endorsements. It shows that since 2006 there has been a gradual decline in the number of teachers opting for the BLE/ESL endorsement, and that teachers are receiving the SEI at double the rate of the BLE or ESL endorsements.

ADE monitors the delivery of the SEI endorsement by specifying the content, delimiting the hours allocated to topics and requiring ADE approval of course syllabi offered by universities and school districts. These official actions by ADE to articulate the curriculum for SEI teacher preparation are an example of implementation of a restrictive language policy in teacher preparation. In the following sections, I review the curricular content of the SEI endorsement and compare it with the recommendations in the literature on preparing quality teachers for ELLs.

The SEI: A Scripted Curriculum for Higher Education

In 2001, Arizona House Bill 2010 required the State Board of Education to adopt an SEI endorsement and provided that universities overseen by the Arizona Board of Regents must require courses necessary to obtain a provisional or full SEI endorsement. These policies established criteria for the content and time to be allocated to the state-approved instructional approach for ELLs: SEI. The requirements for the endorsement were highly controversial and roundly criticized as inadequate (Mahoney et al., 2005; Wright, 2005). In fact, a majority of the professional Judgment Panel interviewed by the National Conference of State Legislatures believed these standards to be 'insufficient' (Mahoney et al., 2005). The endorsement recognized only one instructional approach for ELLs, (SEI), thus precluding teachers from gaining a comprehensive understanding of instructional approaches, methods and strategies used with ELLs at different levels of proficiency and age.

Guidelines for the SEI endorsement were issued in 2006 by Board Rule (R7-2-613) which defined the criteria and content for teachers to obtain the mandated endorsement. The Board Rule articulated a scripted curriculum for higher education courses which specified the time to be allotted to the topics of foundations of SEI, assessment, strategies and standards for ELLs. This scripted curriculum left little room for instructors to include components that the research reports to be high-quality education for teachers of ELLs, such as the development of language-related attitudes and beliefs (Gándara et al., 2005; Lucas & Grinberg, 2008). Rather than provide a comprehensive overview of language acquisition, and methods of teaching a second language, the SEI curriculum promotes a 'one-size-fits-all' instructional approach. The Board Rule limited content to immersion strategies and foundations of SEI limiting rather than expanding teacher understanding.

In 2006, the ADE began implementation of a requirement that all educators in schools possess a SEI. This endorsement requirement was phased in between 2006 and 2009, and gradually doubled in credit requirement or seat hours requirements. The SEI was developed by the ADE in two phases. In the first phase, a 45-hour curriculum (three credit hours) was developed focusing on foundations, strategies, standards and assessment. The bulk of the hours were dedicated to instructional strategies and the most minimal time was allocated to foundations (one hour). The SEI 1 curriculum was followed by SEI 2, which also required 45 hours (three credit hours) and focused on additional foundations, strategies, standards and assessments.

Undergraduates in teacher preparation programs are required to complete 90 hours in two courses for the SEI; in-service teachers are required to complete 90 hours of professional development from state-approved delivery teams. At the university level, syllabi for both SEI courses required ADE approval, before students could be given credit for the endorsement. Critiques of the delivery of the SEI endorsement have emphasized the unevenness in the delivery of this content (see Moore, this volume).

A review of Table 1.3 shows the range of content areas covered by the SEI endorsement. There are six SEI objectives covered by the state-mandated curricular framework: (1) ELL standards; (2) data analysis and application; (3) formal and informal assessments; (4) SEI foundations; (5) SEI strategies; and (6) parent/home/school scaffolding. The minimum hours required for each objective include; a minimum of one hour of instruction on using the Arizona State-mandated ELL standards; a minimum of 3 h on data analysis and application (e.g. using AZELLA results to track student proficiency); at least one hour on SEI Foundations (legal, historical and educational reasons for SEI); three hours on formal and informal assessments (language acquisition assessment, creating multiple classroom assessments, using assessment results for placement decisions); at least three hours on parent/home/school scaffolding (cultivating home/school relationships, identifying community supports for parents to learn English, identifying the sociocultural influences on ELLs and discussing the impact of bilingualism and home language use). The bulk of the time allocation (25 hours) is dedicated to SEI Strategies including instructional methods for beginning English language development, materials and developing vocabulary. There are nine flex hours that can be spent on any of the six SEI objectives for a total of 45 hours of instruction. Every syllabus submitted to the ADE for approval must reflect this time allocation.

Table 1.3 Comparison of SEI/BLE/ESL endorsement requirements

SEI endorsement requirements	SEI I augmented	SEI II	Total hours	BLE/ESL Endorsement (Undergraduate)
ELL proficiency standards (h)	3	1	4	Foundations of instruction for ELLs 3 credits 45 h
Data analysis and application (h)	0	3	3	Language arts methods in BLE/ESL settings 3 credits 45 h
Assessment (h)	3	3	6	SEI for linguistically diverse students 3 credits
SEI foundations (h)	3	1	4	Social studies methods in BLE/ESL settings 3 credits 45 h
SEI strategies (h)	24	25	49	Science methods in BLE/ESL settings 3 credits 45 h
Parent/Home/ School scaffolding (h)	0	3	3	School community/ Family culture/ Parental involvement 3 credits
Flex hours (h)	12	9	21	Mathematics methods in BLE/ESL settings 3 credits 45 h
Total hours (h)	45	45	90	Practicum

As mentioned above, at the university level, the SEI endorsement consists of two 3-credit hour courses focusing on SEI foundations, strategies, standards and assessment. However, as mentioned above, the literature on essential knowledge for mainstream teachers of ELLs (Lucas & Grinberg, 2008) indicates that teachers preparing to work with ELL need to develop language-related experiences, attitudes and beliefs and language-related knowledge. Contrasting the contents of the SEI endorsement with what the literature recommends, we see that completion of the SEI endorsement may reduce rather than augment teacher quality. The SEI endorsement is limited in both the quantity (time) and quality (content) that it allocates to teacher preparation for ELLs. Clearly, there is not sufficient time allowed for teachers in preparation to explore contact with non-English speakers, develop awareness of the sociopolitical dimension of language use, affirm linguistic diversity and develop knowledge of the connection between language, culture and identity. The exclusion of these important components of teacher preparation for ELLs renders the SEI inadequate for quality teacher preparation. Furthermore, the imposition of the SEI scripted curriculum upon university faculty, limits instructors in the provision of what the research finds appropriate.

Summary and Conclusion

The SEI transmits the state's restrictive language policy promoting a lack of tolerance for alternative approaches for ELL instruction to teacher preparation. Restrictive language policies can contribute to molding teacher beliefs that can lead to deficit views of students speaking a language other than English. Not only can teachers develop deficit views of ELLs, they will be left without alternative approaches to understand their background knowledge, experience and strengths. Furthermore, the courses required by ADE for SEI are a noteworthy intrusion into the teacher preparation curriculum. Unlike other teacher preparation courses which are developed by the faculty, the SEI courses must be reviewed and approved by ADE. The ADE (not the university) establishes credentials for approved instructors of SEI courses, and it is them (not the university) who define the major topics to be covered for ADE approval. The requirements of the SEI courses in the teacher preparation curriculum is a direct imposition of restrictive language policy on higher education limiting instructors' ability to adequately prepare teachers for ELLs.

As teacher educators concerned with ELL access and equity, we need to inform policy makers of the critical role that LEP plays in teacher preparation. Teacher preparation programs must address the responsibility 'to inform teachers about the ways in which they may become conflicted by or complicit in, promoting policies that disadvantage or discriminate against language minority children' (Wiley, 2008: 233). The consequences of implementing a restrictive policy in schools and classrooms must be critically examined, especially for teachers working with ELLs. As Wiley suggests, 'given the negative legacy of discriminatory language policies in education for language minorities, some focus on the history of educational language policies to the detriment of language minority students should be a part of teacher preparation' (Wiley, 2008: 238). The SEI does not allow a space for teachers in preparation to understand the legacy of linguistic discrimination, or that language choice is not a neutral or impartial activity, or that there are alternatives to English-only SEI.

As teacher educators, what can we do to address the imposition of this detrimental state requirement? Cochran-Smith has noted: 'What is the college/university role in teacher education at a time when many states are taking unprecedented actions to control the coursework, the subject matter, the time spent in school, and every other aspect of teacher education?' (Cochran-Smith, 2006: 217). It is our responsibility to prepare teachers in ways that are critical, culturally responsive and potentially transformative. Yet, teacher preparation as defined by SEI in Arizona limits the scope of information needed by teachers to be effective with ELLs. The implementation of this SEI in the teacher preparation curriculum transmits restrictive language policy values to pre-service teachers. As teacher educators we need to validate teacher agency, to help them recognize that they are the 'final arbiters of language policy implementation' (Menken & Garcia, 2010: 233).

There is a new wave of LEP research that recognizes the importance of agency in implementation. As teacher educators we have agency to find the implementational and ideological opportunities to combat restrictive language policies in our university classrooms. Johnson and Freeman have noted that even within 'ostensibly restrictive language policies, there is often implementational space that local educators and language planners can work to their advantage and ideological space in schools and communities, which open education and social possibilities for bilingual learners and potentially challenges dominant/hegemonic educational discourses' (Johnson & Freeman, 2010: 15). Now that we are studying language policy in teacher education, we need to continue to study how instructor agency mediates the delivery of stated language policy.

Note

(1) Linguicism—Beliefs, attitudes, and actions whereby differences of language serve to structure inequality between linguistic groups; ideologies, structures, and practices used to legitimate, effectuate, regulate, and reproduce an unequal division of power and resources between groups defined on the basis of language (Skutnabb-Kangas, 1988: 13).

References

Achinstein, B., Ogawa, R. and Spiegelman, A. (2004) Are we creating separate and unequal tracks of teachers? The effects of state policy, local conditions, and teacher characteristics on new teacher socialization. *American Educational Research Journal* 41, 557–603.

Arizona Department of Education (ADE) (2007) Curricular framework for (SEI) endorsement training. Office of English language acquisition services. Online document, accessed 15 March 2007. http://www.ade.state.az.us/asd/lep/downloads/ SBEapprovedSEIcurriculaframewok.pdf

Arizona Department of Education (ADE) (2009) Structured English immersion (SEI) fast facts. Online document, accessed 16 January 2009. http://www.ade.state.az.us/ certification/downloads/SEIFacts.pdf

Arizona Revised Statutes, Title 15, Article 3.1, §15-751–17.755 (2000).

Auerbach, E. (1995) The politics of the ESL classroom: Issues of power in pedagogical choices. In J. Tollefson (ed.) *Power and Inequality in Language Education* (pp. 9–33). New York: Cambridge University Press.

Bartolome, L. (1998) *The Misteaching of Academic Discourse: The Politics of Language in the Classroom*. Boulder, CO: Westview Press.

Christ, H. (1997) Language policy in teacher education. In D. Corson (ed.) *Encyclopedia of Language and Education* (Vol. 1, pp. 219–227). Dordrecht: Kluwer.

Cochran-Smith, M. (2006) *Policy Practice and Politics in Teacher Education*. Thousand Oaks, CA: Corwin Press.

Combs, M.C., Evans, C., Fletcher, T., Parra, E. and Jiménez, A. (2005) Bilingualism for the children: Implementing a dual-language program in an English-only state. *Educational Policy* 19, 701–728.

Corson, D. (1999) *Language Policy in Schools: A Resource for Teachers and Administrators*. Mahwah, NJ: Lawrence Erlbaum.

Crawford, J. (1997) The campaign against Proposition 227: A post mortem. *Bilingual Research Journal* 21 (1), 1–29, February.

Crawford, J. (2004) *Educating English Learners: Language Diversity in the Classroom* (5th edn). Los Angeles, CA: Bilingual Educational Services.

Datnow, A., Hubbard, L. and Mehan, H. (2002) *Extending Educational Reform: From One School to Many*. London: Routledge.

de Jong, E.J. (2008) Contextualizing policy appropriation: Teachers' perspectives, local responses, and English-only ballot initiatives. *Urban Review* 40, 350–370.

de Jong, E.J., Gort, M. and Cobb, C.D. (2005) Bilingual education within the context of English-only policies: Three distinct responses to Question 2 in Massachusetts. *Educational Policy* 19, 595–620.

Evans, B. and Hornberger, N. (2005) No child left behind: Repealing and unpeeling federal language education. *Policy in the U.S. in Language Policy* 4, 87–106.

Gándara, P., Maxwell-Jolly, J. and Driscoll, A. (2005) *Listening to Teachers of English Language Learners: A Survey of California Teachers' Challenges, Experiences, and Professional Developmental Needs*. Santa Cruz, CA: The Center for the Future of Teaching and Learning.

Garcia, E.E. and Curry-Rodriguez, J.E. (2000) The education of limited English proficient students in California schools: An assessment of the influence of Proposition 227 in selected districts and school. *Bilingual Research Journal* 24, 15–36.

Harper, C. and de Jong, E. (2004) Misconceptions about English-language learners. *Journal of Adolescent & Adult Literacy* 48, 152–162.

Hornberger, N.H. (2002) Multilingual language policies and the continua of biliteracy: An ecological approach. *Language Policy* 1 (1), 27–51.

Johnson, D.C. and Freeman, R. (2010) Appropriating language policy on the local level: Working the spaces for bilingual education. In K. Menken and O. Garcia (eds) *Negotiating Language Policy in School: Educators as Policymakers*. New York: Routledge.

Kloss, H. (1977) *The American Bilingual Tradition*. McHenry, IL: Delta Systems.

Lucas, T. and Grinberg, J. (2008) Responding to the linguistic reality of mainstream teacher: Preparing all teachers to teach English language learners. In M. Cochran-Smith, S. Feiman-Nemser, D.J. McIntyre and K.E. Demers (eds) *Handbook of Research on Teacher Education: Enduring Questions in Changing Contexts* (3rd edn, pp. 606–636). New York: Routledge.

Mahoney, K., MacSwan, J., Thompson, M. and Rolstad, K. (2005) The condition of English language learners in Arizona in 2005. In D.R. Garcia and A. Molnar (eds) *The Condition of PreK-12 Education in Arizona*. Tempe, AZ: AERI.

McCarty, T. (2004) Dangerous difference: A critical–historical analysis of language education policies in the USA. In J.W. Tollefson and A.B.M. Tsui (eds) *Medium of Instruction Policies: Which Agenda? Whose Agenda?* (pp. 71–93). Mahwah, NJ: Lawrence Erlbaum Associates.

Menken, K. (2008) *English Learners Left Behind: Standardized Testing as Language Policy*. Clevedon: Multilingual Matters.

Menken, K. and Garcia, O. (2010) *Negotiating Language Policy in School: Educators as Policymakers*. New York: Routledge.

Milk, R., Mercado, C. and Sapiens, A. (1992) *Rethinking the Education of Teachers of Language Minority Children: Developing Reflective Teachers for Changing Schools*. Washington, DC: National Clearinghouse for Bilingual Education.

National Comprehensive Center for Teacher Quality (2009) Certification and licensure for teachers of English language learners, by state. (na) Washington, DC. Online document, accessed 16 January 2009. http://www.tqsource.org

Ogawa, R., Sandholtz, J.H., Marinez-Flores, M. and Scribner, S. (2003) The substantive and symbolic consequences of a district's standards based curriculum. *American Educational Research Journal* 40, 146–176.

Ricento, T. and Hornberger, N. (1996) Unpeeling the onion: Language planning and policy and the ELT professional. *TESOL Quarterly* 30, 401–427.

Rowan, B. and Miskel, C. (1999) Institutional theory and the study of educational organizations. In J. Murphy and K.S. Louis (eds) *Handbook of Research on Educational Administration* (2nd edn, pp. 359–384). San Francisco: Jossey-Bass.

Schmoker, M. and Marzano, R.J. (1999) Realizing the promise of standards-based education. *Educational Leadership* 56, 17–21.

Shohamy, E. (2006) *Language Policy: Hidden Agendas and New Approaches*. New York: Routledge.

Skutnubb-Kangas, T. (1988) Multilingualism and the education of minority children. In T. Skutnabb-Kangas and J. Cummins (eds) *Minority Education: From Shame to Struggle* (pp. 9–44). Clevedon: Multilingual Matters.

Spolsky, B. (2004) *Language Policy*. Cambridge: Cambridge University Press.

Stritikus, T. and Garcia, E.E. (2003) The role of theory, policy and educational treatment of language minority students: Competitive structures in California. *Educational Policy Analysis Archives* 11, 29–52.

Tsui, A.B.M. and Tollefson, J.W. (2004) The centrality of medium of instruction policies in sociopolitical processes. In J.W. Tollefson and A.B.M. Tsui (eds) *Medium of Instruction Policies: Which Agenda? Whose Agenda?* (pp. 1–18). Mahwah, NJ: Lawrence Erlbaum.

Varghese, M. and Stritikus, T. (2005) Nadie me dijo (Nobody told me): Language policy negotiation and implications for teacher education. *Journal of Teacher Education* 56, 73–87.

Wiley, T. (2002) Revisiting the mother-tongue question in language policy, planning and politics. *International Journal of the Sociology of Language* 154, 83–97.

Wiley, T. (2007) Accessing language rights in education: A brief history of the U.S. context. In O. García and C. Baker (eds) *Bilingual Education: An Introductory Reader* (pp. 89–109). Clevedon: Multilingual Matters.

Wiley, T. (2008) Language policy and teacher education. In S. May and N. Hornberger (eds) *Encyclopedia of Language and Education* (Vol. 1, pp. 229–241). New York: Springer.

Wong-Filmore, L. and Snow, C. (2002) What teachers need to know about language. In C.T. Adger, C.E. Snow and D. Christian (eds) *What Teachers Need to Know about Language* (pp. 7–53). Washington, DC: Center for Applied Linguistics.

Wright, W.E. (2005) The political spectacle of Arizona's Proposition 203. *Educational Policy* 19, 662–700.

Wright, W.E. and Choi, D. (2005) *Voices from the Classroom: A Statewide Survey of 3rd Grade English Language Learner Teachers on the Impact of Language and High-Stakes Testing Policies in Arizona*. Tempe, AZ: Language Policy Research Unit, Education Policy Studies Laboratory, Arizona State University. Online document, accessed 14 February 2005. http://www.asu.edu/educ/epsl/EPRU/documents/EPSL-0512-104-LPRU.pdf

2 Research-based Reform in Arizona: Whose Evidence Counts for Applying the Castañeda Test to Structured English Immersion Models?

Christian Faltis and M. Beatriz Arias

In 2006, the Arizona legislature passed House Bill 2064, and in doing so created the English Language Learner (ELL) Task Force (ARS 15-756.01), whose primary charge was to 'develop and adopt research based models of Structured English Immersion (SEI) programs for use by school districts and charter schools'. House Bill 2064 was in response to Proposition 203, a bill passed by Arizona voters which effectively restricted the use of non-English languages for instruction, and mandated SEI programs to teach English to English learners within a one-year time period.

Background of the ELL Task Force

The ELL Task Force was comprised of nine members: three appointed by the State Superintendent of Instruction, two by the Governor, two by the President of the State Senate and two by the State Speaker of the House. On the nine members, one was a university researcher with a long and distinguished career in bilingual and ESL education; another was a well-respected superintendent with experience in language minority schooling. Two members were former high school ESL teachers who were closely involved in the English for Children campaign to support Proposition 203. The Chair of the

ELL Task Force was an engineer with no classroom or educational research experience. The remaining four Task Force members had minimal or no classroom experience or had they worked in schools with ELLs. The goal of the ELL Task Force was to develop and adopt an SEI program model based on sound educational theory and research. To accomplish this goal, the Task Force relied on a series of experts, consultants, school personnel and university faculty, who had worked in the field of ELL education.

It took the Task Force a year to develop and adopt an SEI program model, which a majority of the Task Force members believed was research-based and supported theoretically. Two Task Force members vehemently objected to the model adopted by the majority, arguing that it was theoretically unsound and pedagogically unsupported by any research conducted in the United States. Three university experts (Christian Faltis, Arizona State University; Richard Ruíz, University of Arizona and Norbert Francis, Northern Arizona University) also testified that the SEI program models were not research based. Notwithstanding these objections and the recommendations of university experts, the Task Force, following the advice of English-only consultants and school authorities, mandated that all English learners scoring below the designation of Intermediate on the State-approved Arizona English Language Learner Assessment (AZELLA) are to be placed in English language development classes (ELD). These students will be placed with other English learners of similar levels of English proficiency for four hours a day for a full year, and up to two years until they score higher than Intermediate on the AZELLA test. The ELD classes are expected to teach English phonology, morphology, syntax and semantics, through activities that engage students in speaking, listening, reading and writing in English. Students are not to be taught academic content; rather the focus is explicitly on development of English language skills only.

How was the ELL Task Force able to create an SEI program for English learners that university experts who gave testimony at Task Force hearings and submitted papers (ELL Summit Participants, 2007; Faltis & Arias, 2007; Krashen *et al.*, this volume) averred to be pedagogically unsound and unsupported in the research? To what standard of admission of expertise are state agencies and school districts held, in making judgments about the relevance of evidence used in decisions about educational plans for English learners?

A large part of the answer stems from the way expertise in judging 'appropriate action' for English learners has developed through court decisions, and subsequently used by state agencies in crafting educational plans. The requirement for determining 'appropriate action' stems from the *Castañeda v. Pickard* (1981) court case, which ruled that academic programs designed to meet the needs of English learners must be determined by qualified experts to be theoretically sound.

The Castañeda Test for Appropriate Action

In 1981, the Fifth Circuit in *Castañeda v. Pickard* established a three-part test for determining whether a school district's program for English learners was 'appropriate action' as required by the Equal Educational Opportunity Act of 1974. The test required that the language program:

(1)   Must be based on (a) sound educational theory that is (b) supported by qualified experts;
(2)   Must be provided with sufficient resources and personnel to be implemented effectively; and
(3)   After a trial period, students must actually be learning English and, to some extent, subject matter content (*Castañeda v. Pickard*, 1981).

This three-pronged test was subsequently adopted by the federal Office of Civil Rights as the primary instrument for enforcing the requirements of *Lau v. Nichols* (1974), a US Supreme Court case, which ruled unanimously that:

There is no equality of treatment merely by providing students with the same facilities, textbooks, teachers, and curriculum; for students who do not understand English are effectively foreclosed from any meaningful education.

Purpose of the Chapter

In this chapter, we focus on the first requirement of *Castañeda v. Pickard* only, that programs for English learners must be based on educational theory and research recognized as sound by qualified experts. We review major court cases that have interpreted the *Castañeda* case to understand how, over time, judges have ruled on who is qualified to be an expert to judge that educational theory pertaining the education of English learners. We apply these rulings, which eventually defer to state agencies and school districts to determine what counts as educational theory and research, to how the Arizona ELL Task Force was able to create and develop SEI program models; models that teachers, university experts and two Task Force members deemed pedagogically unsound and unsupported in the academic literature by leading experts in the field of English learner education. In particular, we argue that the ELL Task Force used school district personnel and anti-bilingual education consultants to serve as expert witnesses to argue for a particular kind of SEI model: one that contradicts 'sound educational theory that is supported by qualified experts' with respect to the following aspects: (1) how SEI program models differ from immersion education used in Canada; (2) how long it takes to learn a second language in school settings; (3) the role of students' first language for learning in a second language; and (4) the effects of segregation of English learners from English speakers on language learning and successful schooling.

How was the ELL Task Force able to rely on expertise that came from people who were not experts? We begin by examining how expertise, in decisions about educational plans, has been interpreted legally. It is the legal interpretation, as it has developed over time, which has given the green light to administrative bodies such as the ELL Task Force to rely on people whose expertise fall well below what we believe is needed to make important decisions about the education of English learners. In the final section of the chapter, we argue for a standard of admission of expertise that approaches or equals that of *Daubert v. Merrill Dow Pharmaceutical* (1993), and that follows the guidelines used in the Federal Rules of Evidence (FRE, 2009). Together, *Daubert* and the FRE require that information provided in support or against a particular educational plan comes from people with the knowledge, skill, education, and experience to accurately distinguish theoretically sound pedagogy and research from politically based reports. Without such a high standard for admission of expertise, individuals who are politically motivated, but without advanced preparation in relevant research, will continue to influence decisions that are not based on what relevant research says about what works best with English learners. When this occurs, there is good reason to argue that the first prong of *Castañeda* test has not been met.

Test Cases and *Castañeda*: Who Counts as an Expert?

We start out by tracing the evolution of how the courts have considered who counts as experts in determining the soundness or unsoundness of a particular educational program for English learners. In the beginning, *Castañeda* required educational programs for English learners to be supported by qualified experts, without defining who qualifies as an expert. Over time, the courts have deferred to school district personnel and consultants working for the school districts, allowing them to be considered as experts on educational theory related to the education of English learners. We now turn to a summary of how this situation came about.

After the *Castañeda* ruling in 1981, the first issue tackled by the courts was how many experts it takes to make a strong argument for or against theoretical soundness. In *U.S. v Texas* (1982), argued in the Fifth Circuit Court, the US government presented a number of experts on English-only approaches to educating English learner to argue that the Texas bilingual program for English learners was pedagogically unsound. The school district put on only one witness, representing the school district, who did not provide any evidence of expertise in the field of bilingual education (Haas, 2005). The court concluded that the school district's bilingual program was not appropriate for remedying the needs of the English learners it served, basing it ruling on the sheer number of experts put on by the plaintiff. The Fifth Circuit did not reveal the standard of proof they used to determine that the plaintiffs provided sufficient evidence using educational theory that the school district's pedagogical approach was unsound (Haas, 2005). An implication of this case, therefore, is that it takes more than one witness to build a case based on expertise about the soundness of a program.

The next major case to rule on the issue of expertise in the matter of determining the soundness of an educational plan for English learners was decided in *Gomez v. Illinois State Board of Education* (1987). In this case, the Seventh Circuit Court decided that school district personnel possess expertise in educational theory and practice. They based their ruling on the argument that school districts are administrative agencies, which under the Administrative Procedures Act (1949), are presumed to possess expertise in their field and to be acting within the scope of their authority (Haas, 2005). This case opened the door for school district personnel and their consultants to act as expert witnesses for determining the soundness of an educational program for English learners, effectively deferring to school district as authorities and experts on what works best for English learners.

This deference to the school districts as authorities and experts in pedagogy for English learners was solidified in two cases, *Teresa P. v. Berkeley Unified School District* (1989) and *Valeria G. v. Wilson* (1998, 2002). These two cases found that one-year, English immersion programs were pedagogically sound under the *Castañeda* test, or at least as sound as the bilingual programs advocated by the plaintiffs. Both cases relied on the *Gomez* case, giving authority to school district staff to act as expert witnesses, whose testimony was based on observations and personal knowledge of the schools in question. In *Teresa P. v. Berkeley Unified School District* (1989), the court ruled that plaintiffs did not convincingly show that the Berkeley Unified School District, which used an English-only immersion approach to teaching English learners, was not pedagogically unsound. The court based its ruling on the testimonies of school district's witnesses, teachers and administrators, who argued that monolingual English teachers were capable of teaching

English learners successfully. The judge in this case – who relied heavily on teachers and administrators as 'experts' in pedagogy – considered less valuable research-based conclusions that bilingual teachers were essential for providing English learners access to academic content, than testimony made by classroom teachers and school administrators.

Valeria G. v. Wilson (1998, 2002) was the first case tried after the implementation of Proposition 227, which banned bilingual education in California and required English learners to be taught English in English. In this case, which eventually made it to the Ninth Circuit Court in 2002, the plaintiffs argued that research and sound educational theory for teaching English to English learners demonstrated through research, (mainly meta-analyses) that bilingual education was pedagogically more effective than English immersion. Meta-analysis enables researchers to express an effect size of a single study in terms of a single number, which when calculated over a number of studies produces a summary effect size. Researchers can then come to conclusions about the relative effectiveness of one educational program over another. The plaintiffs also argued that using the students' first language was effective for literacy development and for providing access to academic content while students were learning English. The plaintiffs presented experts who testified that the school plan failed the *Castañeda* test requiring theoretically sound research-based programs for English learners.

To counter the plaintiffs' arguments, the defendants relied on their own experts, who presented research evidence from several countries, mainly Canada, to argue that immersion education was effective for learning a second language and for learning academic content. This was the first time that defendants drew on research from Canadian immersion programs to argue the soundness of English immersion programs. Below, we compare Canadian immersion programs with SEI programs used in Arizona. The defendants were able to convince the judge that since immersion had been successful in Canada, their plan for teaching English was supported by research. Accordingly, the judge ruled that as long as defendants can point to evidence that somewhere in the world immersion education has been successful, this would suffice as meeting the first test in *Castañeda*. This means that defendants need not be experts themselves, but rather they can refer to any sound educational program, which appears similar to theirs, and use this as expert evidence. This places a nearly insurmountable burden on plaintiffs, because it yields expertise to school authorities who are not experts themselves, allowing them to rely on research conducted in entirely different contexts from the educational realities of English learners in the United States.

Are School Authorities and Teachers Reasonable Experts?

Since *Castañeda*, the courts have slowly, but surely deferred to school districts as experts in determining appropriate action for English learners (Haas & Gort, 2009). This is remarkable because the very reason that judges in the *Castañeda* case created the three-prong test for appropriate actions was due to the Supreme Court decision in *Lau v. Nichols*, which noted that school districts have created educational programs for English learners that are both unsound and ineffective. As a result of the *Lau* decision, the government created the *Lau* Remedies and passed the Title VII, also known as the Bilingual Education Act. These two actions came about because school districts were not meeting the needs of English learners by merely immersing them in English, without support in their first language. As Haas points out, 'It appears likely that if there were to be any legal presumption for most, if not all, school districts, it would be that they do *not* (emphasis in original) employ sound education theory in devising their programs for second language assistance' (Haas, 2005: 379). In other words, school districts have a long history of providing poorly designed programs for English learners; to believe that they are now experts in designing new ones based on Canadian programs or the anecdotal observations of administrators and teachers is unjustifiable. If the Administrative Procedures Act were in fact truly carried out in deferring to school districts as experts, school districts would need to spell out their assumptions, explain inconsistencies, disclose methodologies, present an extensive review of the literature, and provide overwhelming support for their conclusions (Jasanoff, 1997; Rodgers, 1979). What has happened instead is that expertise in cases and actions involving school districts (and most recently, the ELL Task Force) has been reduced to opinions of individuals who hold certain perspectives about the role of non-English languages in learning English, with a clear disregard for the findings based on research and sound theoretical principals about how children and adolescents learn a second language in school.

The ELL Task Force's Interpretation of the Research

In the following sections, we present four areas of research that the Arizona ELL Task Force of English chose to ignore in creating and developing their version of SEI English learners in Arizona. The four areas are: (1) the comparison between the Canadian immersion programs and SEI programs, (2) the amount of time it takes to learn English, (3) the role of students' first language in learning a second language and (4) issues of segregation of English learners relating to language learning and school success.

Canadian immersion programs and SEI programs: A comparison

In *Valeria G.*, the court deferred to the authority of school district personnel to act as experts on what works with English learners. The school district argued that immersion education in Canada had been and continues to be a sound program for teaching a second language and teaching in a second language. If it worked successfully in Canada, and the program goals and designs for English immersion are the same, then the English immersion program promoted by the school district must also be pedagogically sound. Moreover, school district personnel testified that in their 'expert' opinions, English learners were making progress in English immersion classes.

Let us take a few moments to examine the similarities and differences between Canadian immersion programs and the newly mandated SEI programs in Arizona. This is important because, as in the *Valeria G.* case, school authorities in Arizona argue that SEI will be successful because French immersion programs in Canada have been successful. We argue that the logic connecting Canadian immersion successes to SEI fundamentally flawed because the goals and designs differ substantially between the two programs.

In Table 2.1, we compare Canadian Immersion programs with SEI programs in Arizona (adapted from Hernández-Chávez, 1984). In Canadian immersion programs, students are expected to become highly bilingual and biliterate; their first language is assessed and valued, and their primary sociocultural identities are recognized and developed (Genesee & Gándara, 1999). Conversely, in SEI programs, students' first language is devalued; language proficiency and academic achievement is assessed in English only; and US culture is stressed. Major differences also exist in program design between Canadian immersion and SEI. In Canadian immersion programs, all teachers are fully bilingual and biliterate in the two languages of the program. Instruction in the second language lasts up to six years, and is gradually decreased to about 40% of the students' daily schedule. Biliteracy is promoted in the Canadian immersion programs (Genesee & Gándara, 1999; Lazaruk, 2007) while only English literacy is developed in SEI. Clearly, Canadian immersion programs have worked because they are based on considerably different goals, and they are designed for different purposes than those embedded in SEI programs.

A key point to stress here is that Canadian immersion programs keep students in second language classes for an average of six years, which is in line with established research on how long it takes to become sufficiently proficient

Table 2.1 Comparison of Canadian immersion and Arizona SEI programs

	Canadian immersion programs	Arizona's SEI programs
Program goals	Enrichment bilingualism and biliteracy; L1 fully developed; L2 developed to a high degree of proficiency. Language proficiency and academic achievement assessed in multiple ways in both L1 and L2. Home culture is recognized and nurtured; French cultural knowledge and practices added for enrichment.	Displacement bilingualism and no L1 literacy; development of academic language and literacy in English; minimal use of L1 for noninstructional purposes. Language proficiency (single measure) assessed for exit purposes; academic achievement assessed n English only. US cultural identities stressed; 'other' cultures to be maintained by the home.
Program design	Instruction begins with L2; L1 is used by students initially; teachers are fully bilingual and biliterate in English and French. Instruction in French as L2 is decreased to about 40% and typically lasts for six years of schooling. L2 methodology aims to make content comprehensible and with opportunities for interaction in the L2, coupled with reading and writing in both languages.	Program begins with English only; teachers are mainly English speakers; students grouped by proficiency levels. Instruction about English for 4 h/day for one year or more; students scoring higher than intermediate are placed in mainstream classes. Instruction about English for 4 h/day for one year or more; students scoring higher than intermediate are placed in mainstream classes. L2 methodology based on comprehensible input and interaction about English phonology, vocabulary, grammar and semantics; students do not study academic content.
Program results	Students are successful academically and fully bilingual in oral and written French and English; high graduation rates.	Students are linguistically and socially isolated for most of the day for oneyear or more; low graduation rates.

Source: Adapted from Hernández-Chávez (1984)

in a second language to be able to participate in and benefit from academic instruction in that language (see below). SEI programs in Arizona are mandated for one year, with the possibility of staying in the program two years, well short of the time needed to be successful in an all-English mainstream classroom. When ELL Task Force testimonies refer to Canadian immersion programs, they gloss over the details of program goals and design: particularly, how long it takes to gain the kinds of proficiency in a second language needed to be successful in classrooms where that language is used for instruction, with little or no accommodations for second language learners.

Amount of time to become proficient in a second language

Supporters of the ELL Task Force SEI models have repeatedly claimed that English learners can become proficient in English within a year, although they admit that some students may take up to two years to reach a level of proficiency that ensures their success in mainstream classes. What does the research say about how long it takes to become proficient?

Canadian studies have shown it takes anywhere from four to seven years of participation in a French immersion program to become academically proficient in French (Genesee, 1987). In US settings, a number of research studies have addressed how long it takes English learners to learn enough English to participate meaningfully in class and to reach parity with English-proficient peers. Controlling for length-of-residence in an English-speaking environment, Cummins (1981) found that older English learners (aged 12–15) required two to three years to approach reasonable fluency in English, but as long as five years to approach grade level on academic measures. Collier (1987) researched the time it takes English learners to learn English to approach grade level academically. She found that it took 8–11 year-old English learners from middle class backgrounds two to five years to reach the 50th percentile on national norms on a standardized achievement test. Younger English learners were one to three years behind the 8–11 year olds, and older English learners required six to eight years to reach grade level in academic achievement. Hakuta *et al.* (2000) found that it took two to five years to develop communicative proficiency in English, while academic English proficiency took four to seven years to develop. MacSwan and Pray (2005) found that English learners in Arizona needed an average of 3.31 years to reach reasonable fluency levels of proficiency in English. Less than 3% of the English learners they studied attained reasonably fluency in one year. After two years in SEI classrooms, only slightly over 20% reached parity with native English-speaking students. The rest took from three to six years.

These studies show conclusively that, although a few English learners can develop conversational English proficiency in a shorter period, the overwhelming majority of English learners require anywhere from three to seven years to reach academic English proficiency, which involved extensive use and interpretation of text, and ways of using oral and written language to acquire new content knowledge. This is especially the case for adolescent English learners, who upon arrival to US schools may have significant gaps in their academic knowledge and may not be strong readers and writers in their primary language. The ELL Task Force chose to ignore this research. The new report on *Improving Educational Outcomes for English Language Learners: Recommendations for the Reauthorization of the Elementary and Secondary Education Act*, states 'the recommended target-goal timeframe to move most students from the lowest levels of language proficiency to the state defined English proficient level ... is *four to five full academic years*' (emphasis in original) (Working Group, 2010: 7).

The role of the students' first language in learning English

One of the most robust and consistent findings in the research on teaching English learners is that students who learn to read and write well in their first language while they are learning English, do as well as or significantly better than English learners who are taught literacy in English only (August & Shanahan, 2006; Genesee *et al.*, 2006; Willig, 1985). The reason we mention these findings is to show the importance of having bilingual teachers to support the literacy development of English learners. In a state like Arizona, where Spanish speakers are the largest and fastest-growing language minority community, teachers who can support literacy development in Spanish while the students are learning English are invaluable. Moreover, bilingual teachers can communicate with parents and family members, inviting them to participate more fully in their children's schooling experiences. There is nothing in the Arizona statues that prohibits using a language other than English to communicate with parents or to advocate for learning to read in Spanish. In fact, Arizona Revise Statute 15-751 defined SEI as 'an English language acquisition process for young children in which *nearly all classroom instruction is in English* (emphasis added) but with the curriculum and presentation designed for children who are learning the language' and '*teachers may use a minimal amount of the child's native language when necessary*' (emphasis added).

The most recent research to report on the value of teaching literacy in the student's first language was conducted by August and Shanahan (2006) for the National Literacy Panel. Their findings led the unequivocal conclusion that students do better in English literacy when they have first developed literacy in their home language. Prior to the National Literacy Panel study, a number of comprehensive studies, relying on meta-analysis research to determine how large of an advantage one educational program has over another; in this case, the extent to which bilingual programs compare with English-only programs for developing literacy, learning English and promoting academic achievement. Meta-analyses conducted by Willig (1985), Greene (1997), Slavin and Cheung (2005) and Rolstad *et al.* (2005) found that students in programs who developed literacy in their home language outperformed students in programs where literacy was developed in English only. The lone study to favor English-only programs was conducted by Rossell and Baker (1996). This was a narrative review (Krashen & McField, 2005) that relies on voting for or against the results of the studies included in the review. Narrative reviews are considered to be the least rigorous form of analysis, because people who conduct them make choices about which studies to include or exclude without conforming to scientific research standards, which call for revealing information about the parameters of the studies included.

Equity issues and the segregation of English learners

When English learners are placed in SEI classes for four hours a day for a year to learn about English, they will fall behind in their core academic classes. This is especially critical for older English learners who must take and pass the Arizona Instrument to Measure Standards (AIMS) writing and content-based exam in order to graduate from high school. While English learners are in SEI classes for four hours per day learning about English, they are missing out on the core academic areas of math, science and social studies. No research or pedagogical theory related to second language acquisition in US settings recommends the segregation of English learners for the majority of the school day into English language classes, where they are kept from participating in and benefiting from core content instruction, modified to ensure their involvement in learning. On the contrary, research by Gifford and Valdés (2006), Valdés (1998) and Valenzuela (1999) has shown that segregating English learners from English speakers for the major part of the school day creates *ESL ghettos*, unsound learning environments where English learners languish and fall further and further behind in school. Not only are English learners excluded from interaction with English speakers when they are placed in classroom with only other English learners, they are segregated for lunch, recess and extracurricular activities.

To further exacerbate the situation of segregation, the SEI programs endorsed by English-only Task Force consultants and school authorities group English learners by proficiency level, so that all English learners at an Emergent level are placed with others at the same level; English learners at the Basic level are placed with others at the same Basic level. English learners who are placed for four hours with others who are at their level of English proficiency, on a long-term basis, are denied opportunities to interact with and learn from more proficient others. One of the Task Force consultants who came up with the grouping arrangements argued that English learners need to be together with students of their same proficiency level, so they can all be taught about English using the same English language standards according to their grade level, a position that contradicts what that same consultant has espoused in an earlier work. Kevin Clark (1999), the English-only 'expert' consultant hired by the Task Force, reported that learning about English for 50 min a day, plus access to modified core content through sheltered content teaching coupled with the *structured mixing* with English speakers led to significant development of English proficiency in five California schools he had visited. Clark's idea of *structured mixing* was based on SLA theory and research, which asserts that English learners show the greatest progress when they are placed into situations where they have to use their developing oral and written English to communicate with more proficient peers and others who are English speakers (see Long & Adamson, this volume). Interestingly, Clark did not refer to this study in his presentations to the ELL Task Force.

Through interaction with English speakers, English learners are obliged to produce language that increasingly approximates English, because English speakers often ask for clarification, check for understanding and rephrase language to confirm understanding. This kind of negotiated interaction pushes English learners to test hypotheses about language and to pay attention to language structure and language meanings. When English learners are provided these rich opportunities for negotiating meaning and using language for communicating with others about school topics and academic content, oral and written English proficiency increases, along with academic learning (Faltis, 2006).

Who the Task Force Listened to

The majority of ELL Task Force members ignored the widely accepted research on sound pedagogy for English learners. These same Task Force members ignored experts with PhDs and extensive experience in language education who presented research to them in person and in written texts. They refused to accept the objections of the two Task Force members with extensive expertise in language education. Lastly, testimonies from ESL specialists from schools throughout the state raised concerns about a one-size-fits-all program and the segregation of English learner for the majority of a school day; these concerns also fell on deaf ears.

Instead, in the summer of 2008, they approved SEI program models based on the opinions of a few teachers, two consultants, and one university person, all of whom were adamantly opposed to any theoretical principles or research that fell outside their own political favoritism toward English-only policies and practices. The SEI experts the majority of the Task Force relied on were Mr Kevin Clark, Dr Rosalie Porter and Dr Ken Noonan, along with several English-only classroom teachers and principals who testified about their experiences teaching English learners. Mr Kevin Clark, who has his own school consultancy business and has worked for the Institute for Research in English and Academic Development (READ), was the main source of expertise for creating and developing the 4-h SEI program models. Dr Rosalie Porter, who works for the READ Institute, a conservative think tank that produces reports touting the effectiveness of English immersion and works for English-only causes nationwide, argued that SEI is the only viable program for English learners, and cautioned the Task Force to be wary of university experts, because they only support bilingual education. Dr Ken Noonan is the former superintendent of Oceanside School District in California and an advocate of English-only immersion. He opined that it only takes a year of good English language development for English learners to be ready for mainstream classrooms.

None of these individuals or the teachers who testified before the ELL Task Force brought up any research to support the ELL programs that Mr Clark eventually created and developed. Instead they mentioned that immersion education worked in many countries, and in their experience had also worked in schools in California and Massachusetts, the two other states with bans on bilingual education. Mr Clark argued that 'SEI is easy to implement' and that 'all students need is lots of work on English morphology, spelling, word lists and grammar practice' (personal notes from ELL Task Force meeting, March 14, 2007). Their 'expertise' sufficed as evidence that SEI programs were theoretically sound and research-based, notwithstanding numerous objections by two members of the ELL Task Force and members of the audience in attendance at Task Force monthly meetings.

What Can be Done to Separate English-only Political Advocacy from Rigorous, Reliable Research and Practice?

There is much to be learned from the legal history involving experts in the education of English learners. From *U.S. v. Texas* to *Valeria G.*, the courts have been soft on deciding who is an expert and therefore, whose expertise counts in the decisions about what works well for English learners. By deferring to school district authorities as experts in educational practices, when school districts have a general history of poorly serving language minority students, administrative bodies, such as the ELL Task Force, have been able to implement educational plans using marginal, discredited and non-peer-reviewed research reports. Moreover, in the case of the ELL Task Force, they have issued a statement that the SEI Models are sound and supported by research, and therefore, are allowed under *Castañeda* (Arizona Department of Education, Frequently Asked Questions, 2008).

What can advocates for English learners do to prevent others from using speculative opinions to further their political views about English-only education? An approach we find appealing is to insist on a standard of expertise for experts who contribute opinions about the pedagogical soundness and research base of educational plans for English learners. For this, following Haas (2005) and Haas and Gort (2009), we recommend the standards set forth in *Daubert v. Merrill Dow Pharmaceutical* (1993), which used the Federal Rules of Evidence (FRE) to determine the admissibility of research-based testimony. The crux of *Daubert* was the credibility of the experts representing each side. Using the FRE, the judge ruled that the substance of an expert must be based on scientific knowledge that assists the court to determine a fact at issue (*Daubert*, 509 U.S. at 592). This requirement, called the *Daubert* test, was developed as a way to ensure 'that any and all scientific testimony or evidence admitted is not only relevant, but reliable' (*Daubert*, 509 U.S. at 589, in Haas, 2005: 382).

To help evaluate the reliability of theory or research methods, the judge recommended a thorough examination of issues such as: (1) whether the research has been published in a peer-reviewed journal; (2) the degree to which the theory or research has been tested; and (3) the level of acceptance within the intellectual research community (see also Jasanoff, 1997). These requirements are similar to those required by the Administrative Procedures Act. The courts in *Daubert* recognized that all experts and their opinions are not equal. Moreover, the courts understood that experts differ in their opinions. What they would not accept, however, is that marginalized, unsubstantiated research reports be accepted as theoretically sound just because an 'expert' declares them so.

If the ELL Task Force were held to the FRE and *Daubert*, there is little doubt that the 'expertise' of Mr Kevin Clark would not have been admissible. His opinions about the soundness of SEI would be deemed unscientific, unreliable and marginal within the larger English learner research community. Neither Dr Porter nor Dr Noonan has ever conducted reliable research on the effectiveness of SEI, and neither has ever published research on SEI or could point to research on SEI in a peer-reviewed journal. Teachers' and ESL teachers' opinions would be noted, but it would be the research-base that would carry the greatest weight. What Clark and his followers presented to the ELL Task Force was opinion based on a political perspective about how to educate English learners in English. This opinion does not stack up the over-whelming evidence by experts, who represent a larger body of knowledge, that the SEI program models adapted the ELL Task Force are pedagogically unsound and without a reliable research base. Under both the Administrative Procedures Act and the *Daubert* test, the experts on both sides of the argu-ment would have been required to show that they possessed a wide range of research experience, and that the information they presented must be reliable and meet criteria for acceptable research practices found in the larger research community. Were this the case, it is likely that English learners in Arizona would not be segregated from English learners by proficiency level to learn about English; nor would they be excluded from learning academic content for a year or more. In concert with Haas and Gort (2009: 116), now is time 'to challenge the application of these English-only education requirements as being so ineffective' that they violate the sound theory requirement of *Castañeda*. However, this time we need to be better prepared to argue that the scientific basis for English-only programs like the one implemented in Arizona must be subjected to the same kind of critical assessment done in other areas.

References

Administrative Procedures Act (1949) Title 5, U.S. Code.
Arizona Department of Education (2008) Structured English immersion frequently asked questions, online document, accessed 25 October 2008. http://ade.state.az.us/oelas/sei/SEIModelsFAQ.doc
Arizona Revised Statute 15-751, online document, accessed 25 October 2008. http://www.azleg.state.az.us/FormatDocument.asp?inDoc=/ars/15/00751.htm&Title=15&DocType=ARS
Arizona Revised Statute 15-756.01, online document, accessed 25 October 2008. http://www.azleg.state.az.us/FormatDocument.asp?inDoc=/ars/15/00756-01.htm&Title=15&DocType=ARS
August, D. and Shanahan, T. (eds) (2006) *Developing Literacy in Second-Language Learners: Report of the National Literacy Panel on Language-Minority Children and Youth*. Mahwah, NJ: Lawrence Erlbaum.
Castañeda v. Pickard (1981) 648 F.2d 989 Fifth Circuit Court.
Clark, K. (1999) *From Primary Language Instruction to English Immersion: How Five California Districts Made the Switch*. Washington, DC: READ (Institute for Research in English Acquisition and Development).
Collier, V. (1987) Age and rate of acquisition of second language for academic purposes. *TESOL Quarterly* 21, 10–34.

Cummins, J. (1981) Age on arrival and immigrant second language learning in Canada: A reassessment. *Applied Linguistics* 11, 132–149.

Daubert v. Merrill Dow Pharmaceutical (1993) 509 U.S. 579, Supreme Court.

ELL Summit Participants (2007) *Educating Arizona's English Language Learners.* Prepared by Alpha School Consortium.

Faltis, C. (2006) *Teaching English Language Learners in Elementary School Communities: A Joinfostering Approach* (4th edn). New York: Merrill/Prentice-Hall.

Faltis, C. and Arias, B. (2007) English language learners task force: A response to the proposed structured English immersion models. Submitted to the ELL Task Force Hearings, Phoenix, AZ, August 2.

Federal Rules of Evidence (2009) Rule 702. Testimony by experts.

Genesee, F. (1987) *Learning through Two Languages: Studies of Immersion and Bilingual Education.* Cambridge, MA: Newbury House.

Genesee, F. and Gándara, P. (1999) Bilingual education programs: A cross-national perspective. *Journal of Social Issues* 55, 665–685.

Genesee, F., Lindholm-Leary, K., Saunders, W. and Christian, D. (2006) *Educating English Language Learners: A Synthesis of Research Evidence.* New York: Cambridge University Press.

Gifford, B. and Valdés, G. (2006) The linguistic isolation of Hispanic students in California's public schools: The challenge of reintegration. *Yearbook of the National Society for the Study of Education* 105, 125–154.

Gomez v. Illinois State Board of Education (1987) 811 F.2d 1030, Seventh Circuit Court.

Greene, J. (1997) *A Meta-Analysis of the Effectiveness of Bilingual Education.* Austin, TX: Tomás Rivera Center.

Haas, E. (2005) The Equal Educational Opportunity Act 30 years later: Time to revisit 'appropriate action' for assisting English language learners. *Journal of Law and Education* 34, 361–387.

Haas, E. and Gort, M. (2009) Demanding more: Legal standards and best practices for English language learners. *Bilingual Research Journal* 32, 115–135.

Hakuta, K., Butler, Y. and Witt, D. (2000) How long does it take English learners to attain proficiency? University of California Linguistic Minority Research Institute Policy Report 2000-1.

Hernández-Chávez, E. (1984) The inadequacy of English immersion education as an educational approach for language minority students in the United States. In California State Department of Education (ed.) *Studies on Immersion Education* (pp. 144–183). Sacramento, CA: California State Department of Education.

Jasanoff, S. (1997) *Science at the Bar.* Cambridge, MA: Harvard University Press.

Krashen, S. and McField, G. (2005) What works? Reviewing the latest evidence on bilingual education. *Language Learner* 1, 7–10, 34.

Lau v. Nichols (1974) 414 U.S. 563, Supreme Court.

Lazaruk, W.A. (2007) Linguistic, academic, and cognitive benefits of French immersion. *The Canadian Modern Language Review* 63, 605–627.

MacSwan, J. and Pray, L. (2005) Learning English bilingually: Age of onset of exposure and rate of acquisition among English language learners in a bilingual education program. *Bilingual Research Journal* 29, 653–675.

Rodgers, W.H. Jr. (1979) A hard look at Vermont Yankee: Environmental law under close scrutiny. *Georgetown Law Journal* 67, 699–716.

Rolstad, K., Mahoney, K. and Glass, G. (2005) The big picture: A meta-analysis of program effectiveness research on English language learners. *Educational Policy* 19, 572–594.

Rossell, C. and Baker, K. (1996) The educational effectiveness of bilingual education: *Research in the Teaching of English* 30, 7–69.

Slavin, R. and Cheung, A. (2005) A synthesis of research on language reading instruction for English language learners. *Review of Educational Research* 75, 247–284.

Teresa P. v. Berkeley Unified School District (1989) 724 F, Supp. 698 N. D. California.

U.S. v. Texas (1982) 680 F.2d 356.

Valdés, G. (1998) The world outside and inside schools: Language and immigrant children. *Educational Researcher* 27, 4–18.

Valenzuela, A. (1999) *Subtractive Schooling: U.S. Mexican Youth and the Politics of Caring.* Albany, NY: State University of New York Press.

Valeria G. v. Wilson (1998, 2002) 12 F, Supp. 2d. 1007 N.D. California, 1998, affirmed 2002, 307 F.3d 1036, Ninth Circuit Court.

Willig, A. (1985) A meta-analysis of some selected studies on the effectiveness of bilingual education. *Review of Educational Research* 55, 269–318.

Working Group on ELL Policy (March 26, 2010) *Improving Educational Outcomes for English Language Learners: Recommendations for the Reauthorization of the Elementary and Secondary Education Act.* Stanford, CA: Stanford University School of Education.

3 SLA Research and Arizona's Structured English Immersion Policies

Michael H. Long and H.D. Adamson

In 2000, Arizona voters passed Proposition 203, amending the Arizona State Constitution to require that English language learners (ELLs) be taught only in English without using their native language and also that in most cases they be allowed to take English as a second language courses for only one year before being enrolled in all mainstream classes [Arizona Revised Statutes, Title 15 (Education), § 3.1 (English Language Education for Children in Public Schools), 751-756.01]. The rules for implementing this law, which are laid down by the Arizona Department of Education, have changed over the years, and continue to change. At first, individual school districts were given considerable freedom regarding how to teach ELL students during the one-year period before mainstreaming, as long as they did not use bilingual education, but beginning in the 2008–2009 school year, the Department has required all districts to abide by a set of uniform guidelines developed by the English Language Learners Task Force (Arizona Revised Statutes (2009). Title15-756.01). As described in Chapter 4 of this book, these guidelines mandate that ELLs receive four hours of ESL instruction per day at the elementary and secondary level. The Department of Education also mandates the teaching approach that will be used, which it calls 'Structured English Immersion' (SEI). This turns out to be traditional ESL instruction, using a structural syllabus to focus on grammar and vocabulary, without attention to the academic content for which students will be held responsible. We believe that this new program, with its use of a synthetic linguistic syllabus, its lack of instruction in content areas, and the lack of opportunity it provides for students to acquire the specialized varieties of English they need for study in academic contexts, conflicts sharply with what we know about how school-age ELL students learn second languages and academic subject matter.

It is expected that after one year, students will test out of the SEI program on the basis of an English proficiency test and be mainstreamed. If they do not test out, they will continue in the same program, but the school will no longer receive additional funds for them. There is no flexibility about gradually mainstreaming students or providing individualized programs of ESL and mainstream courses according to individual students' abilities and needs. In practical terms, this will be a disaster because the ELLs have to take the same standardized tests in science, social studies, math and so on, as the native English speakers [Arizona Revised Statutes (2009). Title15-756.01], but they will not be taught those subjects (Arizona Department of Education, 2009). This is a practice that will effectively further undermine public education. It also wastes a valuable national resource, knowledge of another language and culture that immigrants offer and on which state and federal governments subsequently have to spend massive amounts of money in an often unsuccessful attempt to replenish in its adult population, often with poor results, given that adults are poorer language learners than children (Hyltenstam & Abrahamsson, 2003).

We begin our discussion by defining and distinguishing two key terms that have been used in the debate on ESL teaching in Arizona and elsewhere in the United States: language submersion programs and language immersion programs.

Submersion, Immersion and 'Structured English Immersion'

Submersion involves placing immigrant children with mother tongues other than English in mainstream classes with native speakers of English without providing any kind of special help. Submersion does not merit the label 'program', in other words, since no program is provided. This approach, often referred to as 'sink or swim', is common around the world, but was ruled illegal by the United States Supreme Court in the 1974 *Lau v. Nichols* decision, when it declared that the result was that 'students who do not understand English are effectively foreclosed from any meaningful education' (quoted in Stein, 1986: 37). If teachers use materials designed for native speakers and speak appropriately for them, ELLs are in danger of not understanding and being left behind. Conversely, if they adapt their language to the ELLs, the native English speakers suffer, as their progress is slowed down.

Immersion programs also teach ELL students using little or none of the native language, but with a crucial difference: *all* students in a class are non-native speakers and at approximately the same English proficiency level. As a result, teachers can employ a variety of techniques, such as demonstrations and visual aids of many kinds, to make sure their students understand the material, and do so without wasting anyone's time. Even more important, because all students in immersion classrooms are non-native speakers and form a relatively homogeneous group, teachers may choose written texts matched to their reading ability and adjust their classroom speech appropriately. They can do this without the risk of diluting syllabus content, as Mackay (1986, 1993) found may happen when teachers achieve comprehensibility by simplifying their speech and restricting the range of productive (speaking and writing) tasks demanded from students.

There are several different types of immersion programs (for discussion, see Brisk, 1998; Cummins, 2009; Faltis & Hudelson, 1998; Genesee *et al.*, 1989), and even similar types may be delivered differentially, on a partial or full-time basis, and starting with children of different ages. One type often described in the literature is 'bilingual structured immersion', used in the Protestant School System of Montreal to teach French to native English speakers. In this program, English-speaking students are separated from native French-speaking students and receive their regular education almost completely in French, taught by bilingual teachers, from kindergarten until third grade. When necessary, teachers can use English for short explanations, and students are allowed to answer questions in English. Beginning in Grade 3, English classes are introduced: 40% in Grade 3, 60% in Grades 4–6 and 80% through high school. Teachers present understandable and interesting input in French, supported by plenty of context. Typical activities include reading stories that are acted out or well-illustrated, role-playing with plenty of props, and field trips. The curriculum covers some of the same academic material studied in the regular French schools; however, French grammar is not emphasized and accuracy is not insisted on at first (Schauber, 1995). By age 18, the French listening and reading abilities of high school graduates emerging from programs like this across Canada are often on par with those of monolingual French age-peers, although many students still exhibit basic errors in speaking and writing (Swain, 1991).

Arizona's SEI program is very different from the successful Canadian immersion model. In Arizona SEI teachers do not have to be bilingual; they and the students are discouraged from using the native language under any circumstances; and the main focus is on the language as object, not medium, of communication, as in true immersion programs.

In theory, SEI emphasizes the importance of providing input from native English-speaking children and of learning content material, as described in the following passage from the book *Structured English Immersion: A Step-by-Step Guide for K–6 Teachers and Administrators*, written by Johanna J. Haver:

> Structured English immersion ... is based on the theory that children learn a second language best when they are integrated with other children who speak that language with native-speaker ability. The beginning English language learners are separated initially – for as short a time as possible – from the other children, to receive English and content-area instruction systematically in a non-threatening setting. However, even at that beginning stage, these children participate in mainstream classes in which language is not necessary for success: hands-on science, music, art, and physical education, for instance. (Haver, 2003: 1)

Haver also notes, 'SEI blends English grammar and vocabulary instruction with the teaching of content ...' (Haver, 2003: xv).

Because Haver was one of the developers of the Arizona Department of Education's SEI guidelines (available from the website of the Arizona Department of Education, http://www.ade.state.az.us/oelas), they might be expected to exemplify, at least, the principles of native-speaker peer input and content-based instruction, but they do not. As mentioned, under the guidelines, ELL students are separated from their native English-speaking peers for four hours a day, and in practice, because students do not move from class to class in elementary schools, but, rather, have one teacher for the entire day, ELLs and native English speakers in many schools will be separated for the entire day. In such cases, immigrant students will be exposed to insufficient native speaker input, most of it the notoriously impoverished kind offered by a diet of ESL teacher speech, and probably make few English-speaking friends, who could otherwise provide much of what is needed outside the classroom. The segregation they experience in school will have negative linguistic and cultural consequences – consequences that, paradoxically, will work against legislators' clearly assimilationist goals for these students. Furthermore, although the SEI curriculum includes a large amount of English grammar and vocabulary, it does not blend this instruction with the teaching of content subjects like social studies, science, and mathematics, which ELL students must know to succeed in school and through which they could acquire academic English.

Nurturing Child Second Language Learning

While much about how children and adults learn second languages, and about how best to teach them, remains unknown, some things are clear. Primary among these is that young children (and some claim, adults, too) do not learn a language the same way they learn content subjects like history, science or geography. Instead of accumulating knowledge *about* English, one fact (vocabulary item, collocation, grammatical or pragmatic rule) at a time, *they learn languages gradually, in context, by experiencing their use, by doing things with and through the language.* Interaction is as crucial a part of child SLA (Oliver, 2009; Philp *et al.*, 2008) as it is of adult SLA (Gass, 1997; Long, 1996a, 2010; Mackey & Goo, 2007). In the case of young children, especially, they rely greatly on their capacity for implicit learning, and acquire the new code incidentally, while doing something else. This does not mean that they do not attend to language or need to do so. Anyone who has been around children who are learning a second language (and has been paying attention) will have been impressed by their uncanny ability to notice all sorts of details in the language they hear around them – evidence that they have been attending to more than the speech addressed specifically to them, and so adapted to their level of understanding. They are better at this than adults, and unlike adults, for whom second language acquisition in or out of classrooms routinely ends in at least partial failure, all but the seriously mentally disabled eventually attain native-like listening and speaking abilities. (For reviews of child–adult differences in ultimate attainment, see, e.g. DeKeyser & Larson-Hall, 2005; Hyltenstam & Abrahamsson, 2003, and for a critique of claims to the contrary and reanalysis of supposed counter-evidence, see Long, 2005.) Given a rich linguistic environment and enough time, the same is true of child second language learning, as seen in the success of true immersion programs (see, e.g. Swain, 1991), although the process can be speeded up, and so made more efficient, if teachers or pedagogic materials draw students' attention to problems when they arise during attempts to communicate – so-called 'focus on form' (Doughty & Williams, 1998; Long, 1991; Long & Robinson, 1998) – often nonsalient linguistic features they might otherwise take a long time to notice, or in the case of adults, not notice at all.

One of the major problems with Arizona's SEI approach is that by employing a traditional grammatical syllabus and focusing on language as object (grammar, vocabulary items, etc.), that is focus on forms, not focus on form, it impedes children's access to the type of classroom linguistic environment they need. Arizona's SEI promises dull, teacher-fronted lessons with their traditional diet of model sentences for repetition and manipulation in drill-like activities, linguistically simplified input, display questions and restricted opportunities for creative student talk. Focus on form, in contrast, involves meaning-focused communicative lessons during which students' attention is drawn to the language itself (pronunciation, grammar, lexis, collocations, etc.) when problems arise, in context. Child or adult learners are more much likely to understand the meaning and function of a new (grammatical, lexical, etc.) item, and remember it later, when they have a felt need for it for whatever they are working on at the time, and are more likely to be attending to the input. With focus on form, instead of trying to impose an external linguistic syllabus on the child (relative clauses because it is 10 o'clock on Monday, when the children are probably not ready to process, so learn, relative clauses), the teacher responds to the learner's internal syllabus. Starting where the child is a generally accepted principle in education, and it should be accepted in language teaching, too.

Far more effective for ELLs, especially in the elementary grades, but not only then, would be a task-based approach (see, e.g. Doughty & Long, 2003; Long, 2009; Long & Norris, 2000), where students learn the new language by doing intellectually stimulating activities (pedagogic tasks) *through* English, with task content drawn from the regular content curriculum the children would be doing at their age if they were native speakers. An age-appropriate task-based approach can provide students with the motivating and attention-holding challenge of meaningful problem-solving, game-like activities, and the opportunities those bring for rich linguistic input, a balance of display and referential questions and genuine two-way communication between teacher and students and among the students themselves. Researchers have long documented the power of 'talking to learn' (Barnes, 1976; Barnes & Todd, 1975) for developing children's mastery of both their first language and school curricular content, and for the symbiotic relationship between exploratory talk and learning, as they work cooperatively in small groups for substantial parts of lessons. There is ample empirical evidence for the facilitating role of conversation in both child and adult second language acquisition (see, e.g. Gass, 2003; Hatch, 1978; Mackey & Goo, 2007; Pica, 1994; Russell & Spada, 2006; Sato, 1986), and of group work in classroom second language learning (see, e.g. Long & Porter, 1985; Pica *et al.*, 1996).

In place of a focus on language as object, the focus in a task-based communicative classroom is on meaning and communication *through* the language. Instead of linguistic simplification, with content, too, being simplified as a result, teachers and texts can employ the many *elaborative modifications* native speakers use routinely, and largely unconsciously, with non-natives inside and outside classrooms. They achieve comprehensibility through the use of numerous devices, including repetition, rephrasing, decomposition, lexical switches, matching order of occurrence with order of mention, a preference for topic-comment over subject–predicate constructions and yes/no and or-choice over wh questions and linguistic redundancy (see Long, 1983a,b, 1996a,b). Compare, for example, the following sentences:

(1) *Genuine native speaker version*: Because he had to work at night to provide for his family, Paco often fell asleep in class.
(2) *Simplified version*: Paco had to make money for his family. Paco worked at night. He often went to sleep in class.
(3) *Elaborated version*: Paco had to work at night to earn money to provide for his family, so he often fell asleep in class next day during his teacher's lesson.

The simplified version results in short, choppy sentences reminiscent of basal readers, loses something of the connections between the events reported, models unnatural use of *go to asleep*, and removes at least two items from the input – *provide for* and *fall asleep* – that students will need to encounter if they are ever to learn them. The elaborated version avoids all those problems, although the intentional redundancy (designed, e.g. to convey the meaning of *provide for*) produces a rather lengthy, syntactically complex sentence. The benefits of elaboration, without the side-effect, can be achieved by modifying the elaborated version, usually, as here, simply by dividing one longer sentence into two shorter ones:

(4) *Modified elaborated version*: Paco had to work at night to earn money to provide for his family. As a result, he often fell asleep in class next day during his teacher's lesson.[1]

Needless to say, provided they are focused on getting their message across and understanding what students are saying to them, teachers will make most of these adjustments spontaneously (for reviews of studies of foreigner talk discourse in and out of classrooms, see Gass, 2003; Long, 1996a), without having to think about the rationale or the changes themselves. Research has shown that elaborative modifications of spoken or written input can achieve virtually the same degree of improvement in student comprehension as simplification, despite the greater linguistic complexity resulting from elaboration (see, e.g. Oh, 2001; Yano *et al.*, 1994). Elaboration provides a more realistic sample of target discourse and, crucially, retains the linguistic items (new vocabulary, collocations, morphology, syntactic constructions, etc.) to which students must be exposed if they are to be acquired, but which are often dropped from simplified versions. Elaborative modifications, moreover, preserve the information in equivalent texts for native speakers that linguistic simplification of the same texts loses (Long & Ross, 1993). This is important because it means that with a task-based communicative program, ELLs can develop their command of English *and* their subject matter knowledge. The English they can acquire this way, moreover, will include another key element missing from Arizona's SEI program, academic English, to which we now turn.

Academic Competence

The goal of most language teaching programs is to produce students who are proficient in the target language.[2] It has proved difficult for scholars to agree on exactly what language proficiency consists of, although everyone agrees that it includes knowledge of phonology, vocabulary and syntactic patterns (linguistic competence), and of when it is appropriate to use particular linguistic forms (pragmatic competence) (see Bachman, 1990). It is also agreed that different kinds of abilities are required for different kinds of language tasks, and that the ability to converse informally is different from the ability to do academic work. This distinction was introduced by Cummins (1979, 1981a,b), who used the terms *Basic Interpersonal Communicative Skills* (BICS) for the first ability, and *Cognitive Academic Language Proficiency* (CALP) for the second. Other scholars (e.g. Bruner, 1975; Gee, 1990) have used similar terms. BICS are considered easier because they involve treating familiar topics and doing so with contextual support, in the here and now. CALP is harder because it involves the ability to produce and understand context-reduced language in learning about what are typically unfamiliar and cognitively demanding topics, often displaced in time and space. Clearly, students must develop CALP as well as BICS if they are to succeed in school.

Students must also know the underlying concepts of academic subjects if they are to read textbooks, and such reading is a critically important activity for students who are acquiring L2 academic competence (Adamson, 1993). Reading specialists describe the comprehension of written language in terms of bottom-up and top-down processing. Bottom-up processing begins with using phonological or spelling rules to put together spoken or written segments in order to form words, using the rules of syntax to put words together to form sentences, and then using rules of discourse to put sentences together to yield an understanding of a coherent text. Phonics instruction teaches reading by means of bottom-up processing. The complementary process of top-down processing allows a reader to take advantage of prior knowledge of a subject to guess the meanings of unknown words and larger chunks of text. These guesses can then be confirmed by bottom-up processing and further reading of the text. Goodman characterized the interactive process of bottom-up and top-down processing as a 'psycholinguistic guessing game' (Goodman, 1967: 126). There is ample evidence that readers who have more knowledge about the topic of a text, and, therefore, can engage in top-down processing, understand the text better (e.g. Bransford & Johnson, 1972; Chiesi *et al.*, 1979; Haenggi & Perfetti, 1994).

In one such study, Perfetti *et al.* (1995) looked at the text-based learning of American history. The topic was the building of the Panama Canal, and the researchers measured how well students understood the causal connections in this historical episode, such as the fact that the United States needed a fast sea route from the West to the East Coast because gold had been discovered in California. The students were provided with short weekly readings and tests. Although none of these students were ELLs, there were considerable differences in their background knowledge (but not in their intelligence). Perfetti *et al.* found that students who had the least amount of background knowledge about the canal and about world events in general learned the least about the canal.

Accessing internal knowledge of a content area in order to fill in gaps in understanding academic material is a form of *scaffolding,* a notion introduced by the cognitive psychologists Wood *et al.* (1976). Another important kind of scaffolding is when a teacher supplies missing background knowledge, in order to help a student understand new concepts. Adamson (2005) describes a case of how scaffolding worked when a Spanish-speaking student was learning the periodic table of the elements. A transcript of a tutoring session revealed that the student could not understand the assigned science text because he lacked some important concepts. The student knew some basic information about chemistry, such as the fact than an atom consists of a central nucleus and orbiting particles, but did not know that the particles in the nucleus are protons and neutrons and that the orbiting particles are electrons. When the tutor supplied this information, the student was able to understand the passage.

Developing knowledge of content areas is important in its own right for ELLs, but also because it is the optimal way for them to develop control of the language that goes with it. A major reason academic competence needs to be distinguished from conversational competence is that language and language use differ in academic and informal conversational language settings. Therefore, students with tolerable abilities in the latter may still be unable to function in the former. Academic vocabulary, for example, differs not only from the common core of high-frequency items in a language, but also varies somewhat from one content area to another (Valdes, 2001). Corson (1997) points out that academic English derives largely from Greek and Latin, whereas the vocabulary of conversational English derives largely from Anglo-Saxon. But vocabulary is only the beginning. Biber (1995; Biber *et al.*, 1998) has done extensive studies of language varieties, comparing features, including syntactic structures, which co-occur in spoken and written English. He found that writing contains higher percentages of passive sentences, conjunctions and subordinate constructions than speaking. So, in order for students to learn academic subjects, they must learn the academic language in which those subjects are taught.

Perhaps most important of all, academic language use involves command of its rhetorical devices: knowing how to present and support an argument, organize a piece of writing (a lab report, essay, letter, etc.) and deal with the complex discourse patterns required when higher-order logical relationships are at issue. In a longitudinal study of selected ELLs in a California middle-school, Zweirs (2007) found academic discourse in lessons in all three content fields he observed to involve extensive use of such higher-order cognitive processes as cause and effect, comparison, persuasion, interpretation and taking other perspectives, with comparison more frequent in history and science, and interpretation more common in language arts. He noted (mostly teacher) use of metaphors for academic purposes, what he calls 'academic idioms', such as 'all boils down to, that answer doesn't hold water, a thin argument, a keen insight, crux of the matter, and on the right track' (Zweirs, 2007: 108). (It is hard to imagine such expressions occurring very often in traditional 'focus on forms' ESL lessons.) Zweirs found students were more likely to attempt to use academic language following teacher provision of models and production opportunities, for example, an invitation to compare two things, with visual language prompts (Zweirs, 2007: 110–111). A common pattern was for teachers to move from facts and concrete ideas, with right and wrong answers to their display questions, to more abstract and complex ideas, through explanation, cause and effect and comparison, to a variety of referential, open-ended (personal, justifying, clarifying, and elaborating) questions to prompt student persuasion, interpretation and perspective-taking (Zweirs, 2007: 101–103).

As first pointed out in Basil Bernstein's ground-breaking work on restricted and elaborated codes (e.g. Bernstein, 1971), middle-class children have more often grown up with both codes at home, whereas working-class children tend to have experienced mostly restricted code, and are at a major disadvantage at school, where elaborated code is the classroom norm and the one primarily used to encode the complex cognitive processes and relationships at issue. Numerous immigrant children in the United States come from very poor, working-class families, where not only is such discourse less common, but where most communication is in the parents' native language, not English. Paraphrasing Gee (1992), such children, like many of their working-class English-speaking classmates, lack important knowledge about social roles, about how to perform appropriately, both behaviorally and cognitively, in order to participate effectively in academic discourse and to learn academic subject matter through it, that is about how to do well at school.

An implication of these ideas and the research findings is that ELL students need to be exposed to, and participate in, academic discourse, both oral and written, if they are to succeed in school. Obviously, this will be more important in the upper grades, but even in elementary school, ELL students will encounter a different variety of language in their social studies, science and math lessons from that on the playground. The English language program must provide the foundation for understanding this variety of English. Yet it is well established that the discourse of traditional ESL (and foreign language) programs, where the target language is the object, not the medium, of instruction, differs markedly from what is required. For example, every study of traditional ESL classes we are aware of that has looked at participation patterns in general, and at teacher questions in particular, has found overwhelming teacher use of display questions throughout, greatly constraining the creativity of students' responses, with attention focused not on the correctness of (typically, minimal) factual content of what they say or write, but on the accuracy with which they say or write it (see, e.g. Early, 1985; Long *et al.*, 1984; Long & Sato, 1983; Wintergest, 1994).

The experience of academic language use required will clearly not occur in the SEI program designed by the Arizona Department of Education. Furthermore, there is a danger that if the only exposure to content area discourse takes place when ELLs are mixed with native speaker age peers, they will not be able to participate in the deeper, productive ways necessary for acquiring academic language in that context, either. Mostly passive exposure to isolated instances of new words in a text results in a roughly 10–15% chance that the word will be acquired (Nagy *et al.*, 1985). Repeated exposure is needed, preferably with plenty of opportunities for attempts to use it productively. There is some evidence from the study by Zweirs (2007) that ELLs are less favored interlocutors in mainstream classrooms, especially for open-ended, creative speaking opportunities. Reminiscent of Mackay's (1993) findings on teachers' use of 'hygienic' pedagogic strategies to 'clean up' problems occurring in content lessons as a result of Inuktituk children's limited English proficiency, Zweirs (2007: 105) found well-intentioned teachers in his California study, wittingly or unwittingly, attempting to prevent problems, for example by treating native speakers and ELLs differentially or by or ignoring problems when they occurred. For example, 55% of all display questions were directed at ELLs, but only 18% of all open questions and only 22% of elaboration questions. Similarly, in a practice Zweirs (2007: 112) labels 'linguistic enabling', teachers allowed ELL students to produce nonacademic responses, and in one case, accepted most of their oral and written work without corrective feedback in an effort to validate the students' home language and culture. Such practices are entirely understandable. Teachers are responsible for completing the curriculum set for their subject, and they cannot simply sacrifice that goal for the native English speakers in their charge in an effort to teach English to the non-native children.

Surely the answer is obvious. ELLs must be allowed to acquire English, including a solid basis in academic English, during the periods when they are taught separately. This will not happen via a traditional grammar-based course, where the focus is on the forms of primarily conversational language, not academic English and the cognitive processes it enables. A focus on *academic tasks* is required, whose academic *content* is that of the mainstream classes the children will encounter when integrated with their English-speaking age peers the rest of the day, and when they are ultimately main-streamed full-time. Hoping ELLs will pick up academic English as an 'add-on' *after* mainstreaming is unreasonable. Conversely, having them participate in their own task-based ESL lessons with appropriate academic content, when they are not competing with native speakers, many of whom already know both conversational and academic English, means they will have every opportunity to acquire the language they need and to fulfill the classroom roles they will be required to perform when mainstreamed.

For most children this will take more than just a year of English language support. Ideally, so that they do not fall behind in their regular studies, children should be covering age-appropriate subject matter in their first language, that is as part of a true bilingual program. As Thomas and Collier put it after reviewing the research findings:

> The first predictor of long-term school success is cognitively complex on-grade-level academic instruction through students' first language for as long as possible (at least through Grade 5 or 6) and cognitively complex on-grade-level academic instruction through the second language (English) for part of the school day, in each succeeding grade throughout students' schooling. (Thomas & Collier, 1997: 15)

Unfortunately, however, bilingual education has been ruled out by the educational policy in Arizona and many other parts of the United States, despite its proven status as the single most effective type of program for immigrant children, and despite the fact that programs that *add* a second language or dialect (Long, 1999; Sato, 1985, 1989), rather than replace one with another, result in individuals and societies that are both linguistically richer and more capable.

In sum, if ELL students are to succeed in school, they obviously need to acquire CALP, but this is a process known to take several years, even for native speakers. Cummins (1981a), for example, noted that immigrant children in English-speaking Canada require between five and seven years to attain comparable vocabularies to English-speaking age peers, and argued, as a result, that the two years of ESL then provided was inadequate for those children. And in another sobering conclusion, Thomas and Collier observed:

> It takes the typical young immigrant schooled all in L2 in the U.S. 7–10 years or more to reach the 50th NCE [roughly the 50th percentile], and the majority of these students do not ever make it to the 50th NCE, unless they receive support for L1 academic and cognitive development at home. (Thomas & Collier, 1997: 36)

Few immigrant families can provide such support, and under Arizona's SEI program it is denied by the schools, as well.

Conclusion

Arizona's new SEI program is fundamentally flawed in at least two ways. First, it is inconsistent with what SLA research has shown about how children learn new languages and about how best to teach them. Second, academic competence is different from conversational competence, and needed by ELLs if they are to succeed in school, but SEI instruction will not develop academic competence. Its instructional materials include neither academic English nor the concepts needed to understand academic materials. For this reason, school districts should have the freedom to discard those parts of the new curriculum they feel are irrelevant or even counter-productive, and to substitute appropriate instructional programs that will meet immigrant children's needs. While no substitute for a true bilingual or immersion program, a carefully designed task-based ESL program would go much of the way to remedying the situation. Any additional costs associated with such programs will be minimal compared to the price of educational failure later for major segments of Arizona's and the country's school-aged population.

Acknowledgments

Thanks to Mary Carol Combs and Pam Selby for enlightening discussions regarding Arizona's SEI policies and practices.

Notes

(1) For detailed discussion of these and other examples, see Long (2007b: 119–138).
(2) It could be argued that some foreign language teaching programs do not aim to instill proficiency in a language but, rather, an appreciation for the culture and literature of target language countries (see Adamson, 2009, Chapter 9). It is clear, in any case, that they do not succeed in developing foreign language proficiency (see Long, 2007b).

References

Adamson, H.D. (1993) *Academic Competence: Theory and Classroom Practice*. New York: Longman.
Adamson, H.D. (2005) *Language Minority Students in American Schools: An Education in English*. Mahwah, NJ: Lawrence Erlbaum Associates.
Adamson, H.D. (2009) *Interlanguage Variation in Theoretical and Pedagogical Perspective*. New York: Routledge.
Arizona Department of Education (2009) *Administrator's model implementation training*. Online document, accessed 17 February 2010. https://www.ade.az.gov/oelas
Arizona Revised Statutes (2009) Title15-756.01. Arizona English language learners task force; research based models of structured English immersion for English language learners; budget requests; definition. Online document, accessed 17 February 2010. http://www.azleg.gov/DocumentsForBill.asp?Bill_Number=HB2064
Arizona Revised Statutes, Title 15 (Education), § 3.1 (English Language Education for Children in Public Schools), 751-756.01.
Bachman, L.F. (1990) *Fundamental Considerations in Language Testing*. Oxford: Oxford University Press.
Barnes, D. (1976) *From Communication to Curriculum*. Harmondsworth: Penguin.
Barnes, D. and Todd, F. (1975) *Communication and Learning in Small Groups. A Report to the Social Science Research Council*. London: Routledge & Kegan Paul.
Bernstein, B. (1971) *Class, Codes and Control* (Vol. 1). London: Routledge & Kegan Paul.
Biber, D. (1995) *Dimensions of Register Variation. A Cross-Linguistic Comparison*. Cambridge: Cambridge University Press.
Biber, D., Conrad, S. and Hakuta, K. (1998) Corpus-based approaches in applied linguistics. *Applied Linguistics* 15, 169–189.
Bransford, J.D. and Johnson, M.K. (1972) Contextual prerequisites for understanding: Some investigations of comprehension and recall. *Journal of Verbal Learning and Verbal Behavior* 11, 117–726.
Brisk, M.E. (1998) *Bilingual Education: From Compensatory to Quality Schooling*. Mahway, NJ: Lawrence Erlbaum Associates.
Bruner, J.S. (1975) Language as an instrument of thought. In A. Davies (ed.) *Problems of Language and Learning* (pp. 61–88). London: Heinemann.
Chiesi, H.L., Spilich, G.J. and Voss, J.F. (1979) Acquisition of domain-related information in relation to high and low domain knowledge. *Journal of Verbal Learning and Verbal Behavior* 18, 257–273.

Corson, D. (1997) The learning and use of academic English words. *Language Learning* 47, 671–718.

Cummins, J. (1979) Cognitive/academic language proficiency, linguistic interdependence, the optimum age question, and other matters. *Working Papers on Bilingualism* 19, 121–129.

Cummins, J. (1981a) Age on arrival and immigrant second language learning in Canada: A reassessment. *Applied Linguistics* 11, 132–149.

Cummins, J. (1981b) *Bilingualism and Minority Language Children*. Toronto: Ontario Institute for Studies in Education.

Cummins, J. (2009) Bilingual and immersion programs. In M.H. Long and C.J. Doughty (eds) *Handbook of Language Teaching* (pp. 161–181). Oxford: Blackwell.

DeKeyser, R. and Larson-Hall, J. (2005) What does the critical period really mean? In J. Kroll and A.M.B. de Groot (eds) *Handbook of Bilingualism: Psycholinguistic Approaches* (pp. 88–108). Oxford: Oxford University Press.

Doughty, C.J. and Williams, J. (1998) Pedagogical choices in focus on form. In C.J. Doughty and J. Williams (eds) *Focus on Form in Classroom Second Language Acquisition* (pp. 197–261). Cambridge: University Press.

Doughty, C.J. and Long, M.H. (2003) Optimal psycholinguistic environments for distance foreign language learning. *Language Learning and Technology* 7, 50–80.

Early, M. (1985) Input and interaction in content classrooms: Foreigner talk and teacher talk in classroom discourse. Unpublished PhD dissertation. Los Angeles: University of California.

Faltis, C. and Hudelson, S. (1998) *Bilingual Education in Elementary and Secondary School Communities: Toward Understanding and Caring*. Boston: Allyn & Bacon.

Gass, S.M. (1997) *Input, Interaction, and the Second Language Learner*. Mahwah, NJ: Lawrence Erlbaum.

Gass, S.M. (2003) Input and interaction. In C.J. Doughty and M.H. Long (eds) *Handbook of Second Language Acquisition* (pp. 224–255). Oxford: Blackwell.

Gee, J. (1992) Reading. *Journal of Urban and Cultural Studies* 2, 65–77.

Gee, J.P. (1990) *Social Linguistics and Literacies: Ideologies in Discourses*. New York: Falmer Press.

Genesee, F., Holobow, N.E., Lambert, W.E. and Chartrand, L. (1989) Three elementary school alternatives for learning through a second language. *Modern Language Journal* 73, 250–263.

Goodman, K. (1967) Reading: A psycholinguistic guessing game. *Journal of the Reading Specialist* 4, 126–135.

Haenggi, D. and Perfetti, C. (1994) Processing components of college-level reading comprehension. *Discourse Processes* 17, 83–104.

Hatch, E.M. (1978) Discourse analysis and second language acquisition. In E. Hatch (ed.) *Second Language Acquisition: A Book of Readings* (pp. 401–435). Rowley, MA: Newbury House.

Haver, J. (2003) *Structured English Immersion: A Step-by-Step Guide for K–6 Teachers and Administrators*. Thousand Oaks, CA: Corwin Press. Accessed 1 March 2010. http://www.azleg.gov/DocumentsForBill.asp?Bill_Number=HB2064

Hyltenstam, K. and Abrahamsson, N. (2003) Maturational constraints in second language acquisition. In C.J. Doughty and M.H. Long (eds) *Handbook of Second Language Acquisition* (pp. 539–588). Oxford: Blackwell.

Long, M.H. (1983a) Native speaker/non-native speaker conversation and the negotiation of comprehensible input. *Applied Linguistics* 4, 126–141. Reprinted in C.N. Candlin and T. Macnamara (eds) (2001) *A Reader in Applied Linguistics*. London: Routledge.

Long, M.H. (1983b) Linguistic and conversational adjustments to non-native speakers. *Studies in Second Language Acquisition* 5, 177–193.

Long, M.H. (1991) Focus on form: A design feature in language teaching methodology. In K. de Bot, R.B. Ginsberg and C. Kramsch (eds) *Foreign Language Research in Cross-cultural Perspective* (pp. 39–52). Amsterdam: John Benjamins.

Long, M.H. (1996a) The role of the linguistic environment in second language acquisition. In W.C. Ritchie and T.K. Bahtia (eds) *Handbook of Second Language Acquisition* (pp. 413–468). New York: Academic Press.

Long, M.H. (1996b) Authenticity and learning potential in L2 classroom discourse. In G.M. Jacobs (ed.) *Language Classrooms of Tomorrow: Issues and Responses* (pp. 148–169). Singapore: SEAMEO Regional Language Centre.

Long, M.H. (1999) Ebonics, language and power. In F.L. Pincus and H.J. Ehrlich (eds) *Race and Ethnic Conflict. Contending Views on Prejudice, Discrimination, and Ethnoviolence* (2nd edn, pp. 331–345). Westview/Harper Collins. Also in R. Blot (ed.) (2003) *Language and Social Identity* (pp. 147–170). Westport, CT: Greenwood.

Long, M.H. (2005) Problems with supposed counter-evidence to the Critical Period Hypothesis. *International Review of Applied Linguistics* 43, 287–317.

Long, M.H. (2007a) Second and foreign language education. In S. Mathinson and W. Ross (eds) *Battleground Schools: An Encyclopedia of Conflict and Controversy* (pp. 249–254). Westport, CT: Greenwood Press.

Long, M.H. (2007b) *Problems in SLA*. Mahwah, NJ: Lawrence Erlbaum.

Long, M.H. (2009) Methodological principles for language teaching. In M.H. Long and C.J. Doughty (eds) *Handbook of Second and Foreign Language Teaching* (pp. 374–393). Oxford: Blackwell.

Long, M.H. (2010) Towards a cognitive-interactionist theory of instructed SLA. Plenary address, 30th Second Language Research Forum. University of Maryland, October 14. To appear in M.H. Long *Second Language Acquisition and Task-based Language Teaching*. Oxford: Wiley-Blackwell.

Long, M.H. and Sato, C.J. (1983) Classroom foreigner talk discourse: forms and functions of teachers' questions. In H.W. Seliger and M.H. Long (eds) *Classroom-Oriented Research on Second Language Acquisition* (pp. 268–285). Rowley, MA: Newbury House.

Long, M.H. and Porter, P. (1985) Group work, interlanguage talk, and second language acquisition. *TESOL Quarterly* 19, 207–227.

Long, M.H. and Ross, S. (1993) Modifications that preserve language and content. In M. Tickoo (ed.) *Simplification: Theory and Application* (pp. 29–52). Singapore: SEAMEO Regional Language Centre.

Long, M.H. and Robinson, P.E. (1998) Focus on form: Theory, research, and practice. In C. Doughty and J. Williams (eds) *Focus on Form in Classroom Second Language Acquisition* (pp. 15–41). Cambridge: Cambridge University Press.

Long, M.H. and Norris, J.M. (2000) Task-based teaching and assessment. In M. Byram (ed.) *Encyclopedia of Language Teaching* (pp. 59–603). London: Routledge. Reprinted in K. Van den Branden, M. Bygate and J.M. Norris (eds) (2009) *Task-Based Language Teaching. A Reader* (pp. 135–142). Amsterdam: John Benjamins.

Long, M.H., Brock, C., Crookes, G., Deicke, C., Potter, L. and Zhang (1984) The effect of teachers' questioning patterns and wait-time on pupil participation in public high school classes in Hawaii for students of limited English proficiency. Technical Report #1, Honolulu, HI: Center for Second Language Classroom Research (Summary in *TESOL Quarterly* 19, 1985, 605–607).

Mackay, R. (1986) The role of English in education in an Eastern Arctic School: An account of success and failure in the Canadian Arctic. PhD dissertation, L'Université de Montréal.

Mackay, R. (1993) Embarrassment and hygiene in the classroom. *ELT Journal* 47, 1.

Mackey, A. and Goo, J. (2007) Interaction research in SLA: A meta-analysis and research synthesis. In A. Mackey (ed.) *Conversational Interaction in Second Language Acquisition* (pp. 407–452). Oxford: Oxford University Press.

Nagy, W.E., Herman, P.A. and Anderson, R.C. (1985) Learning words from context. *Reading Research Quarterly* 20, 233–253.

Oh, S-Y. (2001) Two types of input modification and EFL reading comprehension: Simplification versus elaboration. *TESOL Quarterly* 35, 69–96.

Oliver, R. (2009) How young is too young? Investigating negotiation for meaning and feedback to children aged five to seven years. In A. Mackey, and C. Polio (eds) *Multiple Perspectives on Interaction* (pp. 135–156). NY: Routledge.

Perfetti, C., Britt, A.M. and George, M.C. (1995) *Text-based Learning and Reasoning: Studies in History*. Hillsdale, NJ: Lawrence Erlbaum Associates.

Philp, J., Oliver, R. and Mackey, A. (eds) (2008) *Second Language Acquisition and the Younger Learner. Child's Play?* Amsterdam: John Benjamins.

Pica, T. (1994) Research on negotiation: What does it reveal about second language learning conditions, processes and outcomes. *Language Learning* 44, 493–527.

Pica, T., Lincoln-Porter, F., Paninos, D. and Linnell, J. (1996) Language learners' interaction: How does it address the input, output, and feedback needs of L2 learners? *TESOL Quarterly* 30, 59–84.

Russell, J. and Spada, N. (2006) The effectiveness of corrective feedback for the acquisition of L2 grammar. In J.M. Norris and L. Ortega (eds) *Synthesizing Research on Language Learning and Teaching* (pp. 133–164). Amsterdam: John Benjamins.

Sato, C.J. (1985) Linguistic inequality in Hawai'i: the post-Creole dilemma. In N. Wolfson and J. Manes (eds) *Language of Inequality* (pp. 255–272). Berlin: Mouton.

Sato, C.J. (1986) Conversation and interlanguage development: Rethinking the connection. In R. Day (ed.) *Talking to Learn: Conversation in Second Language Acquisition* (pp. 23–45). Rowley, MA: Newbury House.

Sato, C.J. (1989) A non-standard approach to standard English. *TESOL Quarterly* 23, 259–282.

Schauber, H. (1995) The second language component of primary French immersion programs in Montreal, Quebec, Canada. *Bilingual Research Journal* 19, 483–495.

Stein, C.B. (1986) *Sink or Swim: The Politics of Bilingual Education*. New York: Praeger.

Swain, M. (1991) French immersion and its off-shoots: Getting two for one. In B. Freed (ed.) *Foreign Language Acquisition Research and the Classroom* (pp. 91–103). Lexington, MA: D.C. Heath.

Thomas, W.P. and Collier, V. (1997) School effectiveness for language minority students. *NCBE Resource Collection Series* 9, 36.

Valdes, G. (2001) *Learning and Not Learning English*. New York: Teachers College Press.

Wintergest, A.C. (1994) *Questions and Answers in ESL Classes*. Toronto: University of Toronto Press.

Wood, D., Bruner, J. and Ross, G. (1976) The role of tutoring in problem solving. *Journal of Child Psychology and Psychiatry* 17, 89–100.

Yano, Y., Long, M.H. and Ross, S. (1994) The effects of simplified and elaborated texts on foreign language reading comprehension. *Language Learning* 44, 189–219.

Zweirs, J. (2007) Teacher practices and perspectives for developing academic language. *International Journal of Applied Linguistics* 17, 93–116.

Part 2

Implementing SEI in Arizona

4 Everything on Its Head: How Arizona's Structured English Immersion Policy Re-invents Theory and Practice

Mary Carol Combs

> *And I remember in frequent discourses with my master concerning the*
> *nature of manhood, in other parts of the world, having occasion to talk of*
> lying *and* false representation *... For he argued thus; that the use of*
> *speech was to make us understand one another, and to receive information*
> *of facts;* now if any one *said the thing which was not, these ends were*
> *defeated ... ... he leaves me worse than in ignorance, for I am led to*
> *believe a thing black when it is white, and* short *when it is* long.
>
> *Gulliver's Travels*, Part IV: Voyage to the
> Country of the Houyhnhnms

In Jonathan Swift's satiric novel *Gulliver's Travels*, Lemuel Gulliver travels to the land of the *Houyhnhnms*,[1] a race of intelligent horses endowed with reason, order and good sense.

The Houyhnhnms rule over a race of creatures called *Yahoos*, who are human in appearance, but are primitive, brutish and incapable of rational thought. Gulliver resembles the Yahoos physically 'in every part', but he is nonetheless profoundly different: he is a Yahoo capable of rational thought. Gulliver gradually learns the language of the Houyhnhnms and discovers that it has no words for lying or deceit. In order to communicate these concepts to the Houyhnhnms, he is forced to construct all manner of distorting circumlocutions to convey ideas that do not exist in the horses' reality. Thus, to describe the English and other European languages' words for lying, he uses a negative definition: *lying* becomes *the thing which was not.*

Gulliver's Houyhnhnm mentor is deeply troubled that words and speech, which are supposed to impart essential truths, could instead be used to misrepresent those truths. For him, uttering *the thing which was not* would be unthinkable, because such a practice leaves us 'worse than in ignorance'. We might be led to believe that something is black when it is white, or *true* when it is really *false*. Gradually, the Houyhnhnms realize that Gulliver is an intelligent Yahoo. Because Gulliver's behavior, thoughts and demeanor challenge the Houyhnhnm perception of other Yahoos in the land, he comes to represent a threat to the social order. The Houyhnhnms fear that he will corrupt the other Yahoos, so they expel him from their country.

I take Swift's fable as a rueful metaphor for the way in which language and education policies governing English language learners (ELLs) have been enacted in the state of Arizona. I argue that state ELL policy is a confusing and contradictory amalgam of numerous *things which are not*, that is, misinformed but authoritative declarations about the way that children learn a second language – in this case English, and how state schools should teach them English. I discuss a number of perplexing *things which are not*, and draw attention to serious contradictions in state ELL program policy and instructional practices. I also focus on the odd convergence of state and federal legislation, case law and policies that both determine and confound educational choices for English learners. This convergence represents a legal and policy conundrum for schools and school districts, one that confuses, challenges and or justifies the educational decisions districts make for their ELL students.

It is regrettable enough that the state policies affecting thousands of English language learners in Arizona have originated from an audacious fiction. It is even more unfortunate that these policies continue to morph into new and more *things which are not*, leaving us in a circumstance, if not entirely worse than ignorance, is one in which we shake our heads in disbelief. Indeed, *things which are not*, once expressed as vaguely worded ballot measures, convoluted legislation and folk beliefs about language acquisition and teaching, have now become codified as state law. As such, they have also become *fact*, however deceptive and hyperbolic.

The Convoluted History of Structured English Immersion in Arizona

Education policy from the Ballot Box: Proposition 203

In November 2000 Arizona voters approved Proposition 203 ('English for the Children-Arizona'), a ballot initiative that severely curtailed the implementation of bilingual education programs in public schools, mandating instead a relatively untested program model known as 'Structured English Immersion' (SEI). Prior to the passage of Proposition 203, SEI had little support in the educational or applied linguistics research literature. Few studies conducted to date on the effectiveness of SEI in improving children's English acquisition or academic achievement have indicated positive outcomes (Combs *et al.*, 2005; Mahoney *et al.*, 2005; Wright & Pu, 2005). Instead, public schools are increasingly contentious and contradictory sites in which the debate about the education of immigrant English language learners plays out (Rabin *et al.*, 2008).

Proposition 203 began as a so-called 'citizen's' initiative. Titled 'English for the Children,' the measure was designed to replace bilingual education programs in public schools with an experimental program known as SEI. In an SEI classroom, instruction typically is in English only but teachers are expected to modify their instruction through 'sheltered' techniques to accommodate students' developing proficiency in English (Combs *et al.*, 2005). The potential superiority of SEI over other approaches to teaching English language learners was largely unknown at the time. Nonetheless, its supporters promoted the program as the most effective way to teach immigrant students (Arizona Secretary of State Voter Education Pamphlet, Arguments for Proposition 203, 2000; Unz, 2001). After its supporters collected the required number of valid signatures, the measure qualified for placement on the November 2000 general election ballot. Proposition 203 was one of a total 14 ballot initiatives that Arizona voters considered that year (Rabin *et al.*, 2008).

The initiative process has become a popular means for creating or changing state policies on many issues. Between 1990 and 2009, for example, the number of initiatives appearing on state ballots nationwide was 746 (Initiative and Reform Institute, 2009). Fifty-four of these measures concerned a wide variety of education policies[2] (National Conference of State Legislatures, 2009). Voters approved 23 of them.

Historically designed as a means of circumventing state legislative special interests, 'direct democracy' ballot initiatives increasingly are being sponsored by special interest groups or wealthy entrepreneurs who exploit their appeal to further personal or political agendas (Broder, 2001; Chávez, 1998; Gamble, 1997; Haskell, 2001; Kraker, 2000). For these individuals, ballot initiatives represent a uniquely effective method for advancing causes that potentially would fail in a state legislature. Thus, the initiative process provides a free-wheeling arena in which almost any measure can qualify for an election ballot, assuming enough signatures are collected to place it there.

Taking an initiative measure all the way to an election requires enormous sums of money, initially to gather signatures, and then to run an effective campaign. Without money, the majority of initiatives never make it to the ballot (Broder, 2001). The relatively few that do are the ones supported by interest groups or individuals with access to big money, often their own. The campaign to pass Arizona's Proposition 203, for example, was bankrolled by a single individual, Ron Unz, a Silicon Valley software entrepreneur who earned millions of dollars after developing a financial software program used by the mortgage departments of banks and other lending institutions (Miller, 1999). Unz provided fully 81% ($186,886) of the total $229,786 spent to bring the measure to state voters (Crawford, 2001). Unz also sponsored antibilingual education ballot initiatives in three other states: California, Massachusetts and Colorado.[3] Ultimately, Arizona voters approved Proposition 203 by 63%.

It is probably not surprising that the majority of Arizona voters appeared to believe claims that SEI would teach English more effectively than bilingual education. The theoretical or practical justifications for bilingual education are unknown to most voters. Whether Ron Unz and other proponents of antibilingual initiatives intentionally took advantage of voter ignorance about bilingual education is debatable. What is not debatable is that the campaign for Proposition 203 was waged primarily through misleading and inflammatory sound bites. In separate analyses of media coverage of the proposition, Johnson (2005) found that supporters of the measure used metaphoric and rhetorical language to disparage bilingual education and educators. Wright (2005) similarly noted that a 'political spectacle' had occurred, rather than a reasoned debate about the educational interests of immigrant English language learners. In fact, the political discourse leading up to the elections in all four states was 'highly contentious and largely unrelated to the practical and pedagogical issues facing public school administrators, teachers, parents, and students' (Mora, 2009: 16). Initiative proponents portrayed bilingual education as a failed and expensive Spanish-only, academic welfare program in which children languished for years, or as an entrenched bureaucracy seeking to preserve its financial stake (Ayala, 1999; Crawford, 2008; English for the Children-Arizona, no date; Unz, 1997).

Applied linguistic research vs. common sense

Research studies in second language acquisition may be a hard sell anyway, especially in political contests. For one thing, conclusions about second language acquisition seem counterintuitive to most voters, especially the consistent finding that learning to read in the first language actually improves proficiency in English, or that the *quality* of exposure to English, rather than *quantity*, is a key factor in English acquisition. For another, elected officials and the voting public seemed unwilling to accept that a program designed to teach English, by teaching in students' first languages, could possibly be effective (Combs *et al.*, 2005). They simply did not believe that students immersed in English actually need *more* time to acquire it than students schooled in their home language and English, although this has been a consistent finding in the research literature on second language acquisition (Collier, 1987, 1995; Cummins, 1991, 1992; Cummins & Swain, 1986; Ramírez, 1992; Ramírez *et al.*, 1991; Wong Fillmore, 1991).

The text of Proposition 203 expresses at least three 'folk theories', or 'cultural models' – simplified versions of complex events or processes (Gee, 2008) – of second language acquisition: (1) that young children learn English better than older students; (2) that immersion in an all English setting would help students acquire the language more rapidly; and (3) that such an approach would teach them enough English in one year to be academically successful in the mainstream classroom.[4] Since the proposition became a law, Arizona Department of Education (ADE) officials have repeated these folk theories in department policy documents, reports, press releases and professional development sessions.

These popular but questionable ideas about how, and how fast, young children can acquire English have influenced the educational programs state policymakers have ordered school districts to implement for English language learners. The consequences for not adhering strictly to state ELL policy are serious: the State Superintendent of Public Instruction, a vociferous supporter of SEI, has threatened to withhold funds from school districts that are slow to implement the law (Horne, 2004a,b).

Arizona Policy: A Palimpsest of *Things Which Are Not*

Flores v. Arizona

Arizona language and education policy is not solely determined by Proposition 203. The federal court resolution of the *Flores v. Arizona* lawsuit actually predated the ballot proposition by almost a year. This lawsuit originated in Nogales, Arizona in 1992 as a class action case in the Nogales Unified School District. In civil rights litigation, a class means a group of people 'similarly situated', that is, people who are similarly affected by a particular policy, law, or practice. Because potentially people share the effects of a policy, law or practice, they may sue for themselves or for themselves and other members of the class (Alexander & Alexander, 1985).

According to Federal law, such a class is legally protected from discrimination. In the *Flores* case, the class would include English language learners in all 15 Arizona counties.[5]

The plaintiffs charged the State of Arizona with violating the Equal Education Opportunities Act (EEOA) by its failure to take 'appropriate action to overcome language barriers that impede equal participation by its students in its instructional programs' [Title 20 U.S.C. § 1703(f)]. Specifically, the plaintiffs charged the state with inadequately funding public school districts that enrolled predominately low-income minority children (the majority of whom in Nogales were English language learners), and whether the lack of funding privileged predominately Anglo schools and resulted in fewer educational benefits and opportunities for low-income ELLs.

What constituted 'appropriate action' and whether the State of Arizona was meetings its responsibilities under the EEOA was a prominent feature in the trial and in subsequent state policy developments. In 1981, the 5th Circuit Court of Appeals had ruled in *Castañeda v. Pickard* that school districts had to a duty to provide assistance to their English language learners. Local education authorities, according to the Court, had to 'make a genuine and good faith effort, consistent with local circumstances and resources, to remedy the language deficiencies of their students and deliberately placed on federal courts the difficult responsibility of determining whether that obligation had been met' (*Castañeda v. Pickard*, 1981). The Court created an analytical framework for determining whether or not school districts were taking 'appropriate action' to help students overcome language barriers (for a description of the Castañeda Test, see Chapter 2, this volume).

Before passage of Proposition 203, school districts in Arizona were implementing four different ELL programs, and the plaintiffs in *Flores* did not challenge them. Thus the State could be said to have passed the theory requirement of the Castañeda Test. It was the second part of framework that plaintiffs charged the State had failed to pass, specifically, that the State's failure to provide adequate funding of schools serving high numbers of English language learners had resulted in many deficiencies, including insufficient numbers of classrooms, qualified teachers and teacher aides, inadequate tutoring programs, and not enough teaching materials for content area and English as a second language classes (Hogan, no date). More important, the Court ruled that the State Legislature's supplementary allocation of funding for ELL education, a paltry $150 to the per-pupil base minimum of $2,410.56 (1992–1993 figures), was 'arbitrary and capricious.' In other words, it was not based on serious study about how much it would truly cost districts to educate children acquiring English as a second language. The case that finally went to trial considered only the funding issues, with both the State and plaintiffs agreeing to negotiate any curricular and instructional issues out of court. In January 2000, Judge Alfredo Marquez decided the case in favor of the *Flores* plaintiffs, agreeing with their claim that the State of Arizona had violated the EEOA (*Flores v. Arizona*, 172F. Supp. 2d 1225, D. Ariz. 2000). Six months later, both parties signed a legally binding Consent Order, which 'acquired the same force and effect as a judgment and became judicially enforceable' (Hogan, no date: 6).

Funding inadequacies were at the heart of the *Flores* case because of their disparate impact on low-income school districts. Nonetheless, the Court's decision had important implications for the kinds of curricular programs that districts implemented for their English learners, as well as the kind of instruction occurring within those programs. Lack of funding prevented districts from providing ELLs 'with a program of instruction calculated to make them proficient in speaking, understanding, reading, and writing English, while enabling them to master the standard academic curriculum as required of all students' (*Flores v. Arizona*, 48 F. Supp. 2d. 937).

The Consent Order squarely addressed this issue with three specific mandates for ELL instruction (*Flores v. Arizona*, Consent Order, CIV 92-596 TUC ACM: 4–5):

(1) English language learners must receive daily instruction in English language development (ELD). The English language instruction shall be appropriate to the level of English proficiency and shall include listening and speaking skills, reading and writing skills, and cognitive and academic development in English.
(2) ELLs must receive daily instruction in basic subject areas that is understandable and appropriate to the level of academic achievement of the limited English proficient student, and is in conformity with accepted strategies for teaching LEP students.
(3) The curriculum of all bilingual education and ELD shall incorporate the [State] Board's Academic Standards and shall be comparable in amount, scope and quality to that provided to English proficient students.

The implications of these mandates were clear. If English language learners had to receive English as a second language instruction together with comprehensible content area instruction *in the same classroom*, ELD 'pull-out' programs were no longer an appropriate means of supporting English language learners. Because pull-out programs were now illegal (at least in theory), all teachers in Arizona potentially were SEI teachers, regardless of content area or grade level.

How the state board of education defines a 'highly qualified' SEI teacher

The Arizona State Board of Education quickly grasped the significance of the Consent Order. Before passage of Proposition 203, the State had offered two specialty endorsements for teachers working with English language learners: an ELD endorsement (18 credit hours, or 6 classes) and a bilingual endorsement (21 credits hours, or 7 classes). The Flores Consent Order now made it necessary for school districts to consider how all teachers in the state could become 'highly qualified' to teach students acquiring proficiency in English. The State Board convened a series of meetings with ADE officials, teachers, administrators, and university teacher educators to consider requirements for the qualifications of ELL teachers.

Along with school district and university colleagues, I participated in one of these meetings. We argued that at minimum, ELL teachers should obtain an ELD endorsement to best prepare them for working with students acquiring English as a second language (we suggested that the Board could even rename it as an SEI endorsement). We were troubled that the Board had proposed a new SEI endorsement of only 15 hours (1 credit) and felt that a one-credit course was simply insufficient time in which to prepare teachers to become highly qualified educators of English language learners. We argued that 15 hours could not possibly cover the pedagogical, theoretical, linguistic, socio-cultural, assessment or literacy issues involved in the education of English learners, all subjects in which highly qualified ELL teachers should be knowledgeable. From our perspective, it made little sense for the Board for select an SEI endorsement of 1 credit over an ELD endorsement of 18 credits, if the Board's goal was to help teachers become highly qualified.

The State Board compromised and established an SEI endorsement of 60 hours, or 4 credits (1 $\frac{1}{2}$ classes), in effect, minimizing the importance of obtaining a specialist endorsement over a more generic one. Of the different endorsement options available, the State Board simply voted to support the least demanding plan (Mahoney *et al.*, 2005). The new endorsement required all individuals with a K–12 Arizona teaching certificate to complete the 1 credit hour course by August 1, 2006, and subsequently, a 3 credit hour by

August 1, 2009. The Board compromise also required any teacher seeking a certificate after August 1, 2006 to complete two SEI courses, or a total of 6 credits.

Universities and community colleges began to create courses focused on sheltered content teaching strategies. At the University of Arizona, where I am an instructor, we have designed SEI courses to address the instructional requirements of the Consent Decree, that is, courses that include a focus on both basic subject area instruction *and* English language development (ELD). SEI courses instruct teachers in principles of first and second language acquisition, the socio-cultural context of ELL education in the Southwest and borderlands, students' cognitive, linguistic, and social development, the role of culture in the classroom, English as a second language and thematic and sheltered instructional approaches to second language teaching in academic settings.

A funding roller coaster

While universities and school districts organized SEI teaching training programs, the Arizona State Legislature had a different agenda. The Flores Consent Order appeared to have little effect on the legislature, which took its time meeting the Court's requirement to provide more funding to school districts. Nearly two years after the *Flores* decision, and only because of additional prodding by the District Court, the legislature agreed to fund a cost study to determine the amount of funding necessary to adequately fund ELL programs. In February of 2001, the Arizona Department of Education contracted the Center for Equal Opportunity and the READ Institute, two well-known opponents of bilingual education, to undertake the task.[6] Three months later, ADE released the 'English Acquisition Program Cost Study', which identified per pupil costs in six English immersion programs in Arizona, Pennsylvania, Texas and Washington State (Porter, 2001). The cost of educating English language learners in these programs ranged from $0 to $4600, a range so vast as to be comparatively unhelpful (Arizona Senate Research Staff, 2008).

In June of 2001, the District Court ordered the legislature to raise its minimum level of funding per English learner to a more realistic amount, that is, one that considered the actual costs needed to help students become fluent in English. This order notwithstanding, the legislative session came to an end without any action. Indeed, it was doubtful the legislature had ever intended to take action (Hogan, no date). The plaintiffs then filed a motion for yet another deadline, which the Court granted. The new deadline date was January 31, 2002, or at the conclusion of any earlier legislative session *'called for any other purpose'* (Hogan, no date: 10, emphasis added). Tim Hogan, attorney for the plaintiffs, noted further ironies:

> As it turns out, the legislature was called into special session by the Governor in December 2001 for a purpose unrelated to *Flores*. Rather than face sanctions from the Court, the legislature enacted legislation that addressed the judgment in *Flores* but only on an interim basis. The interim legislation, House Bill 2010, was premised on the notion that the state still did not have reliable cost data to establish appropriate funding levels for ELL programs. Given the data that was available, the legislature determined that doubling ELL funding was appropriate until more reliable cost data could be obtained. (Hogan, no date: 10)

The resulting temporary legislation raised the funding appropriation per English language learner – from approximately $179 to $340. HB 2010 also appropriated additional money for teacher training, instructional materials and another cost study (Arizona Senate Research Staff, 2008), although it postponed the deadline for the study for another two and a half years.

Not surprisingly, the *Flores* plaintiffs argued that like the earlier figure of $150, the new total of $340 was arbitrary and capricious. The District Court agreed and ordered the state to complete the second cost study by January 1, 2003 and by June to have complied with the Court order by producing a funding plan that actually satisfied the findings of the cost study (Arizona Senate Research Staff, 2008; Hogan, no date). The State returned to District Court, arguing that the new total did in fact satisfy the January 2000 ruling. This time however, the Court accepted HB 2010, perhaps hoping that the State would finally address its obligations to English language learners. This particular ruling also ordered the State to complete the second cost study by August 2004 so that the legislature could address whatever recommendations the study made in its January 2005 legislative session.

The contract for the second cost study was awarded to a less partisan entity, the National Conference of State Legislatures (NCSL). NCSL conducted a survey of 39 school districts across the state, of which 18 responded, to determine the costs of their ELL programs. This time the difference in ELL program expenditure ranged from $670 to $2571 per pupil. The figures were still widely divergent, but all 18 districts reported they spent more than the $340 appropriated by the state legislature (Arizona Senate Research Staff, 2008; Hogan, no date). The legislature responded with HB 2718, which provided a temporary increase in 'Group B' weight funding for English language learners, and created an English language learner 'task force'. But the bill also declared 'grave concerns' about the validity and reliability of the NCSL cost study because the study relied upon the judgments of educational professionals to identity ELL strategies, 'rather than research that actually shows a linkage between the strategy and student performance' (HB 2718, Sec. 17A, Intent). Instead of raising the amount of funding for English language learners, the legislation funded the development of cost effective 'research based models of structured English immersion.' The bill was unequivocal in stating that until the task force developed these models, the legislature would be unable to determine the costs of implementing ELL programs (HB 2718, Sec. 17C, Intent). According to Hogan, HB 2718 provided an increase of only $75 per English learner, and after one year would be eliminated altogether (Hogan, no date). Governor Janet Napolitano vetoed this bill in May 2005, proposing an alternative version that increased the funding level to $1289 per English language learner. Tim Hogan described what happened next:

> The legislative majority's reaction to the Governor's proposal was instantaneous. The Speaker of the House declared that Arizona would become 'Mexico's best school district north of the border.' Other legislators denied that the state had any responsibility for educating noncitizens and insisted that children born in the United States to parents who had immigrated illegally were not citizens despite the U.S. Constitution's explicit language to the contrary. One legislator suggested that the children 'should be deported, along with their parents'. (Hogan, no date: 16)

Million dollar fines

After five years of noncompliance with the original consent order, the judge in this protracted legal drama was increasingly frustrated by the legislature's recalcitrance. In late 2005, after yet another motion by plaintiffs to force a funding resolution, Judge Raner Collins quipped that he 'might have to jail the governor and legislative leaders to secure proper funding for English-language learners' (Fischer, 2005: A1). Hogan, doubtful about the Court's ability to do this, suggested that incarceration would only work if the governor and legislators were put in the same cell and told they would not be released until they resolved the funding dilemma. Less drastic, but possibly more effective, according to Hogan, would be to withhold more than $500 million in federal highway funds allotted to the state (Fischer, 2005; Judge gives Arizona education ultimatum, 2005; Scutari, 2005).

Ultimately, the Judge imposed a series of fines against the State, beginning with $500,000 a day for every day after the beginning of the 2006 legislative session. The fines would increase to $1,000,000 a day if the legislature still had not complied within 30 days of the lower fine amount; then $1,500,000 and $2,000,000 million a day until the State met its funding mandate. In the strongly worded Order for sanctions, Judge Collins expressed his frustration with the State:

> The Court can only imagine how many students have started school since Judge Marquez entered the Order in February 2000, declaring these programs were inadequately funded in an arbitrary and capricious manner that violates ELL students' rights under the EEOA. How many students may have stopped school, by dropping out or failing because of foot-dragging by the State and failure to comply with the original Order and compliance directives such as the Order issued on January 28, 2005? Plaintiffs are no longer inclined to depend on the good faith of the Defendants or to have faith that without some extraordinary pressure, the State will ever comply with the mandates of the respective Orders issued by this Court. (*Flores v. Arizona*, 'Order W,' 2005: 3)

The legislature scrambled to pass *something*, which minimally raised the Group B weighted funds but also included extraneous corporate tax credits for private school vouchers. Governor Napolitano vetoed this bill, calling the legislature into special session; the very next day, it passed an *identical* bill, but one which imposed a $50 million cap on the corporate tax credits (Arizona Senate Research Staff, 2008). After the governor vetoed this bill as well, the legislature passed HB 2064. By this time, the court ordered fines totaled $21 million. The governor did not veto this bill but refused to sign it. Some of HB 2064's provisions eventually took effect, but the funding saga continues in court, at least as of this writing. Ultimately, HB 2064 profoundly altered the way that school districts were serving English language learners in SEI classrooms.

SEI 'models': Super pullout?

Like earlier ELL funding legislation, HB 2064 authorized an English Language Learners Task Force, which among other duties was charged with 'developing and adopting research-based models of structured English immersion' (HB 2064, 15-756.01.C)[7] The legislative mandate to establish 'research-based models' was an ironic one given that state officials had touted the SEI model – with its combined sheltered content and ELD instruction – as

Table 4.1 Arizona ELLs task force SEI models

AZELLA Pre-emergent & emergent	AZELLA basic level	AZELLA intermediate level
For the Elementary Grades (K-5)		
45 minutes Oral english	30 minutes Oral english	15 minutes Oral english
60 minutes Grammar	60 minutes Grammar	60 minutes Grammar
60 minutes Reading	60 minutes Reading	60 minutes Reading
60 minutes Vocabulary	60 minutes Vocabulary	60 minutes Vocabulary
15 minutes Pre-writing	30 minutes Writing	45 minutes Writing

the most effective means of curing limited English proficiency. The new models ordered a minimum of four hours per day of ELD and limited a student's participation in the program to a period 'not normally intended to exceed one year'. According to the Task Force, English language development instruction would focus on phonology, morphology, syntax, vocabulary and semantics. In effect, the Task force transformed SEI classrooms into four-hour grammar blocks. With the typical school day comprising 6 to $6\frac{1}{2}$ hours per day, four hours of English grammar instruction is a significant portion. Table 4.1 indicates how the Task Force conceptualized the blocks for the elementary grades (K-5). The learners' English proficiency levels, as measured by the Arizona English Language Learner Assessment (AZELLA) instrument, determine the amount of time they receive oral English development and writing instruction.

Scheduling of the four hour grammar blocks at the middle and high school levels are relatively similar (Table 4.2).

Table 4.2 Arizona ELLs task force SEI models

AZELLA Pre-emergent & emergent	AZELLA Basic level	AZELLA Intermediate level
For the Secondary Grades (6–12)		
60 minutes Conversational english and academic vocabulary	60 minutes Conversational english and academic vocabulary	2 hours Language arts
60 minutes English reading	60 minutes English reading	
60 minutes English writing	60 minutes English writing	60 minutes Academic english reading
60 minutes English grammar	60 minutes English grammar	60 minutes Academic writing and grammar

The 'time-on-task' principle

One justification for such a prescriptive approach, according to state officials, was that districts were not providing enough direct instruction in English to ELLs and that schools implemented too many different programs. A uniform approach to ELL education was therefore necessary to ensure students acquired enough English in one year to master other subjects (Kossan, 2007). Another explanation for the new approach was based on the 'time-on-task' or 'maximum exposure' principle, that is the belief that the more time students spend learning something the better they will learn it.

Time-on-task principles underlie much of the traditional opposition to bilingual education (see, e.g. the time-on-task arguments against bilingual education in Chavez, 1991; Clark, 2000; Epstein, 1977; Imhoff, 1990; Porter, 1990; Rossell, 1990; Walberg, 1986). With regard to the acquisition of English, time-on-task principles advance three general assumptions: (1) that immersion in English is more effective than other alternatives; (2) that immersion settings will enable English language learners acquire the language in one or two years; and (3) that young children are ideally suited for immersion because they are better at learning languages than older children or adults (and therefore immersion should begin as early as possible) (Baker, 1998; Porter, 1990, 2000; Siano, 2000).

In Arizona, time-on-task assumptions fundamentally underlie imposition of the four-hour English language development block. The notion that more exposure to English will yield greater fluency in English reflected the attitudes of the majority of members of the ELL Task Force created by H.B. 2064. Alan Maguire, an economist and investment banker and head of the Task Force, justified the state's approach this way: 'More time on task. That's a tried-and-true educational standard. If you want to learn how to play the piano, what do they tell you to do? They tell you to practice' (quoted in Kossan, 2007: A1).

As noted earlier, the time-on-task adage seems logical and likely makes sense to many individuals, including members of the ELL Task Force. However, second language acquisition is a much more complex process. The relative speed of English acquisition as well as the degree of proficiency acquired by English learners depends on many factors, including importantly, how one actually defines *proficiency*. Applied linguists and second language acquisition researchers generally agree that there are different dimensions of English proficiency and that children acquire these dimensions at different speeds. For example, children tend to acquire *social* or conversational language more rapidly than *academic* language. The former is aided by numerous contextual clues, like nonverbal communication in face-to-face interactions, visual or graphic support in a classroom, and is generally thought to less cognitively demanding (Cummins, 1996). Academic language, on the other hand, is characterized by fewer contextual clues and relies on more advanced knowledge of English vocabulary, word order, grammar and pragmatics, or knowing how to act and interact in the second language in different environments (Kasper & Roever, 2005; Wong Fillmore & Snow, 2000). On average, English language learners tend to acquire social language in one to three years and academic language in four to seven years (Hawkins, 2005).[8]

Children's acquisition of English also depends on other variables, for instance, whether they can read and write in their first language (which has implications for their acquisition of written English), whether their parents are educated and literate in the home language (and thus able to assist their children in first language literacy development[9]), or whether children receive first language support in an instructional program at school. Students' socio-economic status may also intervene either positively or negatively as a predictor of student achievement, according to several researchers (Hakuta *et al.*, 2000; Krashen, 1996). With regard to a time limit on support for English language acquisition, children from working class families 'are the ones who on average are learning English more slowly and thus would be most ... adversely affected by a time limit policy, whether it be one, two, three years or more' (Hakuta *et al.*, 2000: 14).

The belief that young children are better at learning a second language than older children and adults also has been contradicted by research in second language acquisition (Collier, 1987, 1988; Hakuta *et al.*, 2000). Young children tend to pick up the social aspects of language relatively quickly and to acquire the language with a native or native-like an accent. Together, these accomplishments may provide the impression that children are fluent in English, but it is not 'the elaborate, syntactically and lexically complex code of the proficient language' (Van Lier, quoted in Hakuta *et al.*, 2000: 2).

No research base for the four-hour language blocks

At one of the ELL Task Force meetings, university researchers pointed out the lack of a research base to justify placing students into a segregated language block. A better approach was to teach English through content subjects, and English grammar should be embedded in context and not taught as a separate phenomenon. They argued for fewer restrictions on the use of students' first languages within the SEI model, and reiterated the positive connection between the academic development of the first language and acquisition of the second language.[10]

Discussion about the need for research justifying the four-hour block occurred from time to time among task force members themselves. One exchange took place on March 14, 2007 between two members, Johanna

Haver, a former high school ELD teacher, and Eugene Garcia, the only university-based researcher on the task force.[11] Garcia was arguing about the need to back up the proposed four-hour block with research supporting its effectiveness in both language acquisition and academic achievement. Haver appeared to argue that the lack of a research base for the new policy was a moot point, because state law required the four-hour block regardless:

Haver: I just wanted to point out to Dr Garcia that ... we do have to follow policy, whether we like it or not.

Garcia: [I've got] no problem with that.

Haver: And the policy has certain principles to it that you have to accept, whether you like it or not.

Garcia: I'll say the same thing about research, whether you like it or not, it tells us something about how kids learn, whether you like it or not. Many times we can make it fit into the policy, but we can't ignore it. That's what I'm saying.

Haver: I'm with you completely ... but we do have differences on principles of learning a second language that the policy pretty much limits, for instance, bilingual education.

Garcia: Yeah, I'm not arguing that at all, but I would certainly argue that we have to lean on whatever policy is good for kids. That's really what our job is.

The lack of a research base for the four-hour block was a serious criticism of Arizona's English language learning policy. Thus it was probably not surprising that shortly after this exchange a literature review justifying the time on task approach to English language teaching appeared on the Arizona Department of Education Website.[12] Drawing largely from time on task studies, the review argued that more exposure to English would logically facilitate proficiency in the language. The review's credibility was challenged in an analysis by Krashen, Rolstad and MacSwan (this volume) because it did not include research that considered the instructional use of students' native languages to aid acquisition of English, and because the studies it cited were based on research with fluent English speakers, not English language learners.

A Prescriptive Teaching Methodology for a Prescriptive Model: The 'Discrete Skills Inventory'

In November of 2006, the English Language Learner Task Force heard a presentation by Kevin Clark, a California-based education consultant and supporter of the four-hour English Language Development block. Clark argued that instruction within the block should focus on the 'discrete skills' aspects of language, that is, phonology, morphology, syntax and vocabulary, because English learners had to learn *about* English before they could effectively learn content *in* English. In a later article justifying the ELD block, Clark reiterated that the central focus should be language itself, 'its rules, uses, forms, and application to daily school and non-school situations'. Academic content played a supporting but subordinate role; English learners had to have a strong understanding of the English language before they were taught grade-level content (Clark, 2009: 3).

Over the following year, Clark spoke at many task force meetings. A dominant theme in his presentations was the urgent need to 'accelerate' the acquisition of English. Because state law specified a one-year time frame for students to learn English, he proposed a methodology that ostensibly would accomplish this: the *Discrete Skills Inventory* (DSI). Designed as 'a sequential series of English language skills', the DSI was a method teachers could use in conjunction with the state English Language Proficiency Standards and the Arizona English Language Learner Assessment instrument (AZELLA). As Clark noted at one of the meetings: 'if the ELL Proficiency Standards are the freeway for gaining English proficiency on AZELLA, then discrete skills are the surface roads' (ELL Task Force meeting minutes, May 3, 2007). The DSI thus would provide students with the grammatical foundations they needed to achieve proficiency in English:

> The skills presented in the DSI make lesson planning easier for teachers. Using the DSI, teachers can fashion lesson plans and implement classroom activities that provide their students with an understanding of the parts of speech, how they combine to form phrases and sentences, and the overarching structure of the English language. For example, if students are expected to describe items in the classroom, they need first to be taught certain parts of speech such as nouns, adjectives, verbs, as well as how to conjugate verbs, and then learn how to assemble different types of words in proper grammatical order. (Discrete Skills Inventory, n.d.: 1)

The task force ultimately adopted the DSI as the prescribed methodology for ELD teachers, with consistent objection from only two of its members.[13]

The Arizona Department of Education subsequently organized DSI training sessions for teachers and administrators in which trainers emphasized the prescriptive nature of the methodology. First, *language* itself was

Table 4.3 English language development components

ELD components:	Non-negotiable SEI model components

• Phonology: Speech, sounds
• Morphology: Parts of words, prefixes, suffixes and roots (base), verb tenses.
• Syntax: Grammar, Sentence structure, language rules
• Vocabulary
  ○ Lexicon: Collection of words you know
  ○ Semantics: Meaning of words or sentences
	• ELLs not mixed with non-ELLs during ELD
	• Provide four (4) hours of ELD per the SEI Models
	• Group by proficiency
	• HQ Teacher
	• ELP standards

ELD is ...	Principles for accelerating English language learning
• NOT a math lesson • NOT a science lesson • NOT a social studies lesson • NOT optional in an SEI classroom	• Error correction • English only in the classroom • Complete sentences • 50/50 Rule

Source: Arizona Department of Education (2009a), Office of English Language Acquisition Services, Administrator's Model Implementation Training, http://www.ade.az.gov/oelas. Accessed 6.07.10.

narrowly defined as comprising five discrete, inter-dependent elements that had to be taught overtly (phonology, morphology, syntax, lexicon and semantics). Second, the four-hour ELD blocks and the segregation of ELLs from non-ELLs within them were non-negotiable, and third, grouping students by proficiency levels (rather than by age or grade levels) was mandatory. Finally, ELD block teachers were to adhere to the following principles for accelerating the learning of English: error correction, English only in the classroom, complete sentences, and the 50/50 rule (teachers speak 50% and students speak 50%). Table 4.3 presents information contained in a Slide Show part of a June 9, 2009 Administrator's training by the Arizona Department of Education); they spell out the non-negotiability of the models.

Failure to Adopt the SEI Models

Most recently, the Department issued a 'zero tolerance' memorandum to school districts ordering rigid compliance with the ELD block adopted by the English Language Learner Task Force (Arizona Department of Education, 2009b). The memorandum stated unambiguously that 'good faith efforts' to implement the four-hour grammar block were unacceptable, and that nothing short of full compliance would be tolerated. The memorandum also threatened the legal sanctions originally introduced in Proposition 203 (and now state law):

> Any school board member or other elected official or administrator who willfully and repeatedly refuses to implement the terms of this statute [ARS 15-752 and 15-753] may be held personally liable for fees and actual and compensatory damages by the child's parents or legal guardian, and cannot be subsequently indemnified for such assessed damages by any public or private third party. Any individual found so liable shall be immediately removed from office, and shall be barred from holding any position of authority anywhere within the Arizona public school system for an additional period of five years.

The timing of the memorandum and the Department's heavy-handed reiteration of sanctions is not surprising given well publicized defiance of the ELD block by several school districts (Fischer, 2008; Sánchez, 2008a, b). In early 2008, the Sahuarita Unified School District publically rejected the state order, fearing it would violate students' civil rights. School officials stated that placing English learners in the four-hour blocks would be discriminatory if they were prevented from receiving the same curriculum as other students (Sánchez, 2008a). The Tucson Unified School District governing board also had been critical of the state order and explored the legal ramifications of ignoring it. Stated one of the members, 'We could send a real message and say we are not going to do it, so sue us.' After being told the district's funding would be jeopardized, the board voted under protest to approve the four-hour English Language Development Blocks (Sánchez, 2008b).

Discussion

How *folk theories* about language acquisition have become *fact* in the State of Arizona

As noted above, state ELL policy (based on Proposition 203) includes several false statements about how children acquire a second language. That these statements sound logical to the uninformed does not make them accurate. Nor does their ubiquitous presence in state government discourse and directives give them credibility. For example, the State Office of English Language Acquisition Services (OELAS) has a website that provides administrative forms, announcements, links to policy and legal documents and training materials. School districts can access these materials as they wish. One of the documents available is a 107-slide PowerPoint presentation called

'Nuts and Bolts,' which OELAS staff has used in periodic seminars through-out the state.[14] The presentation explains state policy mandates as deriving from case law (*Lau v. Nichols, Castañeda v. Pickard, Flores v. Arizona*), Proposition 203 and House Bill 2064. Only two slides reference research in any form: the first states that the Task Force 'identified critical research based components on which to build the models'. The second slide

lists four broad principles which ostensibly justify the four-hour English Language Development block, but without attribution: (1) English is funda-mental to content area mastery; (2) Language ability based grouping facilitates rapid language learning; (3) Time on task increases academic learning; and (4) a discrete language skills approach facilitates English language learning (Office of English Language Acquisition Services, 'Nuts & Bolts,' slides #39 & #40). Another slide, titled 'One Year to Proficiency,' advances the idea that students can become fluent in English in one year through prescriptive means[15]:

One (1) year to proficiency

Task Force charged to produce models that will lead to proficiency in one (1) year

- Demands PRESCRIPTIVE models;
- Prescriptive curriculum developed in DSI;
- Prescriptive time allocations;
- Prescriptive class content;
- Prescriptive training.

Arizona Department of Education, Office of English Language Acquisition Services, Administrator's Model Implementation Training, http://www.ade.az.gov/oelas.

Arizona language policy: The reification of *things which are not*

In Swift's fable of the Houyhnhnms, Gulliver converses with his mentor about life among the Yahoos (humans). He is forced to invent all manner of lexical circumlocutions to convey the meaning of behavior completely unfa-miliar to the Houyhnhnms. These strenuous discourses focus mostly on the commission of crimes and the practice of certain vices. Such an endeavor takes several days to accomplish, but eventually he manages:

> To clear up which I endeavoured to give him some ideas of the desire of power and riches; of the terrible effects of lust, intemperance, malice and envy. All this I was forced to define and describe by putting of cases, and

making suppositions. After which, like one whose imagination was struck with something never seen or heard of before, he would lift up his eyes with amazement and indignation. (Swift, 2003 [1726]: 244)

Comparing Arizona language policy to crimes and vices might be a stretch. Yet there is undeniably a Gulliverian feel to the discourse of Proposition 203 and the policy documents arising from the Flores case. The paradox is that the text of the proposition, once expressed as part of a vaguely worded measure later approved by voters, is now codified in the Arizona Revised Statutes as law. And as law, the statements – misleading and false though they may be – have become part of the official state discourse about the education of English language learners. And as official discourse, *cum* law, these statements have become fact.

I would also argue the presence of legal *things which are not* in Arizona language policy. For example, state education officials have used the *Castañeda v. Pickard* decision to justify segregating English learners into four-hour English language blocks. They specifically invoke the Court's finding that grouping children into 'language remediation programs is unobjectionable ... so long as such a practice is genuinely motivated by educational concerns and not discriminatory motives'. Officials also routinely remind us that the *Castañeda* Court gave school systems free reign to 'employ ability grouping, even when such a policy has a segregative effect' (*Castañeda v. Pickard*, 648 F.2d 989; 1981).

Indeed, *Castañeda* authorizes a degree of latitude in school district selection of instructional programs for English language learners. School systems also can decide whether to teach language and content *simultaneously* or *sequentially*. However, the legal reasoning in the case is far more nuanced and cautionary. For one, the Court acknowledged the claim that 'pressing English on the child is not the first goal of language remediation'. For another, the Court also affirmed that the Equal Educational Opportunities Act imposed upon school systems an obligation to 'provide limited English speaking ability students with assistance in other areas of the curriculum where their equal participation may be impaired because of deficits incurred during participation in an agency's language remediation program'. In other words, the 'appropriate action' school districts undertake to help English language learners overcome language barriers must be 'reasonably calculated to enable these students to attain parity of participation in the standard instructional program within a reasonable length of time after they enter the school system' (*Castañeda v. Pickard*, 648 F.2d 989; 1981).

The Arizona state legislature and education officials may believe that one year is a reasonable length of time for ELLs to acquire enough English to perform well in the mainstream classroom, but no one familiar with the research on second language learning and teaching does. There is still no evidence that children can learn a second language well in just one year, regardless of the approach used. As noted earlier, the typical public school day is approximately $6 - 6\frac{1}{2}$ hours, and four hours of English language development instruction is a significant portion. If the rest of the day is divided between lunch, recess and math (the other assessed content area on the state's high stakes test), there is little time for science, social studies, music or art. State Education documents make plain that English learners will remain in SEI/ELD classrooms until they reach the 'proficient' level on the state's proficiency test.[16] If students do not achieve proficiency in one year, however, they could remain segregated in remedial classrooms a second, third, even fourth year.

Let us return for a moment to the 'time on task' argument made by members of the ELL Task Force. One of the Task Force members suggested that learning English was like learning to play the piano, that is, the more one practices, the more skilled one becomes. While logical, maximum exposure to English in a short amount of time does not result in full acquisition of English. The applied linguistics literature is clear about this. Still, there is an equally powerful argument to be made against the blanket imposition of ELD policies for all English language learners in the state. Consider, for instance, that practicing the piano for hours and hours may lead *some* students to virtuosity, but it could just as easily frustrate and discourage others. What if two students were forced to practice in the same way for four hours a day? What if one student had an aptitude for music but poor dexterity? What if the other had a Steinway Baby Grand rather than an upright? Or a family with the economic means to afford lessons from a concert pianist? What if one student preferred baseball? Or the other came to the lesson hungry? What if both students were the same age but different in their maturity levels?[17] And so on. The point is that a 'one size fits all' model for any discipline is counterproductive. It may ultimately be harmful. In the end, like Gulliver's Houyhnhnm mentor, we can only react with amazement and indignation.

Acknowledgment

I am grateful to William Combs and Sal Gabaldón for reviewing earlier drafts of this chapter.

Notes

(1)   Pronounced 'hwi-hn'm' (Oxford English Dictionary, 1989), an onomatopoetic combination of letters meant to resemble the whinnying of a horse.
(2)   In addition to ballot initiatives regulating the language of instruction in public schools were others covering a wide range of topics, including teacher salaries,

charter schools, vouchers, testing, curriculum content, funding, school start dates, affirmative action and so on.

(3) The measures passed in California, Arizona and Massachusetts and failed in Colorado.

(4) From the Findings and Declarations of Proposition 203: 'Young immigrant children can easily acquire full fluency in a new language, such as English, if they are heavily exposed to that language in the classroom at an early age.' Now officially part of Arizona Revised Statutes, Title 15, Section 752: English Language Education: 'Children who are English learners shall be educated through sheltered English immersion during a temporary transition period not normally intended to exceed one year (Arizona Revised Statutes, Title 15, Section 752: English Language Education).

(5) The U.S. District Court, District of Arizona certified the class in August of 1997, defining it as 'all minority "at risk" and limited English proficient children (LEP), now or hereafter, enrolled in Nogales Unified School District (NUSD), as well as their parents and guardians'. As a class action lawsuit that challenged the State of Arizona's school funding formula, the Court at trial determined that the State had failed to provide adequate funding for minority at risk LEP students 'attending public school systems in districts like NUSD'. (*Flores v. Arizona*, 48 F. Supp. 2d. 937: 2).

(6) At the time of the cost study, CEO was headed by Linda Chavez, former President of U.S. English, a national organization dedicated to making English the official language of the US. The READ Institute was funded by U.S. English (Crawford, 2008).

(7) The English Language Learner Task Force was composed of nine members, three of whom were appointed by the Superintendent of Public Instruction, two appointed by the governor, two by the President of the Senate, and two by the Speaker of the House. Of the nine individuals, only one had extensive research expertise in the education of English language learners: Arizona State University professor and College of Education Dean Eugene Garcia.

(8) These are estimates. Some researchers posit that the acquisition of social language actually requires up to three years, and even from three to five years (Hakuta *et al.*, 2000).

(9) Steve Krashen (1996) calls this phenomenon 'de facto bilingual education', that is, when students learn English at school but continue to develop L1 literacy at home.

(10) Richard Ruiz from the University of Arizona, Christian Faltis from Arizona State University, and Norbert Francis from Northern Arizona University. They spoke at the November 20, 2006 Task Force meeting. The minutes of that meeting are available on-line at http://www.ade.az.gov/ELLTaskForce/2006/minutes/11-20-06-MinutesELLTaskForce.pdf. Last accessed 21.06.10.

(11) The entire meeting is streamed on the Arizona State Government website: http://azleg.granicus.com/MediaPlayer.php?view_id=3&clip_id=731. Last accessed 2.06.10.

(12) 'Research Summary and Bibliography for Structured English Immersion Program Models,' available on-line at http://www.ade.az.gov/oelas/downloads/modelcomponentresearch.pdf. Last accessed 2.06.10.

(13) Dr Eugene Garcia, from Arizona State University, and Dr John Baracy, Superintendent of Scottsdale Unified School District.

(14) Available from the website of the Arizona Department of Education, http://www.ade.state.az.us/oelas. Last accessed 2.06.10.

(15) Retrieved 4 November 2009 from http://www.ade.state.az.us/oelas. Last accessed 2.06.10.

(16) Nuts and bolts: Structured English Immersion models, round #1. Powerpoint slides #45 & 46. Online document: http://www.ade.state.az.us/oelas. Accessed 5 June 2010.

(17) I thank Sal Gabaldón for suggesting this useful analogy.

References

Alexander, K. and Alexander, M.D. (1985) *American Public School Law* (2nd edn). St. Paul, MN: West Publishing Company.

Arizona Department of Education (n.d.) Discrete skills inventory. Online document, accessed 2 June 2010. https://www.ade.az.gov/oelas/downloads/DSIAllLevels.pdf

Arizona Department of Education (2009a) Administrator's model implementation training. Online document, accessed 5 June 2010. https://www.ade.az.gov/oelas

Arizona Department of Education (2009b) Guidance on SEI model implementation for 2009–2010. Memorandum to Superintendents and School Administrators from John A. Stollar, Jr., Superintendent for Accountability, May 7. Online document, accessed 2 June 2010. http://www.ade.state.az.us/oelas/downloads/GuidanceonSEIModel Implementationfor2009–2010.pdf

Arizona Revised Statutes, Title 15 (Education), § 3.1 (English Language Education for Children in Public Schools), 751-756.01.

Arizona Revised Statutes (2009) Title15-756.01. Arizona English language learners task force; research based models of structured English immersion for English language learners; budget requests; definition. Online document, accessed 2 June 2010. http://www.azleg.gov/DocumentsForBill.asp?Bill_Number=HB2064

Arizona Secretary of State (2000) Voter education pamphlet: 2000 Ballot propositions. Online document, accessed 5 June 2010. http://www.azsos.gov/election/2000/Info/pubpamphlet/english/contents.htm

Arizona Senate Research Staff (2008) Issue paper: *Flores v. Arizona*. August 27. Online document, accessed 5 June 2010. http://www.azleg.gov/briefs/Senate/FLORES%20 V.%20ARIZONA.pdf

Ayala, H. (1999) Congressional testimony on bilingual education. House Committee on Education and the Workforce, June 24.

Baker, K. (1998) Structured English immersion: Breakthrough in teaching limited-English-proficient students. *Phi Delta Kappan* 80, 199–204.

Broder, D. (2001) *Democracy Derailed: Initiative Campaigns and the Power of Money*. Boston: Mariner Books.

Castañeda v. Pickard, 648 F.2d 989 (5th Cir. 1981).

Chavez, L. (1991) *Out of the Barrio: Toward a New Politics of Hispanic Assimilation*. New York: Basic Books.

Chávez, L. (1998) *The Color Bind: California's Campaign to End Affirmative Action*. Berkeley: University of California Press.

Clark, K. (2000) The design and implementation of an English immersion program. In K. Clark (ed.) *The ABC's of English Immersion: A Teacher's Guide* (pp. 24–30). Washington, DC: Center for Equal Opportunity.

Clark, K. (2009) The case for structured English immersion. *Educational Leadership* 66, 42–46.

Collier, V. (1987) Age and rate of acquisition of second language for academic purposes. *TESOL Quarterly* 21, 617–641.

Collier, V. (1988) *The Effect of Age on Acquisition of a Second Language for School.* Washington, DC: National Clearinghouse for Bilingual Education. Online document, accessed 5 June 2010. http://www.eric.ed.gov/ERICDocs/data/ericdocs2sql/content_storage_01/0000019b/80/ 1d/a9/40.pdf

Collier, V. (1995) *Promoting Academic Success for ESD Students: Understanding Second Language Acquisition for School.* Elizabeth: New Jersey Teachers of English to Speakers of Other Languages-Bilingual Educators.

Combs, M.C., Evans, C., Fletcher, T., Parra, E. and Jiménez, A. (2005) Bilingualism for the children: Implementing a dual language program in an English only state. *Educational Policy* 19, 701–728.

Crawford, J. (2001) Proposition 203: Anti-Bilingual initiative in Arizona. Online document, accessed 2 July 2010. http://www.languagepolicy.net/archives/az-unz.htm

Crawford, J. (2008) *Advocating for English Learners.* Clevedon: Multilingual Matters.

Cummins, J. (1991) Interdependence of first- and second-language proficiency in bilingual children. In E. Bialystok (ed.) *Language Processing in Bilingual Children* (pp. 70–89). Cambridge: Cambridge University Press.

Cummins, J. (1992) Bilingual education and English immersion: The Ramírez Report in theoretical perspective. *Bilingual Research Journal* 16, 91–104.

Cummins, J. (1996) *Negotiating Identities: Education for Empowerment in a Diverse Society.* Ontario, CA: California Association for Bilingual Education.

Cummins, J. and Swain, M. (1986) *Bilingualism in Education: Aspects of Theory, Research, and Practice.* London: Longman.

English for the Children (n.d.) English for the Children-Arizona: An organization to eliminate bilingual education. Campaign Brochure.

Epstein, N. (1977) *Language, Ethnicity, and the Schools: Policy Alternatives for Bilingual-Bicultural Education.* Washington, DC: Institute for Educational Leadership.

Equal Education Opportunities Act of 1974 ('EEOA'), 20 U.S.C. § 1703(f).

Fischer, H. (2005) Politicians locked up? English case vexes judge. *Arizona Daily Star* November 1, A1.

Fischer, H. (2008) Schools seek delay in English-learner requirement. *Arizona Daily Star* March 7, B6.

Flores v. Arizona, 48 F. Supp. 2d. 937, U.S. District Court, District of Arizona, 1999.

Flores v. Arizona, 172 F. Supp. 2d 1225 (D. Ariz. 2000).

Flores v. Arizona, 405 F. Supp. 2d 1112, (D. Ariz. 2005) ('Order W').

Gamble, B.S. (1997) Putting civil rights to a popular vote. *American Journal of Political Science* 4, 245–269.

Gee, J. (2008) *Social Linguistics and Literacies: Ideology in Discourses* (3rd edn). New York: Routledge.

Hakuta, K., Butler, Y.G. and Witt, D. (2000) *How Long Does it Take for English Learners to Attain Proficiency?* Santa Barbara, CA: University of California, Linguistic Minority Research Institute. Online document, accessed 2 July 2010. http://www.lmri.ucsb.edu/publications/00_hakuta.pdf

Haskell, J. (2001) *Direct Democracy or Representative Government?* Boulder, CO: Westview Press.

Hawkins, M. (2005) ESD in elementary education. In E. Hinkel (ed.) *Handbook of Research in Second Language Teaching and Learning* (pp. 25–43). Mahwah, NJ: Lawrence Erlbaum, Inc.

Hogan, T. (n.d.) *Flores v. State of Arizona*: History, status and implications. Online document, accessed 2 July 2010. http://www.nsba.org/SecondaryMenu/CUBE/Conferences Meetings/CUBEMeetingsHeldin2006/CUBE38thAnnualConferenceBuildingCulturally

CompetentGovernanceforUrbanSchools/FloresvArizonaSchoolFinanceLawsuitand
Proposition203ArizonasEnglishOnlyLaw/FloresvStateofArizona.aspx
Horne, T. (2004a) English immersion works fine. *Arizona Republic* August 19, B9.
Horne, T. (2004b) *First Annual State of Education Speech*, January 6. Online document,
accessed 5 June 2010. http://www.ade.az.gov/administration/superintendent/
articles.asp
Imhoff, G. (1990) The position of U.S. English on bilingual education. In C.B. Cazden
and C.E. Snow (eds) *English Plus: Issues in Bilingual Education* (pp. 48–61). The Annals
of the American Academy of Political and Social Science. Newbury Park, CA: Sage
Publications.
Initiative and Reform Institute (2009) Ballotwatch. Online document, accessed 5 June
2010. http://www.iandrinstitute.org/ballotwatch.htm
Johnson, E. (2005) Proposition 203: A critical metaphor analysis. *Bilingual Research Journal*
29, 69–84.
Judge gives Arizona education ultimatum: Aid English learners or face big fines, State is
told (2005) *Arizona Republic* December 17, A1.
Kasper, G. and Roever (2005) Pragmatics in second language learning. In E. Hinkel (ed.)
Handbook of Research in Second Language Teaching and Learning (pp. 317–334). Mahwah,
NJ: Lawrence Erlbaum, Inc.
Kossan, P. (2007) New learners must spend 4 hours a day on English. *The Arizona Republic*
July 15, A1.
Kraker, D. (2000) Ugly initiatives show democracy's allure. *Arizona Daily Star* November
23, B7.
Krashen, S. (1996) *Under Attack: The Case Against Bilingual Education*. Culver City, CA:
Language Education Associates.
Miller, K.P. (1999) The role of courts in the initiative process. Paper presented at the
American Political Science Association Meeting, Atlanta.
Mora, J.K. (2009) From the ballot box to the classroom. *Educational Leadership* 66, 14–19.
Mahoney, K., MacSwan, J. and Thompson, M. (2005) *The Condition of English Language
Learners in Arizona: 2005*. Tempe: Arizona State University, Education Policy Studies
Laboratory.
National Conference of State Legislatures, Ballot Measures Database (2009) Online docu-
ment, accessed 2 June 2010. http://www.ncsl.org/Default.aspx?TabId=16580
Oxford English Dictionary (1989) Oxford: Oxford University Press.
Porter, R. (1990) *Forked Tongue: The Politics of Bilingual Education*. New York: Basic Books.
Porter, R. (2000) The benefits of English immersion. *Educational Leadership* 57, 52–56.
Porter, R. (2001) Introduction. The cost of english acquisition programs: The Arizona
Department of Education English acquisition cost study. *READ Perspectives* 8, 5–10.
Rabin, N., Combs, M.C. and González, N. (2008) Understanding *Plyler's* legacy: Voices
from border schools. *Journal of Law and Education* 37, 15–82.
Ramírez, J.D. (1992) Executive summary. *Bilingual Research Journal* 16, 1–62.
Ramírez, J.D., Yuen, S.D. and Ramey, D.R. (1991) *Executive Summary of the Final Report:
Longitudinal Study of Structured English Immersion Strategy, Early-Exit and Late-Exit
Transitional Bilingual Education Programs for Language-Minority Children* (Contract No.
300-87-0156; submitted to the U.S. Department of Education). San Mateo, CA: Aguirre
International.
Rossell, C. (1990) The effectiveness of educational alternatives for limited English profi-
cient children. In G. Imhoff (ed.) *Learning in Two Languages: From Conflict to Consensus*

in the Reorganization of Schools (pp. 71–122). New Brunswick, NJ: Transaction Publishers.

Sánchez, G. (2008a) Sahuarita rebuffs state on ELL. *Arizona Daily Star* May 24, 1.

Sánchez, G. (2008b) Board OKs English-learner program. *Arizona Daily Star* January 23, B1.

Scutari, C. (2005) Judge: State shorting English ed: Lawyer wants court to hold road funds if spending doesn't rise. *Arizona Republic* January 26, A.1.

Siano, J. (2000) Teaching Juan and Maria to read. In *The ABC's of English Immersion: A Teacher's Guide* (pp. 16–19). Washington, DC: Center for Equal Opportunity.

Swift, J. (1726) *Gulliver's Travels*. New York: Barnes and Nobles Classics Edition, 2003.

Unz, R. (1997) Bilingualism vs. bilingual education. *Los Angeles Times* October 19, M6.

Unz, R. (2001) Rocks falling upward at Harvard University. *National Review On-line* October 26. Online document: http://www.onenation.org/0110/102601.htm

Walberg, H.J. (1986) Letter to Frederick Mulhauser, September 22. In U.S. General Accounting Office (1987) *Bilingual Education: A New Look at the Research Evidence* (pp. 71–72). Washington, DC: Author.

Wong Fillmore, L. (1991) Second language learning in children: A model of language learning in social context. In E. Bialystok (ed.) *Language Processing in Bilingual Children* (pp. 49–69). Cambridge: Cambridge University Press.

Wong Fillmore, L. and Snow, C.E. (2000) What teachers need to know about language. U.S. Department of Education's Office of Educational Research and Improvement, ED-99-CO-0008. Online document, accessed 30 July 2010. http://faculty.tamu-commerce.edu/jthompson/Resources/FillmoreSnow2000.pdf

Wright, W. and Pu, C. (2005) *Academic Achievement of English Language Learners in Post Proposition 203 Arizona*. EPSL-0509-103-LPRU. Tempe, AZ: Language Policy Research Unit (LPRU)/Education Policy Studies Laboratory. Arizona State University.

Wright, W.E. (2005) The political spectacle of Arizona's Proposition 203. *Educational Policy* 19, 662–700.

5 Teachers' Sheltered English Immersion Views and Practices

Wayne E. Wright and Koyin Sung

Arizona's Proposition 203, passed by voters in 2000, was designed to restrict bilingual education programs by mandating an approach called Sheltered English Immersion (SEI).[1] The Superintendent of Public Instruction who took office in 2003 ran on a platform of strictly enforcing Proposition 203. He made good on his promise by appointing one of the local chairs of the Proposition 203 'English for Children' campaign as his Associate Superintendent over the state's ELLs programs. Together they have enforced a narrow and strict interpretation of Proposition 203 (see Wright, 2005c for details).

The US Supreme Court Case *Lau v. Nichols* and federal policy outlined in the Equal Educational Opportunities Act of 1974 make it clear that ELLs cannot simply be thrown into a regular, mainstream English-only classroom and left to sink-or-swim. Rather, schools must provide a program which ensures ELLs learn English and are given equal access to the core curriculum. Unfortunately, the distinction made in Proposition 203 between SEI and mainstream classrooms is not precise. It defines a mainstream classroom as one where '[s]tudents are native English speakers or already have acquired reasonable fluency in English'. The law declares that in an SEI classroom, books and instructional materials are in English, and all reading, writing, and subject matter are taught in English, however this is no different than in mainstream classrooms. Proposition 203 only provides two criteria that distinguish SEI from mainstream classrooms: (1) The curriculum and presentation are designed for ELLs, and (2) *Nearly* all classroom instruction is in English.

To comply with federal policy, a curriculum designed for ELLs would, at minimum, require explicit instruction in English as a second language (ESL) or English language development (ELD), and content-area instruction that is specially designed to make it comprehensible for ELLs when taught in English. The latter is referred to in the literature as Specially Designed Academic Instruction in English (SDAIE) or simply as Sheltered Instruction (Echevarria, 2002). The stipulation that *nearly* all instruction is in English reflects Proposition 203's allowance for teachers to 'use a minimal amount of L1 [students' first language] when necessary'. The use of students' L1 in this manner to help make English instruction comprehensible is referred to in the literature as primary language support (Wright, 2008, 2010). Thus, the three distinguishing factors that separate SEI from mainstream classrooms are (1) ESL/ELD instruction, (2) sheltered content instruction and (3) primary language support. With the restrictions placed on bilingual education, it is imperative that teachers in SEI classrooms understand and include these critical components in order for their ELLs to successfully learn English and academic content taught in English.

This chapter presents the findings from studies which address the following research questions: How do classroom teachers of ELLs view SEI policies and practices? How much information and guidance have they received, and how is SEI being implemented in their schools? How effective is SEI instruction in meeting the linguistic and academic needs of ELL students? Methods used to answer these questions include a state-wide survey of 3rd grade ELL teachers, and case studies conducted in two 3rd grade SEI classrooms.

The Arizona Context: NCLB, High Stakes Testing and School Labels

Discussions of SEI implementation and effectiveness requires an understanding of the educational context in Arizona where school reform efforts focusing on high stakes testing and accountability are being driven by the federal No Child Left Behind Act (NCLB) of 2001, and state-level testing and accountability policies, including the practice of labeling schools based on test scores. The logic behind these school reform efforts is very simple – establish standards to identify what students need to know, measure student attainment of the standards through high-stakes standardized tests and then use the results to hold schools accountable (Barton, 2006; Ravitch, 1997). One common way to hold schools accountable is to convert complicated sets of test scores into a single label which depicts the 'quality' of the school. In Arizona these labels are organized in a hierarchy from least to most desirable: failing, underperforming, performing, highly performing and excelling (Arizona Department of

Education, 2003). Under a separate federal system, NCLB requires states to identify 'failing' schools that do not make 'adequate yearly progress' toward the goal of all of students passing their state's exam by 2014 (Abedi, 2004; Darling-Hammond, 2004; Wright, 2005b). Under both NCLB and Arizona's account-ability programs, schools with low labels are required to improve their test scores; if they do not the school faces a series of sanctions, including the ulti-mate take-over of the school by the state or a private company (de Cohen *et al.*, 2005; Valenzuela, 2004). Thus, school labels – and the high-stakes tests scores used to calculate them – are taken very seriously by the schools.

In the midst of this these requirements for accountability is the fact that there is rapidly growing population of ELL students (National Clearinghouse for English Language Acquisition, 2006). There has been much debate over how to best meet the language and academic needs of ELL students (Baker, 2006; Crawford, 2003, 2004; Krashen, 1996; Porter, 1990; Rossell, 2002). There has also been debate over NCLB's requirements that all ELL students be tested and included in state accountability programs (Abedi, 2003; de Cohen *et al.*, 2005; Wright, 2005a, b; Wright & Choi, 2006). NCLB sets up an unusual situation in which ELL students are defined as students who will have difficulty meeting state standards due to their lack of proficiency in English, but the law nonetheless requires that they meet these standards anyways as evidenced by passing test scores, and schools are held accountable if they do not (Wright, 2005b, 2006).

The use of high-stakes tests and school labels as part of the accountability program has been very controversial. There is a growing body of research which provides evidence that the focus on high-stakes testing is actually decreasing the quality of instruction (Haney, 2002; Kohn, 2000; McNeil, 2000; Popham, 2001; Sacks, 1999; Valenzuela, 2004; Wright, 2002; Wright & Choi, 2006). Some scholars have argued that the basic logic behind the school labeling process – designed to 'shame' low-performing schools into doing better – is deeply flawed and not producing the intended results (Fuller *et al.*, 2006; Mintrop, 2003; Popham, 2004). Nonetheless, school labels are often taken at face value. Policy makers, educators, parents and the general public typically accept the labels as accurate depictions of a school. However, when it comes to ELL students, some research has suggested that these labels may be highly misleading (Wright, 2005a; Wright & Pu, 2005).

Methodology

The survey results reported here are selected from an earlier study (Wright & Choi, 2006) in which 40 third-grade ELL teachers from different school districts across the state with large numbers of ELL students participated in telephone surveys and interviews. These 40 teachers represent 11 out of Arizona's 15 counties, and provided direct instruction to 878 ELL students in the 2004–2005 school year. Furthermore, the 40 school districts represented by these teachers provided instruction to three-fourths of all 3rd grade ELLs in the state in 2004 (see Wright & Choi, 2006, for further details on sample, methodology and analysis).

For the case study, two Phoenix-area elementary schools in different school districts were selected: a school labeled as 'performing' from the West Valley (hereafter Westside school), and a school labeled as 'Underperforming' in the East Valley (hereafter, Eastside school). Data were collected through participant observations of a 3rd grade SEI classroom at each school, and interviews with the classroom teachers. While observations were conducted throughout the 2003–2004 school year, the data presented here focus on classroom observations collected across a single representative week of instruction toward the end of the first semester in the 2003–2004 school year. Fieldnotes were kept during the observations. Classroom instruction was digitally audio-recorded and used as a reference to aid fieldnote accuracy and subsequent data analysis.

Data analyses utilized the Sheltered Instruction Observation Protocol (SIOP) developed by Echevarria *et al.* (2007) in response to the need for an organizational framework for planning, delivering, and evaluating sheltered English instruction. The SIOP is a popular model and is used widely in programs for ELLs across the country. It is aligned with the type of instruction mandated by Arizona's Proposition 203 for ELL students. The SIOP consists of 30 specific observable items indicative of the quality of sheltered instruction. Each item is scored on a Likert-type scale of 0–4. While the highest possible score is 120 points, some SIOP items may not be applicable to certain lessons. To account for the exclusion of nonapplicable items, percentages are calculated from the ratios of points/total possible points.

Analyses of observational and interview data was conducted with the aid of NVivo, a qualitative research software program. We used the 30 items on the SIOP model as our main coding scheme for all data. In addition we identified and scored individual lessons taught in each classroom on three comparable days during the weeks' observations using the SIOP. A total of 36 lessons were evaluated, 15 in Mrs Charles classroom at Westside, and 21 lessons in Mrs Silvers classroom at Eastside. Where field notes were not sufficient to evaluate the lessons, we listened to the original recordings. To ensure inter-rater reliability of these evaluations, we cross-checked a sample of each other's SIOP evaluations to ensure consistency in the scoring of the 30 items.

Survey Findings

Teacher's views on bilingualism, bilingual education, Proposition 203 and sheltered English immersion

The teachers throughout the state who participated in the survey were given several statements related to language issues and instructional models, and were asked to indicate their level of agreement. The results appear in Table 5.1. These results indicate that these teachers of ELL students value

Table 5.1 Third-grade ELL teachers' views on bilingualism, bilingual education, Proposition 203 and SEI

	Agree/Strongly agree (%)	Neutral (%)	Disagree/Strongly disagree (%)
ELLs need to learn English to succeed in this country	95	5	0
ELLs should abandon their home language and speak only English	0	0	100
ELL students should become fully bilingual in both English and their home language	98	3	0
Schools should help students become proficient in both English and their home language	78	13	10
When properly implemented, bilingual education programs are effective in helping ELL students learn English and achieve academic success	95	5	0
SEI is a better model for ELLs than bilingual education	30	30	40
Proposition 203 has resulted in more effective programs for ELL students	10	13	70
Proposition 203 is too restrictive in terms of approaches schools can take to help ELL students learn English	73	15	8

Note: $N = 40$; Figures may not add up to exactly 100% due to rounding bilingualism, and nearly all agreed or strongly agreed that bilingual education is effective for helping ELLs learn English and achieve academic success when it is properly implemented. Only 30% felt SEI was a better model for ELLs than bilingual education, and only 10% felt Proposition 203 resulted in more effective programs. The majority (73%) felt that Proposition 203 is too restrictive in terms of approaches schools can take to help ELLs learn English. Thus, these teachers' views differ substantially from the premises of Proposition 203.

Information, guidance, implementation and effectiveness of SEI

The majority of schools represented in the survey went through a major transition following Proposition 203–27 (68%) had bilingual programs before the law passed, but only 4 (10%) had programs at the time of the survey. In the four schools where bilingual education survived, their programs were substantially reduced and changed (e.g. only in the upper grades, only serving English-proficient students, etc.). While the schools were mandated to place ELLs in SEI classrooms, the teachers described receiving little to no information about the SEI model, or how to implement it in their classrooms. A couple of teachers described SEI as a default label for any classrooms with ELLs in it. Two other teachers claimed the difference between mainstream and SEI classrooms had been explained to them, but were unable to articulate these differences. One teacher explained that SEI means you cannot help the students in Spanish. Ironically, as noted above, this is one of the characteristics which actually distinguishes SEI from mainstream instruction. Nonetheless, most teachers were under the impression – or were explicitly told by an administrator – that use of a student's primary language was not allowed. A few teachers had never even heard of SEI. A couple of teachers familiar with SEI acknowledged that in practice it was no different from mainstream sink-or-swim instruction.

As described above, SEI classrooms must include explicit ELD or English as a second language (ESL) instruction. However, 83% of the teachers reported that their students did not receive any ESL instruction (in-class or pull-out). The teachers explained there was little emphasis on providing ESL instruction, and 68% reported that their schools had not even purchased ESL instructional materials. Finally, while SEI requires content-area instruction that has been specially designed to make it comprehensible for ELLs, many of the teachers expressed frustration over being able to provide such instruction given the immense pressure they were under to narrow their instructional focus to preparing ELLs for the Arizona Instrument to Measure Standards (AIMS), the state's high-stakes test. The overwhelming majority of teachers reported that the emphasis on high-stakes tests was driving instruction that was inappropriate for ELLs (80%), that the focus on testing has not helped them become a more effective teacher of ELLs (75%), and that the focus on test preparation has prevented them from focusing on the linguistic and cultural needs of their students (93%). Despite the mandates for SEI, given the lack of information and guidance on SEI from the state, it is not surprising that half of the teachers surveyed reported most ELLs in their schools were placed in mainstream classrooms, or were not sure what type of program they were in. Even in the SEI-designated classrooms, the lack of ESL/ELD instruction and primary language support, and the instructional focus of high-stakes test preparation meant that in practice there was little difference between SEI and mainstream instruction.

Case Study Findings

To further understand the issues raised in the survey research, case studies were conducted in two 3rd grade SEI classrooms at two elementary schools on different sides of the Phoenix valley. As described above, Eastside school, where Mrs Silvers' classroom was observed, had been rated as 'Underperforming', while Westside School, where Mrs Charles' classroom was observed, had been rated as 'Performing'. We will first describe the differences in the demographics and achievement between the two schools. Next we will describe findings from the qualitative data regarding the quality of instruction. Finally, we will describe the findings related to the evaluation of classroom instruction using the SIOP.

Demographic Differences and Academic Achievement of ELLs

Table 5.2 highlights the demographics of Eastside and Westside elementary schools. As shown in this table, the student population at Westside is smaller and more diverse compared to Eastside. Most of the students at Eastside are Hispanic (90%) while Hispanics only make up 39% of the population at Westside. This difference is important as nearly all of the ELLs in both schools are Hispanic. Nearly half of the students at Westside are White (49%) while Asians, African Americans and Native Americans make up 12% of the population compared to only 3% at Eastside.

Table 5.2 Demographics of Eastside and Westside Schools (2004–2005)

	Eastside School	Westside School
Total students	909	655
Asian	1%	2%
African American	1%	7%
Hispanic	90%	39%
Native American	1%	3%
White	7%	49%

Source: www.greatschools.net

Figure 5.1 provides the 3rd grade ELL test scores from the state's AIMS test for Eastside and Westside schools from 2002 to 2004. Note that a much higher percentage of ELL students at Eastside passed the AIMS tests compared to the ELLs at Westside in all three subject areas across all three years except for Writing in 2003, where scores at Eastside scores were slightly lower than Westside's. These results are surprising in light of the fact that Eastside had been labeled as 'Underperforming' while Westside had been labeled as 'Performing'. There are two factors which may explain the disconnect between the school labels and ELL student achievement: (1) Most ELL test scores are removed from the formulas to determine a school's label (Wright, 2005a), and (2) Westside had a much larger proportion of White English-proficient students whose achievement was able to make up for the school's low ELL test scores.

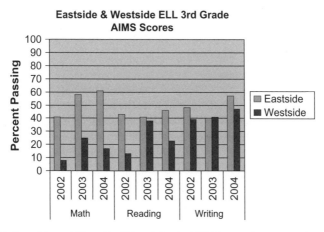

Figure 5.1 Eastside and Westside ELL 3rd Grade AIMS Scores (2002–2004)

Qualitative Observations of the Quality of Instruction

The 3rd grade SEI classrooms at Eastside (Underperforming) School and Westside (Performing) School, were vastly different. The teacher of the 3rd grade classroom observed at Eastside, Mrs Silvers, is a veteran teacher with over 15 years of experience, while Mrs Charles, at Westside, was a first-year teacher, though she had been a long-term substitute at the school for last five months of the prior school year.[2] Both teachers were ELL certified. Mrs Charles completed her ESL certification through her teacher credential program at a local university, while Mrs Silvers earned hers as an endorsement after teaching for several years. Mrs Silvers' class contained students with a wide range of English proficiency, from newcomers who spoke little or no English, to former ELLs redesignated as English proficient. Mrs Charles' class consisted of ELLs who had been in the United States for two years or less, and were designated as beginning-level ELLs. Nearly all of the students in both classrooms were Latino.

The two classrooms had much different curricular foci. In Mrs Silvers class at Eastside, the school was designated as a Reading First school, and thus there was a heavy focus on reading as driven by curriculum mandated by this federal grant program targeting 'low performing' schools. Mrs Silvers used the school's mandated basal reading series, which included homogeneous intervention reading groups of students at about the same reading levels. Students were accessed regularly using the DIBELS (Dynamic Indicators of Early Basic Literacy Skills) test to measure their attainment of discrete reading skills, such as phonemic awareness and phonics skills. Mrs Silvers also utilized the Accelerated Reader program, wherein students read books and took computerized comprehension quizzes. Her students were expected to read at least one book a day and pass the quiz for each book read.

At Westside School, Mrs Charles' students were required by the school to spend the majority of their morning in the computer lab working with a computer program called *FastForward*, which was designed for special education students with cognitive reading disabilities. The appropriateness of this software program for ELLs is questionable; however, the students spent the first four months of school in the lab, and spent hours each day interacting with the program while Mrs Charles sat in the lab with little to do. In addition to content-areas taught by specialists (i.e. art, music, PE, science, library), Mrs Charles only had her students for less than two hours in the afternoon to provide any of her own instruction. At the time of observation, the FastForward sessions had just ended and Mrs Charles was finally given full control over her instructional day.

There was a large observable difference in terms of the quality of instruction between these two classrooms. At Eastside, Mrs Silvers was very structured. Students were well trained in classroom routines, and there was quick and smooth transitions between well-planned lessons and structured learning activities. There was a clear curriculum in Mrs Silver's class, and she drew from a wide variety of purposefully chosen instructional resources with a clear academic focus. In contrast, Mrs Charles' classroom at Westside was very unstructured, with long transitions between lessons and activities as she decided what to do next. There was a clear lack of planning. A daily posted schedule was not followed. Lessons ideas hastily written in her plan book were not taught. Much of the instruction is best described as 'spur of the moment' or 'winging it'. Thus, at Westside, there was no clear curriculum. In Mrs Charles classroom there was little to no use of school-adopted curricular programs, and an overuse of disconnected worksheets copied from supplemental workbooks, as will be described below.

In Mrs Silver's classroom, there were high expectations and students were held accountable for their daily work. Mrs Silver's checked students work as soon as they completed it. If there were any errors, she brought these to the students' attention and required them to re-do it until they got it right. Students had to earn their recess each day and their free time on Friday afternoons by meeting reading goals (Accelerated Reader). Mrs Silvers closely monitored her students' progress with constant on-going assessment. In contrast, at Westside there were unclear expectations and low accountability in Mrs Charles' classroom. It was unclear when she assessed the work students completed or if she reviewed it with the students at a later time. The only assessment observed was a spelling test.

Mrs Charles herself admitted that she was unclear on 'what a 3rd grade classroom really looks like'. She also made several comments during classroom observations or in interviews revealing the unstructured and chaotic nature of the instruction in her classroom:

'I'm all over the board. I know why people quit teaching. ... OK, we're going to get this under control one of these days!'

'Today is kind of a crazy day ...'

'Today is Friday, so we're going to take it easy.'

Even less structure was observed in Mrs Charles classroom at the end of the year after students had taken the TAKS test. Mrs Charles explained to me during an observation, 'Now that testing is over, we're basically just kicking back, watching videos, reading stories ...'.

In the sections that follow, details on the quantity and quality of instruction based on the observational data are provided.

Quantity and quality of reading instruction

Table 5.3 shows the amount of different types of reading instruction that took place during the observations in the two classrooms. Both Mrs Silvers and Mrs Charles read aloud to their students and provided instruction in smaller reading groups. While the amount of read aloud time was similar, the small reading groups in Mrs Charles class did not cover all the students in the class, in contrast to Mrs Silver's classroom. Most significant, there was little whole reading group instruction and no independent reading done by students in Mrs Charles class, whereas in Mrs Silver's class, these were a major focus of instruction.

The quality of the instruction differed dramatically. In Mrs Silver's class, spelling instruction, daily oral language, whole group reading lessons and small group reading texts and lessons were all aligned in terms of theme and content with a focal story in the basal reader. Most students received instruction on their own level through the small group instruction, and, as noted above, students were constantly engaged in independent reading with books at their appropriate levels. Independent reading took place not only in designated silent reading times, but also any time students completed other work and had some spare time. In contrast, the spelling, daily oral language, read alouds, reading groups and reading instruction in Mrs Charles class were not aligned, and thus did not build upon or reinforce each other. The reading groups were highly disorganized, as only two groups out of five or six actually

Table 5.3 Quantity of reading instruction

	Mrs Silvers (Eastside)	Mrs Charles (Westside)
Read aloud	26 minutes	20 minutes
Whole group reading Instruction/Guided Practice/Assessment	1 hour 42 minutes	9 minutes
Reading Group Instruction	45 minutes to 1 hour 50 minutes (all students covered)	44 minutes (Only some students covered)
Independent Reading	1 hour 40 minutes to 2 hours	None

Table 5.4 Quantity of writing instruction

	Mrs Silvers (Eastside)	Mrs Charles (Westside)
Spelling	1 hour, 15 minutes	45 minutes
Modeled writing	None	50 minutes
Student independent writing	1 hour 8 minutes	20 minutes
Daily oral language	17 minutes	47 minutes

met with the teacher. As noted above, students in Mrs Charles' classroom did not engage in any independent reading whatsoever.

Quality and quantity of writing instruction

Table 5.4 shows the quantity of writing instruction in the two classrooms. Both teachers engaged students in spelling, independent writing and writing/grammar instruction through Daily Oral Language. Spelling instruction in Mrs Silver's class entailed structured lessons and practice, and also incorporated cursive writing instruction and practice, whereas in Mrs Charles class, most of the time was simply spent reviewing, and then taking a spelling test. Mrs Charles spent more time on Daily Oral Language instruction, her lessons were a bit long and drawn out, whereas Mrs Silvers provided more focused lessons, keeping within a more reasonable time frame for an activity designed for quick review and practice. Mrs Charles did some good modeled writing lessons, which Mrs Silvers did not do. The modeled writing lessons, however, seemed to be more spur of the moment than carefully planned instruction. Mrs Silvers' students spent much more time doing their own independent writing by responding to specific prompts (related to their reading lessons) in their journals. Mrs Charles' modeled writing lesson in the morning was to serve as a model for students' own independent writing, however, rather than give students specific time to focus on their writing, the writing task was delayed to the afternoon and was lumped together during a long stretch of time where students were given other 'jobs' mainly consisting of worksheets to keep them busy.

Quantity and quality of math instruction

As shown in Table 5.5, there was a much greater amount and wider variety of math instruction in Mrs Silvers' class than in Mrs Charles' class. All of the math lessons in Mrs Charles class focused on the completion of worksheets consisting of simple computational facts. Students were loaded with math worksheets with just a little introduction and review. In stark

Table 5.5 Quantity of math instruction

	Mrs Silvers (Eastside)	Mrs Charles (Westside)
Math lesson/Guided practice	2 hours 6 minutes	50 minutes
Math tests/assessments	50 minutes	None
Math independent work	Included in guided practice/test prep	55 minutes
Math test prep	36 minutes	None

contrast, the math lessons in Mrs Silvers' classroom covered a broad range of grade-level math concepts and skills, and students were engaged in a variety of math lessons and activities. Most of these were guided practice where Mrs Silvers' walked students through new concepts and problem-solving strategies, had students try the new concepts on their own, and then followed up with a thorough review. AIMS test prep also was included in Mrs Silvers' instruction, but this was not the sole focus of her math instruction. Even with the AIMS test prep, Mrs Silvers utilized pre-teaching, independent practice and review.

Quantity and quality of other instruction

In Mrs Charles' classroom in Westside Elementary across the three days of observation, students spent 3 hours and 40 minutes on what the teacher called 'jobs'. These 'jobs' were mainly completing worksheets. Students were given a random collection of four to six worksheets at a time to work on independently covering various concepts such as math computation, phonics or basic reading comprehension. There did not appear to be any rhyme or reason to the selection of the worksheets. Mrs Charles attempted to differentiate the instruction by dividing students into two groups – A and B with Group A given easier worksheets, and Group B given slightly more difficulty worksheets. However, for both groups, the worksheets were below the 3rd grade level. While Mrs Charles went over each 'job' before students began their work, it was quick, and covered multiple unrelated concepts given the diversity of the content of the worksheets. The whole purpose of the 'jobs' was to keep students busy so Mrs Charles could meet with her small reading groups. However, during the observation period, she only met once with two different groups, and some days she did not meet with any groups.

In contrast, Mrs Silvers' class was highly structured, and her instruction was well organized. Even though she had a prescribed curriculum, she did her best to make it as appropriate for her students as possible. She resisted some components of the program, and brought in pieces of other programs and curricular materials she felt were more appropriate. Mrs Silvers' had access to a part-time bilingual paraprofessional, and maximized the use of her time to read with students and lead the small group reading lessons. While it would have been preferable for Mrs Silvers' to run the small reading groups herself, students were at least afforded this opportunity to work in a small group, and she provided the appropriate materials and text, and carefully monitored the paraprofessional's instruction. Earlier in the year Mrs Charles also had a bilingual paraprofessional, but she got rid of her because she did not feel she was able to effectively manage her work and interactions with the students.

SIOP observation scores

While the qualitative analysis provides substantial evidence of the differences in the quality of instruction in these two classrooms, we felt it was important to apply the use of a specific observational protocol to evaluate specific individual lessons taught in the two classrooms. As described above, the Sheltered Instruction Observational Protocol (SIOP) was used for this purpose, and enabled us to establish quantifiable scores indicative of the quality of sheltered English instruction in the two classrooms.

Tables 5.6 and 5.7 illustrate the SIOP observation scores received by Mrs Charles at Westside and Mrs Silvers at Eastside across the three full

Table 5.6 SIOP observation scores, Mrs Charles, Westside Elementary School

December 1, 2003			December 3, 2003			December 5, 2003		
Lesson	Score	%	Lesson	Score	%	Lesson	Score	%
Daily oral language	61	51	Calendar	53	44	Daily oral language	53	44
Shared writing	67	58	Alphabet activity	50	42	Phonics	51	43
'Jobs' – worksheet	14	12	'Jobs' – overview	40	33	'Jobs' – independent work	39	33
Read aloud	36	30	Reading Group #1	39	33	Spelling review with Group A	55	46
Math	58	48	Reading Group #2	50	42			
			Math	45	38			

Table 5.7 SIOP observation scores, Mrs Silvers, Eastside Elementary School

November 17, 2003			November 19, 2003			November 21, 2003		
Lesson	Score	%	Lesson	Score	%	Lesson	Score	%
Daily oral language	61	51	Spelling	51	43	Daily oral language	71	59
Reading lesson – the talent show	78	65	Daily oral language	70	58	Journal writing	52	43
Math review	69	58	Journal writing	62	52	AIMS math practice	53	44
Gourmet reading	46	38	Reading lesson	70	58	Engineering math	76	63
AIMS math practice	55	46	AIMS math practice	75	63	White board math review	76	63
Engineering math	62	52	Engineering math	69	58	Gourmet reading	50	42
			Math mini lesson	65	54			
			Gourmet reading	62	52			
			Cursive writing	70	58			

instructional days. Table 5.6 shows that the SIOP score percentages of the 15 lessons taught by Mrs Charles mostly fell into the range of 30–46%, with 12% being the lowest and 58% being the highest.

The 21 lessons taught by Mrs Silvers across the three full instructional days, as shown in Table 5.7, received higher SIOP scores compared to those of Mrs Charles. The SIOP score percentages of Mrs Silvers' lessons mostly ranged between 42% and 63% with 38% being the lowest and 65% being the highest.

Table 5.8 shows the average SIOP score of each instructor on the three instructional days. The comparison of the average daily score demonstrates that Mrs Silvers' instruction was of higher quality and thus more appropriate for ELLs than that of Mrs Charles'. Mrs Silvers' average daily SIOP score exceeded those of Mrs Charles's by more than 10 percentage points each day.

Table 5.9 ranks the top and bottom five SIOP items for Mrs Charles and Mrs Silvers. The table shows that all of the two teachers' top five SIOP items are identical, even though the rank order of the five items is different, and that Mrs Silvers' top five items have higher average score than those of

Table 5.8 Comparison of average daily SIOP scores at Westside and Eastside Schools

Mrs Charles (Westside)			Mrs Silvers (Eastside)		
Lesson	Score	%	Lesson	Score	%
12/01	47	39	11/17	62	52
12/03	46	38	11/19	66	55
12/05	50	42	11/21	63	53

Table 5.9 Top and bottom five SIOP items at Westside and Eastside Schools

Mrs Charles (Westside)		Mrs Silvers (Eastside)	
Top SIOP Items	Average	Top SIOP Items	Average
Speech appropriate for students' proficiency level	3.2	Speech appropriate for students' proficiency level	3.8
Students engaged	3.1	Content concepts appropriate	3.5
Pacing	2.8	Students engaged	3.4
Content concepts appropriate	2.7	Pacing	3.4
Explanation of academic tasks clear	2.7	Explanation of academic tasks clear	3.1
Bottom 5 SIOP Items		Bottom 5 SIOP Items	
Clearly defined language objectives	0.0	Clearly defined content objectives	0.3
Language objectives supported by lesson delivery	0.0	Clearly defined language objectives	0.3
Clearly defined content objectives	0.1	Language objectives supported by lesson delivery	0.3
Clarify key concepts in L1	0.2	Clarify key concepts in L1	0.5
Review of key vocabulary	0.4	Content objectives clearly supported by lesson delivery	0.5

Mrs Charles'. Both instructors used appropriate speech according to their students' English-proficiency level, their students were highly engaged, the pacing of the lessons were appropriate to students' levels, the content concepts were appropriate for the students' age and background, and the academic tasks were explained clearly.

Four out of the five items in the two instructors' bottom five are identical. The instructors did not clearly define content and language objectives in the evaluated lessons, and since the language objectives were not defined, we were not able to determine whether the objectives were supported by lesson delivery. In addition, both instructors rarely clarified key concepts using students' first language. Finally, Mrs Charles frequently ended the lessons without a comprehensive review of key vocabulary taught in the lessons.

Conclusion

Despite Proposition 203's restrictions on bilingual education, many ELL teachers throughout the state value bilingualism and agree that bilingual education, when properly implemented, is effective in helping ELLs learn English and achieve academic success. The 3rd grade ELL teachers participating in a state-wide survey revealed that in the years following Proposition 203's mandates for SEI, teachers received little guidance on what SEI is or how to implement it in their classrooms. Despite the ill-defined difference between SEI and Mainstream classrooms in Proposition 203, a close reading reveals that an SEI classroom should provide, at a minimum, direct ESL/ELD instruction, sheltered English content-area instruction, and primary language support. However, the survey participants revealed that in most of their schools, ESL/ELD instruction was not being provided, primary language support was not allowed, and that the pressure related to high stakes testing and accountability was driving instruction that is inappropriate for ELLs and which made it hard for them as teachers to focus on the unique linguistic and academic needs of their ELL students. Thus, in practice, SEI classrooms in Arizona have differed little, if any, from mainstream classrooms.

The case study of two 3rd grade SEI classrooms revealed that the elementary school labeled as 'Underperforming' (Eastside) was actually providing much higher quality instruction for their ELLs than the elementary school labeled as 'Performing' (Westside). This was evidenced by findings that at Eastside: (1) there were higher ELL test scores, (2) there was a greater amount of instructional time in key content areas, (3) there was better classroom management, (4) there was an aligned curriculum and (5) there were higher SIOP scores on observed lessons. These findings reveal that school labels do not correspond to the quality of education a school provides for their ELLs. Factors such as the elimination of many ELL test scores from school accountability formulas, and school demographics can function in a manner such as at Westside Elementary School where a good school label can mask poor quality teaching of ELLs.[3]

While the quality of the SEI instruction was much higher at Eastside, the SIOP evaluations were still lower than needed to fully address the linguistic and academic needs of the ELL students. The pressure to raise the schools' test scores at Eastside led to a highly prescribed curriculum. Mrs Silvers found this curriculum – much of which was driven by Reading First – quite frustrating as she questioned its appropriateness for her ELL students. She attempted to minimize the least appropriate components and utilized good sheltered instruction strategies to make other parts comprehensible for her ELLs; however, this took time away from the type of instruction she felt would be more appropriate for meeting her students' linguistic and academic needs.

Absent from both Westside and Eastside was explicit ESL/ELD instruction, content-area lessons which had clear language objectives, content-area lessons that were specially designed for ELL students, and ample primary language support. Thus, in both schools, the SEI Model, as mandated by Proposition 203 and enforced by state education leaders, has been insufficient to ensure that ELLs learn English and receive equal access to the core curriculum. Out of frustration, both Mrs Charles and Mrs Silvers quit teaching in SEI classrooms the year following this study. Mrs Charles decided to try teaching in a regular mainstream classroom, and Mrs Silvers decided to become a reading specialist.

As of this writing, the state is just beginning to enforce a new model of SEI which requires four hours of English language development each day. The state has provided a highly prescriptive model outlining discrete skills to be taught and set amounts of time for specific isolated language skills. The model's design has little to no basis in what is known from research about effective language instruction for ELL students (Wright, 2010), and thus has been found to be highly questionable by language learning experts (see also Chapters 3, 4 and 9, this volume). Schools have reported great difficulty in implementing the model. One issue is the high costs of implementing the model and the lack of resources needed to fully comply with the program's demands. This is significant given that Arizona's policymakers have to date resisted a federal court order, stemming from the case *Flores v. Arizona* – to increase funding for ELL students (Wright, 2005a). Another issue is the model leaves little time left for content-area instruction critical to ELLs' academic success. It is unfortunate state education leaders do not take into consideration the views and experiences of teachers who are much more attuned to the strengths and needs of ELL students. The masking of good instruction for ELLs by misleading school labels is also preventing the state's ability to identify and replicate effective practices.

Acknowledgments

The case study research was supported by a grant from the Academy for Teacher Excellence (ATE) at the University of Texas, San Antonio. We are grateful for this support and the encouragement of ATE faculty members and staff as we conducted this study. We also wish to thank the principals and the teachers at Eastside and Westside who were gracious enough to open up their classrooms to allow us to understand how they are dealing with state policies and implementing SEI instruction in their own classrooms.

Notes

(1) Structured English Immersion and Sheltered English Immersion are often used inter-changeably, though a case could be made that there is a difference. I use Sheltered English Immersion in this chapter as this is the wording of the mandate in Proposition 203, and because 'sheltered' instruction is the commonly accepted and widely used term in the literature and in the field to refer to instruction in English that has been modified to make it more comprehensible for ELLs.

(2) While it may seem unfair to compare a veteran teacher with a new teacher, the issue at hand is whether or not the school labels provided an accurate depiction of the quality of instruction for ELL students at each school.

(3) In making these comparisons, it was not our purpose to disparage Mrs Charles' as a teacher. She was a deeply caring brand-new teacher who was trying her best, and showed great potential in many areas. It became clear that she was not receiving the support and mentoring she needed. Furthermore, the school's requirement that her students spent their mornings in the first part of year in the computer lab was beyond her control, and made it difficult for her to establish regular classroom routines by the time of our observations.

References

Abedi, J. (2003) Reporting adequate yearly progress for English language learners: Linguistic and psychometric issues. Paper presented at the Language Minority Research Institute, San Diego, CA.

Abedi, J. (2004) The no child left behind act and English language learners: Assessment and accountability issues. *Educational Researcher* 33, 4–14.

Arizona Department of Education (2003) AZ Learns achievement profiles. Online document, accessed 6 March 2010. http://www.ade.state.az.us/profile/publicview/AZLEARNSSchoolList.asp

Baker, C. (2006) *Foundations of Bilingual Education and Bilingualism* (4th edn). Clevedon: Multilingual Matters.

Barton, P. (2006) Needed: Higher standards for accountability. *Educational Leadership* 64, 28–31.

Crawford, J. (2003) *Hard Sell: Why is Bilingual Education so Unpopular with the American Public?* Tempe, AZ: Language Policy Research Unit, Education Policy Studies Laboratory, Arizona State University.

Crawford, J. (2004) *Educating English learners: Language Diversity in the Classroom* (5th edn). Los Angeles: Bilingual Education Services, Inc.

Darling-Hammond, L. (2004) From 'separate but equal' to 'No Child Left Behind': The collision of new standards and old inequalities. In D. Meir and G. Wood (eds) *Many Children Left Behind: How the No Child Left Behind Act is Damaging Our Children and Our Schools* (pp. 3–32). Boston: Beacon Press.

de Cohen, C.C., Deterding, N. and Clewell, B.C. (2005) *Who's Left Behind? Immigrant Children in High and Low LEP Schools*. Washington, DC: The Urban Institute.

Echevarria, J. (2002) *Sheltered Content Instruction: Teaching English Language Learners with Diverse Abilities* (2nd edn). Boston: Allyn & Bacon.

Echevarria, J., Vogt, M. and Short, D. (2007) *Making Content Comprehensible for English Learners: The SIOP Model* (3rd edn). Boston: Pearson.

Fuller, B., Gesicki, K., Kang, E. and Wright, J. (2006) *Is the No Child Left Behind Act Working? The Reliability of How States Track Achievement*. Berkeley, CA: Policy Analysis for California Education, University of California, Berkeley.

Haney, W. (2002) Revealing illusions of educational progress: Texas high-stakes tests and minority student performance. In Z.F. Beykont (ed.) *The Power of Culture: Teaching across Language Difference*. Boston: Harvard Education Publishing Group.

Kohn, A. (2000) *The Case against Standardized Testing: Raising the Scores, Ruining the Schools*. Portsmouth, NH: Heinemann.

Krashen, S.D. (1996) *Under Attack: The Case against Bilingual Education*. Culver City, CA: Language Education Associates.

McNeil, L.M. (2000) *Contradictions of School Reform: Educational Costs of Standardized Testing*. New York: Routledge.

Mintrop, H. (2003) *Schools on Probation: How Accountability Works (and Doesn't Work)*. New York: Teachers College Press.

National Clearinghouse for English Language Acquisition (2006) The growing number of limited English proficient students 1993/94–2003/04. Online document, accessed 19 February 2010. http://www.ncela.gwu.edu/policy/states/reports/statedata/2003LEP/GrowingLEP_0304_Dec05.pdf

Popham, W.J. (2001) *The Truth about Testing: An Educator's Call to Action*. Alexandria, VA: Association for Supervision and Curriculum Development.

Popham, W.J. (2004) *America's 'Failing' Schools: How Parents and Teachers Can Cope with No Child Left Behind*. New York: Routledge.

Porter, R.P. (1990) *Forked Tongue: The Politics of Bilingual Education*. New York: Basic Books.

Ravitch, D. (1997) The fight for higher standards. *Forbes* 160, 106.

Rossell, C.H. (2002) Dismantling bilingual education, implementing English immersion: The California Initiative, online document, accessed 18 November 2010. http://www.bu.edu/polisci/CROSSELL/Dismantling%20Bilingual%20Education,%20July%202002.pdf

Sacks, P. (1999) *Standardized Minds: The High Price of America's Testing Culture and What We Can Do to Change It*. Cambridge, MA: Perseus Books.

Valenzuela, A. (2004) *Leaving Children Behind: How 'Texas-Style' Accountability Fails Latino Youth*. New York: State University of New York Press.

Wright, W.E. (2002) The effects of high stakes testing on an inner-city elementary school: The curriculum, the teachers, and the English language learners. *Current Issues in Education* 5. Online document, accessed 6 March 2010. http://cie.asu.edu/volume5/number5

Wright, W.E. (2005a) English language learners left behind in Arizona: The nullification of accommodations in the intersection of federal and state policies. *Bilingual Research Journal* 29 (1), 1–30.

Wright, W.E. (2005b) *Evolution of Federal Policy and Implications of No Child Left Behind for Language Minority Students* (No. EPSL-0501-101-LPRU). Tempe, AZ: Language Policy Research Unit, Education Policy Studies Laboratory, Arizona State University. Online document, accessed 19 February 2010. http://www.asu.edu/educ/epsl/EPRU/documents/EPSL-0501-101-LPRU.pdf

Wright, W.E. (2005c) The political spectacle of Arizona's Proposition 203. *Educational Policy* 19, 662–700.

Wright, W.E. (2006) A Catch-22 for language learners. *Educational Leadership* 64, 22–27.

Wright, W.E. (2008) Primary language support. In J.M. Gonzalez (ed.) *Encyclopedia of Bilingual Education* (Vol. 2, pp. 666–668). Thousand Oaks, CA: Sage Publications, Inc.

Wright, W.E. (2010) *Foundations for Teaching English Language Learners: Research, Theory, Policy, and Practice*. Philadelphia: Caslon.

Wright, W.E. and Choi, D. (2006) The impact of language and high-stakes testing policies on elementary school English language learners in Arizona. *Education Policy Analysis Archives* 14, 1–56. Online document, accessed 6 March 2010. http://epaa.asu.edu/epaa/v14n13/

Wright, W.E. and Pu, C. (2005) *Academic Achievement of English Language Learners in Post Proposition 203 Arizona*. Tempe: Language Policy Research Unit, Educational Policy Studies Laboratory, Arizona State University. Online document, accessed 19 February 2010. http://www.asu.edu/educ/epsl/EPRU/documents/EPSL-0509-103-LPRU.pdf

6 Review of 'Research Summary and Bibliography for Structured English Immersion Programs' of the Arizona English Language Learners Task Force

Stephen Krashen, Jeff MacSwan and Kellie Rolstad

The 'Research Summary and Bibliography for Structured English Immersion Programs' of the Arizona English Language Learners Task Force purports to present a scholarly and balanced review of current scientific knowledge regarding effective programs for English language learners (ELLs) in general and structured English immersion (SEI) in particular. However, we find that the review neglects to reference significant research bearing on the questions raised, and frequently draws inappropriate conclusions from the research presented. Perhaps most disappointing is the tendency in the review to neglect important conceptual distinctions which could have usefully guided the research summary. Below we address each area of literature review in turn, pointing out significant limitations and incorrect interpretations as they arise.

What is the Current State of Scientific Research in the Area of Effective Instruction for English Learners?

The review cites references to make the point that there are relatively few high-quality studies regarding program effectiveness for ELLs, with estimates ranging from 5 (Gersten & Baker, 2000) to 50 (Genesee *et al.*, 2006). While any empirical question of significance might benefit from additional research, experts widely believe that an adequate number of program effectiveness studies have been carried out to provide solid guidance to policy makers.

Several recent research syntheses have been conducted which the Task Force document fails to reference and which bear directly on the question of program effectiveness. In a recent narrative synthesis of research, funded by the US Department of Education's Institute for Education Science, Slavin and Cheung (2005) reviewed 16 studies they found to be methodologically rigorous comparing SEI to better established alternative programs which used a combination of English Language instruction and native language academic support such as Transitional Bilingual Education (TBE). Slavin and Cheung (2005) found that most of these studies favored TBE over SEI. Although some studies found no difference, a significant finding in their report was that no study reviewed significantly favored SEI programs. Another research summary conducted by Rolstad *et al.* (2005a) used meta-analysis to compare SEI to TBE. Meta-analysis is a widely used and highly regarded statistical method used for comparing and synthesizing a corpus of studies addressing a single research question, such as the effectiveness of program alternatives for English learners; meta-analysis was developed by Gene Glass in 1974, and is routinely used in medicine, psychiatry and the traditional academic disciplines. Rolstad *et al.* (2005a) found clear evidence that native language instructional support is a more beneficial treatment for ELLs than SEI, and that children in long-term developmental bilingual programs benefited even more from academic support in their native language than did children in either TBE or SEI. In a separate study, Rolstad *et al.* (2005b) reviewed a subset of studies conducted in the Arizona context to assist Arizona policymakers in drawing conclusions regarding program effectiveness for English learners locally. The authors found that the subsample of studies conducted in the Arizona context showed even stronger positive effects for TBE over SEI than studies in the larger national sample. Finally, another significant and very extensive review of research on educating ELLs was published last year by the National Literacy Panel, a project of the US Department of Education's Institute for Education Science. The report found that instructional programs for ELLs which include the use of children's home language for instructional support improved academic achievement outcomes for ELLs (Francis *et al.*, 2006).

The current state of knowledge regarding this question is relatively rich. As in any area of research, some studies are better than others, and the proportion of studies conducted under ideal methodological conditions is relatively small. Nonetheless, in just the last two years, three distinct research teams independently concluded that SEI is an inferior instructional approach in comparison to more traditional programs which teach ELLs in both English and the native language, and a research synthesis focused solely on studies conducted in Arizona drew similar conclusions.

A review of the evidence suggests that the development of scientifically sound programs for ELLs involves curricular and pedagogical activities which use children's native language to enrich their understanding of school content and academic subject matters while they are learning English.

What Research Supports the Time-on-Task Principle?

The Task Force document reviews research relevant to the time-on-task principle, the notion that time spent engaged in learning is positively related to learning outcomes. We have no disagreement with the Task Force document regarding these generalizations, and agree that time spent engaged in learning will positively impact learning outcomes, as concluded by ample research. However, an unstated assumption in the Task Force document may potentially misguide readers regarding the implication of these conclusions. Regrettably, the Task Force document reviews time-on-task studies situated in environments in which children are learning academic subject matter, but does not take note of the advantage children in these studies have from learning in a language they understand (English, their native language, in the studies reviewed). It is now taken for granted among neuroscientists that language acquisition takes place in a specialized center of the mind/brain, in relative isolation from the central processes which concern general academic learning (Gallistel, 2000; MacSwan & Rolstad, 2005). We therefore expect achievement in mathematics, for instance, to be positively affected by time spent engaged in learning mathematics. However, the question of whether the child understands the language of instruction will surely affect engagement, and engagement of mathematics in instructional contexts can result in any linguistic medium comprehensible to the child. Unfortunately, those who reference research evaluating the time-on-task principle as support for the idea that maximum instructional time should be spent in English fail to conceptually distinguish between subject matter content and its linguistic medium.

A recent study funded by the US Department of Education's Institute of Education Science was designed to specifically evaluate the Time-on-Task Theory in relation to the education of ELLs, among other questions (MacSwan et al., 2008). Based on adjusted R^2 indices in a hierarchical regression analysis, researchers found that, after controlling for English literacy (due to overlap with the outcome variables), the addition of English oral proficiency did not contribute significantly to the prediction of achievement. Effect sizes were generally small for the addition of oral language to literacy, with incremental R^2 indices never exceeding 0.05. However, Spanish literacy measures contributed significantly to language, mathematics and reading achievement over and above the set of English oral proficiency measures ($\Delta R^2 = 0.12$, 0.08 and 0.13, respectively). Among these Spanish-speaking children, the combined English oral proficiency and Spanish literacy sets of measures were statistically significant and accounted for 29% of the variance in language, 27% of the variance in mathematics and 32% of the variance in reading.

A review of the evidence suggests that the Time-on-Task Theory, which urges maximal time in English in instructional contexts, is not supported. Rather, the evidence supports an alternative view, sometimes called the Facilitation Theory, which posits that academic content knowledge acquired through use of the native language transfers to and thereby facilitates academic growth in the second language (English) environment.

What Empirical Research Supports the Teaching of Discrete English Language Skills in a Particular Order?

Studies show, as the Task Force document indicates, that we appear to acquire aspects of language in a predictable order. It must be pointed out, however, that this observation alone does not imply that we should attempt to teach children grammatical morphemes (what the Task Force document presumably means by 'functors') along the lines of the attested order, and no evidence is cited to suggest that such teaching strategies should be effective. Rather, the findings regarding the predictable order of acquisition of grammatical morphemes are widely interpreted quite differently: The natural order (and other evidence) suggests that the acquisition of language, along with the order of acquisition of grammatical morphemes, appears to be biologically rooted, and learners are competent to structure and acquire input according to their own internal timetable; therefore, we should not attempt to order linguistic input according to order of acquisition but should rather provide meaningful, comprehensible input accessible to developing language learners.

It should be noted, as further support for these conclusions, that the evidence of a predictable morphological order is attested in first language acquisition at least as robustly as in second language acquisition, and appears to hold regardless of whether a second language was acquired at school or in a nonacademic setting. However, parents are not generally advised to attempt to structure language input according to the order of acquisition of grammatical morphemes in order to facilitate or expedite first language acquisition. Roger Brown, who conducted the initial studies on order of acquisition of grammatical morphemes, addressed the question, 'How can a concerned mother facilitate her child's learning of language?' with this advice:

> Believe that your child can understand more than he or she can say, and seek, above all, to communicate. To understand and be understood. To keep your minds fixed on the same target. In doing that, you will, without thinking about it, make 100 or maybe 1000 alterations in your speech and action. Do not try to practice them as such. There is no set of rules of how to talk to a child that can even approach what you unconsciously know. If you concentrate on communicating, everything else will follow. (Brown, 1977: 26)

Indeed, researchers in the field of child language acquisition have found direct instruction to have no effect whatsoever on rate or quality of acquisition (Berko-Gleason, 1997; Pinker, 1994). One imagines that it could actually be harmful: If a parent insisted that a child first learn each vocabulary item or rule of grammar in a prescribed sequence before moving on to the next, significant language-related disabilities might result (assuming a child had no other linguistic input), because she is deprived of the language-rich environment typically associated with linguistic development.

Perhaps more importantly, while it is reasonably clear that children and second language learners acquire language in a predictable order, relatively little is known about the elements that are acquired. For instance, English has only a handful of grammatical morphemes but a large number of phonological and syntactic rules. The precise nature of these rule systems is not well understood, much less the exhaustive order in which they are learned. Hence, it is not possible to construct a curriculum of English which accurately reflects the order of acquisition of English in a scientifically rigorous way, as the order is not known in detail.

A review of the evidence does not suggest that language development curricula should be structured to focus on order of acquisition of English morphemes or any other aspect of language. Rather, language curricula should support second language learners with rich, meaningful and highly contextualized instruction to provide comprehensible linguistic input.

What Empirical Research Supports the Need for Allocating Fixed Periods of Time to Teaching Certain Elements of the English Language?

The Task Force maintains that ELLs benefit from the allocation of discrete blocks of instructional time devoted to English language and literacy instruction, but oversimplify the issue by ignoring the crucial issue of comprehensibility. Beginning second language acquirers will obviously profit from having a separate time set aside for English language class, because mainstream classroom teaching is incomprehensible to them. As soon as instruction becomes comprehensible, such classes should include subject matter teaching, beginning with subjects that are easier to contextualize for lower-level ELLs (science and math), and gradually moving to more abstract subjects, such as social studies. Ideally, students move into mainstream classes as they become comprehensible. See Krashen (1996) for further discussion.

What Empirical Research Supports the Explicit Teaching of Discrete English Language Skills (in the Domains of Morphology, Syntax, Phonology, Vocabulary)?

A wide variety of studies have pointed to the conclusion that the explicit teaching of discrete English language skills has a very weak effect on English acquisition. However, the Task Force document indicates that explicit teaching of English is of benefit in essentially all domains of linguistic competence.

The studies included in the Task Force review have several things in common: (1) They show very modest effects for grammar study; (2) the conditions hypothesized for the use of consciously learned language (Krashen, 2003) are met (focus on form, time, know the rule) on the measure used; (3) students were experienced language 'learners' and believed in direct teaching; (4) the effect fades with time. These studies thus actually confirm that the effect of teaching grammar is weak (Hillocks, 1986; Krashen, 2003; Truscott, 1998, 2004).

More significantly, the research findings reported in the Task Force document are frequently incorrectly presented. For instance, The Task Force document cites Saunders *et al.* (2006) as showing that including the teaching of 'discrete language skills' in the curriculum resulted in superior achievement in reading for ELLs. However, this study is devoted to the effects of having a separate time block for English Language Development (ELD) and does not mention the specific interventions discussed by the Task Force.

In another instance, the Task Force document cites Fotos and Ellis (1991) as showing that learners who are made aware of certain structures are more likely to notice them in subsequent input. However, this study actually showed that learning grammar rules by problem-solving was slightly less effective than traditional grammar study and did not deal with 'noticing'. The Task Force document further claimed that Robinson (1996: 3–4) 'reported similar findings' but Robinson's study also had nothing to do with 'noticing'. Like other studies, Robinson's results showed a small effect for instruction when conditions for the use of grammar were met.

The Task Force document presents experimental studies to support its claim for the efficacy of the direct teaching of phonology. In all cases, students were focused on form in the measure, and had time to apply the rules they learned. In Derwing et al. (1998), classical pronunciation training had an effect only on a test in which subjects were heavily focused on form. Most importantly, Derwing and colleagues did not present raw data or descriptive statistics describing their results, making it impossible to determine the size of the effect of global pronunciation training. In another study cited, Perlmutter (1989), no comparison group was used, so we cannot tell whether these new US immigrants would have improved in this early stage of acquisition with or without instruction.

The Task Force document further claims that evidence supports the explicit teaching of verb tenses; however, the research reviewed does not support this conclusion. Rather, the studies cited provided evidence for the contrary view: Those who arrive as new immigrants speaking their second language as children typically show full acquisition of verb tenses, and even adult second language acquirers are very good at the acquisition of verb tenses. In Johnson and Newport (1989), for example, adult second language learners only had problems with three of the 13 grammatical forms tested, and even for those three, performance was far from zero, ranging from about 70% to 80% correct. Those who arrived in the United States as children performed very well on all aspects of grammar tested.

Furthermore, contrary to statements made in the Task Force document, Krashen and Pon (1975) did not show that classroom learners could not monitor their language. In fact, it showed the opposite: The one subject who was the focus of the study had achieved a very high level of competence in English morphology and was highly effective in supplying those few forms she had not acquired when focused on form. Furthermore, the brief literature review regarding acquisition of verb tense does not mention the many cases of adults who have successfully acquired verb tenses, as well as other complex aspects of grammar, and who have done so without extensive formal instruction (e.g. Ioup *et al.*, 1994; Krashen, 2000).

Also not mentioned in the Task Force document is the fact that grammar and vocabulary teaching can, at best, cover only a small percentage of what needs to be acquired because the systems that people acquire are large and complex, and the precise character of these systems is not well understood. Thus, even if children in direct instruction learned school lessons with 100% accuracy and retention, they still would not know enough to communicate in English or use it effectively, as there is vastly more to the rule systems underlying English (or any language) than could be presented in class. This argument has been made for the acquisition of grammar, spelling, phonics, writing style and vocabulary (Krashen, 1982, 1984; Nagy *et al.*, 1985; Smith, 1988, 1994).

Grammar-based approaches are also not supported in multivariate correlational studies. The amount of formal study of a language is generally less significant in multivariate studies than the amount of free reading, and is often not found to be a significant predictor of second language competence when free reading is included in the analysis (Gradman & Hanania, 1991; Lee *et al.*, 1996). In Stokes *et al.* (1998), the amount of reading done was the only significant predictor of mastery of the subjunctive in Spanish, with both total formal study and specific instruction on the subjunctive failing as predictors.

Studies do indeed show a positive relationship between reading ability and syntactic competence. A reasonable interpretation of the finding is that reading is the cause of growth in syntactic competence, not that teachers should teach children word order rules to help them in reading. Similarly, studies show that vocabulary size and reading ability are correlated. A reasonable interpretation of this finding is that reading is the source of much of our vocabulary knowledge in school settings. These interpretations are suggested by the many experimental studies which show that students who do more reading outperform the comparison group on tests of reading, writing, grammatical accuracy, vocabulary and spelling.

Research has shown repeatedly that students in comprehension-based classrooms, where the instructional focus is on comprehension of messages of interest and not formal grammar instruction, acquire as much or more of the second language than students in traditional grammar-based classrooms. These findings hold at both the beginning and intermediate levels (Asher, 1994; Hammond, 1988; Isik, 2000; Nicola, 1989; Nikolov & Krashen; 1997; Swaffer & Woodruff, 1978; Winitz, 1996; Wolfe & Jones, 1982;).

A series of studies, dating from 1935, confirms that grammar instruction has no impact on reading and writing development (see reviews by Hillocks,

1986; Krashen, 1984). In a study conducted in New Zealand (Elley *et al.*, 1976), high school students were divided into three groups: One group studied traditional grammar in English class, a second studied generative grammar, and a third studied no grammar. Students were tested every year for three years. The researchers found no differences in reading comprehension, writing style, writing mechanics or vocabulary among the groups, and a follow-up done one year after the project ended also showed no differences among the groups. The authors concluded that 'it is difficult to escape the conclusion that English grammar, whether traditional or transformational, has virtually no influence on the language growth of typical secondary students' (Elley *et al.*, 1976: 17–18). The study of complex grammatical constructions does not help reading (or writing); rather, mastery of complex grammar is a result of reading.

A review of the evidence does not suggest that language is best taught with a focus on discrete forms, but rather that children will acquire a second language naturally in a setting in which rich and meaningful contexts provide support for language acquisition. While some attention to grammar instruction may be minimally beneficial to some students, it should not dominate the language education curriculum.

What Empirical Research Supports Reducing Class Size as a Way of Improving Achievement for ELLs?

The Task Force document suggests that reducing class size will have positive effects on academic achievement for ELLs. Although there is an absence of research directly relating to this question, we agree that a consideration of related evidence suggests that this outcome is likely.

However, other factors of perhaps equal or greater importance are not mentioned in the Task Force document, such as teacher qualifications, the availability of reading materials and texts, funding and coherent programs for ELLs. Research suggests that factors such as these – teacher qualifications and program funding, in particular – deserve significantly more positive consideration than they are presently receiving in Arizona policy contexts.

Conclusions

The Task Force document presents an incomplete view of the research, limiting its citations to studies that appear to support its position. Studies providing counter-evidence are not mentioned, and in many cases the studies that are cited are incorrectly described. A consideration of a wider body of research and more accurate reporting of studies actually supports positions far different from what the Task Force proposes, including the use of the child's first language to accelerate the development of English literacy and academic knowledge and the limited role of direct teaching of the discrete elements of language.

References

Asher, J. (1994) *Learning Another Language through Actions: The Complete Teacher's Guidebook*. Los Gatos, CA: Sky Oaks Productions.

Berko-Gleason, J. (ed.) (1997) *The Development of Language*. Boston: Allyn and Bacon.

Brown, R. (1977) Introduction to Snow and Ferguson. In C. Snow and C. Ferguson (eds) *Talking to Children* (pp. 1–27). New York: Cambridge University Press.

Derwing, T.M., Munro, M.J. and Wiebe, G. (1998) Evidence in favor of a broad framework for pronunciation instruction. *Language Learning* 48, 393–410.

Elley, W., Barham, I., Lamb, H. and Wyllie, M. (1976) The role of grammar in a secondary school curriculum. *Research in the Teaching of English* 10, 5–21.

Fotos, S. and Ellis, R. (1991) Communicating about grammar: A task-based approach. *TESOL Quarterly* 25, 605–628.

Francis, D., Lesaux, N. and August, D. (2006) In D. August and T. Shanahan (eds) *Developing Literacy in Second-Language Learners: Report of the National Literacy Panel on Language-Minority Children and Youth* (pp. 365–413). Mahwah, NJ: Lawrence Erlbaum.

Gallistel, C.R. (2000) The replacement of general-purpose learning models with adaptively specialized learning modules. In M.S. Gazzaniga (ed.) *The Cognitive Neurosciences* (2nd edn, pp. 1179–1191). Cambridge, MA: MIT Press.

Genesee, F., Lindholm-Leary, K., Saunders, W. and Christian, D. (2006) *Educating English Language Learners: A Synthesis of Research Evidence*. New York: Cambridge University Press.

Gersten, R. and Baker, K. (2000) What we know about effective instructional practices for English-language learners. *Exceptional Children* 66, 454–470.

Gradman, H. and Hanania, E. (1991) Language learning background factors and ESL proficiency. *Modern Language Journal* 75, 39–51.

Hammond, R. (1988) Accuracy versus communicative competency: The acquisition of grammar in the second language classroom. *Hispania* 71, 408–417.

Hillocks, G. (1986) *Research on Written Composition. New Directions for Teaching*. Urbana, IL: ERIC.

Ioup, G., Boustagui, E., El Tigi, M. and Moselle, M. (1994) Re-examining the critical period hypothesis: A case study of successful adult SLA in a naturalistic environment. *Studies in Second Language Acquisition* 16, 73–98.

Isik, A. (2000) The role of input in second language acquisition: More comprehensible input supported by grammar instruction or more grammar instruction? *ITL: Review of Applied Linguistics* 129–130, 225–274.

Johnson, J.S. and Newport, E.L. (1989) Critical period effects in second language learning: The influence of maturational state on the acquisition of English as a second language. *Cognitive Psychology* 20, 60–99.

Krashen, S. (1981) *Second Language Acquisition and Second Language Learning*. New York: Prentice-Hall.

Krashen, S. (1982) *Principles and Practice in Second Language Acquisition*. New York: Prentice-Hall.

Krashen, S. (1984) *Writing: Research, Theory and Applications*. Torrance: Laredo.

Krashen, S. (1996) *Under Attack: The Case against Bilingual Education*. Burlingame, CA: Language Education Associates.

Krashen, S. (2000) What does it take to acquire language? *ESL Magazine* 3, 22–23.

Krashen, S. (2003) *Explorations in Language Acquisition and Use: The Taipei Lectures*. Portsmouth, NH: Heinemann.

Krashen, S.D. and Pon, P. (1975) An error analysis of an advanced ESL learner: The importance of the monitor. *Working Papers on Bilingualism* 7, 125–129.

Lee, Y.O., Krashen, S. and Gribbons, B. (1996) The effect of reading on the acquisition of English relative clauses. *ITL: Review of Applied Linguistics* 113–114, 263–273.

MacSwan, J. and Rolstad, K. (2005) Modularity and the facilitation effect: Psychological mechanisms of transfer in bilingual students. *Hispanic Journal of the Behaviorial Sciences* 27, 224–243.

MacSwan, J., Thompson, M., de Klerk, G. and McAlister, K. (2008) Facilitation theory and the time-on-task principle: A structural equation modeling approach to evaluating bilingual and English-only instructional policies. Paper presented at the annual meeting of the American Association of Applied Linguistics, Washington, DC.

Nagy, W.E., Herman, P.A. and Anderson, R.C. (1985) Learning words from context. *Reading Research Journal* 20, 233–253.

Nicola, N. (1989) Experimenting with the new methods in Arabic. *Dialog on Language Instruction* 6, 61–71.

Nikolov, M. and Krashen, S. (1997) Need we sacrifice accuracy for fluency? *System* 25, 197–201.

Perlmutter, M. (1989) Intelligibility rating of L2 speech pre- and postintervention. *Perception and Motor Skills* 68, 515–521.

Pinker, S. (1994) *The Language Instinct: How the Mind Creates Languages*. New York: William Morrow and Company.

Robinson, P. (1996) Learning simple and complex rules under implicit, incidental rule-search conditions, and instructed conditions. *Studies in Second Language Acquisition* 18, 27–67.

Rolstad, K., Mahoney, K. and Glass, G.V. (2005a) The big picture: A meta-analysis of program effectiveness research on English language learners. *Educational Policy* 19, 572–594.

Rolstad, K., Mahoney, K. and Glass, G.V. (2005b) Weighing the evidence: A meta-analysis of bilingual education in Arizona. *Bilingual Research Journal* 29, 43–67.

Saunders, W., Foorman, B. and Carlson, C. (2006) Is a separate block of time for oral English language development in programs for English learners needed? *Elementary School Journal* 107, 181–198.

Slavin, R. and Cheung, A. (2005) A synthesis of research of reading instruction for English language learners. *Review of Educational Research* 75, 247–284.

Smith, C.B. (1988) Does it help to write about your reading? *Journal of Reading* 32, 276–277.

Smith, F. (1994) *Understanding Reading*. Hillsdale, NJ: Lawrence Erlbaum Associates.

Stokes, J., Krashen, S. and Kartchner, J. (1998) Factors in the acquisition of the present subjunctive in Spanish: The role of reading and study. *ITL: Review of Applied Linguistics* 121/122, 19–25.

Swaffer, J. and Woodruff, M. (1978) Language for comprehension: Focus on reading. *Modern Language Journal* 6, 27–32.

Truscott, J. (1998) Noticing in second language acquisition: A critical review. *Second Language Research* 14, 103–135.

Truscott, J. (2004) The effectiveness of grammar instruction: Analysis of a meta-analysis. *English Teaching and Learning* 28, 17–29.

Winitz, H. (1996) Grammaticality judgments as a function of explicit and implicit instruction in Spanish. *Modern Language Journal* 80, 32–46.

Wolfe, D. and Jones, G. (1982) Integrating total physical response strategy in a level 1 Spanish class. *Foreign Language Annals* 14, 273–280.

Part 3

Arizona Teacher Preparation for SEI

7 'They're Just Confused': SEI as Policy into Practice

Sarah Catherine K. Moore

In 2004, the Arizona Department of Education (ADE) took several steps toward compliance with Proposition 203, a law severely limiting access to bilingual education for English learners (ELs) and naming in its place, Structured/Sheltered English immersion (SEI) as the primary means of educating ELs. One piece of several changes included a new mandate that all certified educational personnel in the state complete mandatory SEI training, consisting of 15 seat hours by August 31, 2006 and an additional 45 hours by August 31, 2009. The curricula for each was outlined by the state in one-page documents and made openly available to the public. Any person or organization was eligible to submit a syllabus fulfilling training requirements based on the state's outlined curricula. This open-access opportunity, along with other characteristics of the mandate including the hyper-abbreviated timeline for completion of training, resulted in an extensive range of sessions/courses, all deemed comparable by state standards.

Context SEI as the primary means for teaching all ELs in Arizona presents a key challenge in terms of implementation. The focus of this study was Arizona's state-wide SEI training mandate for pre and in-service certified educational personnel. As SEI is projected from policy into practice, teachers themselves, navigating its requirements and context, ultimately become the negotiators of informal policymaking related to SEI in their own classrooms. Essentially, teachers function as final decision-makers in terms of what SEI looks like and how it plays out after having been projected from policy into practice (McCarty, 2002). Arizona's curriculum for mandated training was clearly outlined by the ADE and required in two forms: first, a 15-hour Curricular Framework, for which the deadline was August 31, 2006; and a 45-hour Curricular Framework, for which the deadline was deadline August 31, 2009.

Several key problems emerge in the context of Arizona's current and past SEI training mandates. First, when an entire state adopts one essentialized framework for teaching each and every English learner, regardless of first and second language proficiency levels, age, and educational history, trainers might not be adequately knowledgeable about research (including, e.g. theories regarding second language acquisition and the relationship between oracy and literacy) beyond the simple transmission of methods through hastily designed and executed teacher training. Second, certain ideological, sociocultural, socioeconomic and sociopolitical issues may or may not be addressed in SEI training sessions depending on trainers' perceptions of them – this background information should represent a foundational aspect of working with language minority populations. Third, the organizations and individuals who conduct training sessions may stand to gain economically and/or politically because of their role in sessions. Fourth, trainers play an integral role in their interpretation of the state framework for defining SEI vís-a-vís explanations of SEI (and more broadly, methods for supporting language learners) in theory, research and practice. Each of these four concerns can clearly be traced to issues related to the role, function and impact of ideology within the contexts of SEI training mandates and the advancement of a 'model' of SEI as a means of instructing ELs. The research questions outlined below are designed to address these problems by tying them together based on ideology, using the notion of narratives and of interpretive policy, which together enable the synthesis of SEI's underlying ideologies.

Understanding SEI Based on the four concerns listed above, the overarching research question for this study was: *Does this SEI policy elicit English-only ideology?* From the outset, the ADE compiled and published the curricular frameworks, granted course and trainer approval, distributed endorsements, and conducted oversight of training implementation using an online survey. Therefore, trainers occupy a key position in policy implementation amidst possible ideological forces – how might trainers from different organizations occupy this positionality?

The first question of this research project was: how are the SEI curricular frameworks interpreted by trainers/instructors from four different organizations: accredited university systems, community colleges, districts and for-profit organizations?[1] Also, from a critical perspective, how do trainers honor what Valdés (2001: 155) terms, 'an ethical understanding of how education is related to broader social and cultural relations' with regard to the ideological, sociocultural and sociopolitical issues that they confront with trainees – how do trainers, as group members from distinct organizations, universities (U); community colleges (CC); districts (D); for-profits (FP), regard sociocultural, socioeconomic, sociolinguistic, sociopolitical issues in

SEI training through *majoritarian* versus *counter narrative* storytelling (Ladson-Billings & Tate, 1995; Solórzano & Yosso, 2002a, b)? Finally, how can SEI training be framed within ideological and political contexts and amidst power structures (Yanow, 2000)? One of my key goals became viewing SEI as existing at the intersection between policy and practice – it was written into policy by English-only advocates (Arizona Revised Statutes, 2000), but is in many ways being implemented by trainers who occupy ideological perspectives at odds with the architects of the training mandate.

Participants and Institutions

During data collection, a key finding emerged in terms of trainers' affiliations with agencies. Many of the participants in my research worked as trainers/instructors for more than one type of institution. Many who had been involved with training at the district level or at universities had been recruited by community colleges and/or for-profit companies, for example. Table 7.1 lists the research participants and their affiliations.

Table 7.1 Participants, affiliations, training type

Pseudonym	Affiliation	Type of training
Katie	U; FP	15; 45
Mary	CC; FP	15; 45
Blanca	U; FP	45
Guillermo	U; CC	15r; 45r
Irma	D	15
Frank	D; FP	15; 45r
Kay	CC	15
Conrado	U	45r
Judy	U	15; 45
Saundra	U	15r; 45
Beth	U	15; 45
Maggie	D; FP	15; 45
Julie	U; FP	15; 45
Armando	D	15

U – University
FP – For-Profit
CC – Community College
D – District

Research included a total of 14 participants, representing varied institutions. An early emergent theme regarded overlap in the institutions for which identified participants worked. For example, those who were instructors at universities tended to also work for for-profit organizations or community colleges. An explanation for this kind of overlap is evident after considering the real-world implementation of state-wide mandates within such a condensed timeframe – logistically speaking, the need for teacher training may have constraints the state's capacity for qualified trainers, thus resulting in the overlapping representation of participants' employment at various institutions.

Framing SEI: Unveiling Narratives and Interpreting Policy

Critical race theory and counter-narratives

A more critical lens provides a means of unveiling the presiding content of SEI courses/workshops. This research then is partly situated within the field of critical race theory and specifically the notion of *storytelling, master narratives* and as an extension *counter-storytelling.* Delgado (1989: 28) maintains that counter-storytelling is essential for minority populations, or what he terms the 'outgroup', stating that, 'The member of an outgroup gains, first, psychic self preservation. A principal cause of the demoralization of marginalized groups is self-condemnation. They internalize the images that society thrusts on them – they believe that their lowly position is their own fault. The therapy is to tell stories. By becoming acquainted with the facts of their own historic oppression – with the violence, murder, deceit, co-optation, and connivance that have caused their desperate estate – members of outgroups gain healing' (Delgado, 1989: 28).

Yosso (2006) looked at critical race counterstories along the Chicana/o educational pipeline. Describing the necessity for counter-storytelling, she writes, 'Indeed, social scientists offer at least two types of stories to explain unequal educational outcomes – *majoritarian stories* and counterstories. A *majoritarian* story implicitly begins from the assumption that all students enjoy access to the same educational opportunities and conditions from elementary through postsecondary school ... the *majoritarian* story faults Chicana/o students and community cultural traditions for unequal schooling outcomes' (Yosso, 2006: 4). Yosso's assertion that Chicana/o students and community cultural traditions are implicitly charged with fault for failing educational outcomes is especially applicable in the case of SEI in

Arizona, because linguists and experts in the field of Second Language Acquisition (SLA) agree (Lightbrown & Spada, 2006) that students minimally need three years to learn a language, rather than the one year prescribed by Arizona's Superintendent of Public Instruction, Tom Horne in immersion settings. Of key importance for this study is gauging how SEI trainers either embrace or deny what Yosso and others term the majoritarian story versus counter-narratives in working with teachers who will ultimately be affecting the lives and learning of ELLs.

Villenas and Dehyle (1999: 413) use 'the lens of Critical Race Theory (CRT) to examine Latino schooling and family education as portrayed in seven recent ethnographic studies'. They reference Trueba's (1993) notion of racism as evidenced in castification, noting that the passage of language policy oriented legislation aimed at Latino/Chicano communities perpetuates the marginalization of target populations, therefore promulgating racism through the maintenance of systems of schooling (Villenas & Dehyle, 1999: 414).

In terms of legislation aimed at the Latino/Chicano communities that Villenas and Dehyle refer to, Propositions 227, 203 and Question 2 (requiring SEI in schools) clearly qualify as functioning to 'perpetuate this castification'.

Interpretive policy analysis

Yanow, discussing policy analysis, asserts that, 'policy analysts work in many capacities: as advisers to policymakers; as advocates for community groups or as community organizers; as staff in nonprofit agencies or lobbying groups' (Yanow, 2000: 3). The conceptual framework of Interpretive Policy Analysis that she presents is partly based on the notion of analyst as adviser and advocate, which represents the opportunity for me to situate research about SEI training and related politics and policymaking within broad contexts that illustrate the political and ideological construction of SEI in Arizona.

A key piece of Yanow's (2000) explanation of Interpretive Policy Analysis is the concept of symbols representing certain meanings (values, beliefs, feelings). She terms these symbols *artifacts*, stating that, 'artifactual symbols include three broad categories of human action: language, objects, acts ... the artifact is the concrete manifestation or expression of the more abstract value, belief, feeling, or meaning' (Yanow, 2000: 15). In this sense, this construct provides an opportunity for research to expand and include symbolic acts, objects and language communicated by the ADE and other related communities of meaning like the appointed ELL Task Force, formed by the Arizona state legislature during the summer of 2006 as a result of

Arizona House Bill 2064. The purpose of the Task Force, as listed on the Senate website is below:

> To develop and adopt research based models of structured English immersion programs for use by school districts and charter schools. The models shall take into consideration at least the size of the school, the location of the school, the grade levels at the school, the number of English language learners and the percentage of English language learners. The models shall be limited to programs for English language learners to participate in a structured English immersion program not normally intended to exceed one year. The Task Force shall identify the minimum amount of English language development per day for all models. The Task Force shall develop separate models for the first year in which a pupil is classified as an English language learner that includes a minimum of four hours per day of English language development. The Task Force shall establish procedures for school districts and charter schools to determine the incremental costs for implementation of the research based models of structured English immersion developed by the Task Force. The Task Force shall establish a form for school districts and charter schools to determine the structured English immersion budget request amount. (Arizona State Legislature, n.d.)

Task Force members were appointed by Superintendent of Instruction Tom Horne, Governor Janet Napolitano, and conservative members of the Arizona's legislature. While teachers were among the appointees, they included only one educational researcher, then Arizona State University Vice President, Eugene Garcia. Members were tasked with the adoption of 'research based models' of SEI, including consideration for key characteristics of program models. The school contexts, amount of English language development allocated, and prescribed hours outlined in the Task Force charter, are examples of factors that directly reflect pedagogical considerations, as well as school-based issues with direct implications for ELs' English acquisition and content learning. Despite the gravity of implications for decisions made by the task force, and the highly specialized nature of qualifications required to adequately weigh school-based, linguistic and other contextual factors, the Task Force was not representative of appointees with experience or expertise in the areas of educational or linguistic research.

The first steps in Interpretive Policy Analysis include the following (Yanow, 2000: 22):

(1)   Identify the artifacts (language, objects, acts) that are significant carriers of meaning for a given policy issue, as perceived by policy-relevant actors and interpretive communities.
(2)   Identify communities of meaning/interpretation/speech/practice that are relevant to the policy issue under analysis.
(3)   Identify the 'discourses': the specific meanings being communicated through specific artifacts and their entailments (in thought, speech and act).
(4)   Identify the points of conflict and their conceptual sources (affective, cognitive and/or moral) that reflect different interpretations by different communities.

According to Yanow (2000: 27), two key first steps to follow in interpretive policy analysis involve the identification of groups and artifacts. Researchers should locate groups sharing a common understanding of policy ideas (which may differ from other groups), along with the concurrent identification of key artifacts through which this shared understanding develops, is expressed, and interpreted.

Yanow's (2000) framework provides a means of situating my research – I was able to integrate information beyond that gleaned from participants. The idea that artifacts (language, objects, acts) reflect and interact with certain meanings (values, beliefs, feelings) was central to analysis using Interpretive Policy Analysis. Yanow contends that, 'we do know a great deal about what others value and believe: although not spoken of directly, others' values, beliefs, and feelings are tacitly known, and communicated through the artifacts that express them—the objects, language and acts of everyday life' (Yanow, 2000: 16). The notion of communicating meaning through artifacts provides an instrument for incorporating a wide range of information that exists outside of trainers/instructors that reflect such tacit knowledge. Yanow's assertion that certain language, objects and acts can be interpreted as representing implicit statements about values, beliefs and feelings allows a deeper analysis of many more pieces of the policy puzzle that reach beyond, but are not unrelated, to SEI training mandates.

Findings

Majoritarian versus counter narratives

For this piece of analysis, I used the notion of *majoritarian* versus *counter narratives* as a means of contextualizing versions of SEI that either align, or are at odds, with English-only/*majoritarian* ideology and storytelling.[2] Table 7.2 illustrates findings given this analytic framing of SEI training.

Table 7.2 Findings comparing majoritarian and counter narratives

	Majoritarian		*Counter*
	FP, D, CC	Vs	U
ADE CF	ADE CF drives course content		Course driven by content outside ADE CF
	FP, CC	Vs	U, D
LI	Restrictive L1 classroom policies; avoiding 'hot topics'; less SLA-related theory; less emphasis on nurturing home culture/language		Discussion of role of L1, culture, schooling; home-school mismatch; bilingualism/biliteracy; sociocultural/sociopolitical contexts of SEI; English-only movement/policies
	FP, D	Vs	CC, U
M-PD	Less construction of knowledge by participants; less critical thinking; engagement; collaboration		More construction of knowledge; inquiry-based; connection to background; engagement; collaboration
	FP, CC	Vs	D, U
M-SEI	Presented SIOP almost entirely independently from outside methods		Used SIOP in addition to other ESL-content material/sheltering

U – University
ADE CF–ADE Curricular Frameworks
FP – For-Profit
LI–Language Ideologies
CC – Community College
M–PD–Methods of Professional Development
D – District
M–SEI–Methods of SEI Instruction

Analysis was based on viewing different characteristics of training sessions: (1) The ADE Curricular Frameworks (ADE CF); (2) Language Ideologies (LI) and (3) Methods for SEI (M).

Note that the table therefore illustrates findings based on each of the three larger characteristics of training, emergent themes from each and whether those themes aligned with majoritarian or counter narratives.

Course content as derived from curricular frameworks

During analysis, salient themes emerged that were coded as aligning more closely with either majoritarian or counter narratives, for example, the trend that course content was often driven almost entirely by the ADE's curricular framework. Regarding the Curricular Frameworks, representatives from all organizations except universities voiced majoritarian narratives, characterized by aligning the overall curricula of SEI courses closely with the ADE. When asked what was included in the workshops at her district, Irma answered blankly, 'Well, you really didn't have much of an option. You had to follow the rubric ... we did all of the training in sections.' Similarly, Frank recalls the scenario at his district in terms of curriculum choices:

F: It was twelve hours of online work and then a three hour project and then a reflection paper and so I graded a third of the papers
           ...
SCKM: What was the curriculum of the online course?
F: It was the state framework. So, legal history, quick and dirty second language acquisition theory, the best practices component was the longest component. There were four modules or whatever they called them on our online thing. It was the legal stuff, SLA, best practices, and they closed it with the SELP ... I'm not a big advocate of online learning, but it was as good as it probably could be'

And further, when asked for a copy of the syllabus to serve as additional archival data, he stopped near short of suggesting that its contents are comparable to that of the ADE frameworks.

SCKM: You don't happen to have that syllabus do you? Could I get that from you?
F: Really what it is, is it's the state framework. The state even wrote out its own syllabus and they put at the head the people who designed the course. It's not much different than what the state said, cuz the state just said, this is what you have to do. Okay, we did it. – Frank (D, FP)

Even though data analysis revealed that university instructors were more likely to stray from the ADE curricular framework, the oversight and attention to alignment is evident in Judy's account, below:

I'm gonna be honest. I stick pretty close to what the state wants. Whether I agree with it or not, I stick with it because I feel a responsibility to my students. I don't want them getting caught, so I go through foundations ... I spend a lot of time doing strategies, a lot of time because that's what they [the state] want – eight hours on that. I don't know. I guess I've become very state regulated, but subversive in my own way. Try to balance it. The students see some lunacy of it but I try to give them something concrete. – Judy (U)

Note that even though Judy claims to 'stick pretty close to what the state wants', later in the interview she also mentioned requiring that her students read Proposition 203, and also incorporating funds of knowledge in course content. This demonstrates that she nevertheless strayed further than her community college, district and for-profit counterparts.

Language ideologies

In terms of language ideologies, both for-profit and community college instructors voiced majoritarian stories, while university and district instructors voiced counter stories. Mary, who worked for both a for-profit and community college, discusses below how she responds to issues related to immigration and politics.

Basically, because I don't like to get into politics. It will not serve the purpose of educating teachers if I turn them off by stating my opinion one way or another, so it's best if I just stick with here's what federal law says and I find that it just puts a pin in it and then there's no problem after that, but they do want to know and they do have a right to know if they're not sure. I think it's important. They're taxpayers, they want to know why and I want to be able to help them understand so that we can move along. It's not that they don't like the kids, it's not that. I think that they're just confused. They're just confused. I think a lot of people right now are confused about immigration issues, so I like to help them understand as best I can with my somewhat limited knowledge what I know about immigration. – Mary (CC, FP)

Mary's discussion of teachers who attend the professional development workshops she provides as 'taxpayers' points to implicitly embracing a majoritarian story that favors mainstream Anglos and marginalizes ELs, communities and undocumented families. A later explanation to participants regarded students' civil right to a public education based on *Plyler v. Doe* (1982), but she did not speak to the sociocultural, sociolinguistic and sociopolitical right to an equal education that a true counter story would reflect. On the contrary, when asked about participants' perceptions of native language use in the classroom during her district trainings, Irma provided a review that reveals an explicit counter story in terms of kids' access to native language maintenance and transference in the classroom.

> Up front we said, any time you can use the native language with the student for the student or have somebody come in and do it. We're not a bilingual [district], we never have been, we have a dual language program we're hoping to increase our language programs, but we've always supported the district and I think more of the teachers realize that this whole thing of English isn't what they thought. You can use supplementals, you can resources, all of these supplies, books, they can take home packets, backpacks with books that parents can use, so they knew that, in the native language, we've had for example in Spanish we've had the math books for the junior high and high school, we've had history books, so they were aware that they were not understanding how it could be used...They were really interested in that. I don't think they were negative as much as not knowing, not realizing – oh, I can do this. So, we try to use the native language as much as we can.
> – Irma (D)

Conversely, when Katie recounts her own training as working for a for-profit in which she was told how best to maintain efficient use of training 'time on task' by avoiding certain topics that veer from a majoritarian version of SEI.

SCKM: Are there questions about language use in terms of native language versus English and how do you address that in the training or do you address it?

K: Well, one of the things that I'll tell you that I've been kind of trained is that there's a lot of what they call hot topics and those are almost diffused immediately or avoided. And one of the reasons –

SCKM: What do you mean as hot topics?

K: If there's something that, an issue that might come up where participants might have varying views or differences of opinion or something that could get into a discussion that would take you away from your intended purpose for that hour and a half break out like if you have something that you need to get to them, some of the presenters there would say, well don't bring that up because if you do, then you're gonna lose them and you're not gonna get through what you need to get through in an hour and a half. – (Katie, U, FP)

Professional development and instructional methodologies

Finally, with regard to PD methodology, or approaches to professional development (PD Methods), for-profits and districts were majoritarian, while community colleges and universities were counter narratives. And with SEI Methods, for-profits and community college trainers reflected majoritarian stories, while districts and university instructors shared counter stories. The response to my question below reflects the misconstrued definitions of SEI in a state with a large population of ELs and a significant population of teachers who had completed SIOP Model training. The Sheltered Instruction Observation Protocol Model, or SIOP Model, is an approach to sheltered instruction that includes eight components and 30 features. In terms of teacher professional development, it has arguably been the most widespread implemented example of an approach or model to sheltered instruction for ELs (Echeverría *et al.*, 2009). While the SIOP Model may be effective in promoting achievement for ELLs, it is not incorporated in the explanations for SEI outlined by the ADE, nor does its adoption reflect a multi-faceted and comprehensive approach to developing and implementing an SEI course.

SCKM: Based on your experiences with [Community College], what was addressed in the training classes, maybe if you could think about maybe 3–5 core areas that were addressed in the course curriculum.

K: They just, they followed the SIOP model, so there were several components to that, so they followed, I can't even remember what they are right this very second. I can grab my – building background was one, comprehensible input was another, strategies like what you can do to in the classroom to meet English language learners' needs, how to change your material to adapt to be more comprehensible and what else? I can't really think right now. I think that was three, wasn't it. – (Kay, CC)

Conrado, teaching at the university level shared a different perspective about the SIOP model and the curriculum of his course. It is notable that later in this account he added that as a principal, he uses the SIOP observation protocol for assessing his teachers. However, this excerpt demonstrates his dedication to providing pre-service teachers in his course with a counter narrative to SEI.

The books and the SIOP model are all very effective, but another big thing is having teachers who will advocate for ELLs, being the positive role models, being the support system for ELLs because coming from schools, I see it firsthand how sometimes an ELL will register and become part of a new class and it's seen as a burden to teachers and administrators instead of being seen as a resource or just seen as a positive challenge for those professionals. It's more of like, 'oh great, I've got another one' that type of a thing, so I tell my classes that you might be if you're in middle school and high school, one of the only periods that your ELL looks forward to so you're the support system. You need to share learning strategies that they can take to other classes where they're not being supported and be their advocate. That would be a major thing too. – (Conrado, U)

Overwhelmingly, university instructors were most likely to offer counter-narrative storytelling in opposition to the majoritarian voice usually sounded by for-profit trainers. There are several plausible explanations for limited presentations of the material. One may be the hyper-abbreviated timeline for mandated completion of the training and limited resources on the part of districts charged with ensuring the maintenance of a certificated teacher core. Unfortunately, findings suggest that the majoritarian story in some cases was one that did not espouse the sort of expertise and training required for teachers to adequately support ELLs in classrooms (Gándara & Baca, 2008; Gándara *et al.*, 2005; Garcia, 2009). Frank describes the quandary faced by the administrators at his district, who were torn between promoting efficacy and meeting state training deadlines.

And we argued long and hard on what the threshold would be for passing or failing [the 15-hour training] and we decided that, well I won't say we, the decision was that this [15-hour training] was getting your feet wet, get your foot in the door of language acquisition and as long as there's some effort shown to get this done, then you pass. In my opinion as a language specialist, it's a bunch of crap, a whole bunch of crap, but we decided that they were gonna have to go through another college course type thing and stuff and that that's gonna hold them to a higher standard and they'll learn the material. This was basically dabble. Try it out, reflect. – Frank (D, FP)

Perhaps a key distinction between university instructors and trainers from the other three institutions lay in their backgrounds. University instructors, given the positionality in a research-oriented context may have a more comprehensive set of knowledge about SEI amidst larger issues related to language minority schooling, both in Arizona and at the federal level. The excerpt below poignantly illustrates a tension given SEI mandates.

... but I would still like to think that we are training people to teach English language learners who truly want to teach them, who wanna work with them specifically and one of the things that I still don't like about SEI is that it sort of assumes that anybody can teach an ELL child and that's not the case at all, so I still think that it's a job for specialists, to use the language of undergrads, you major in ELLs because you want to be there, not because you have to and that hasn't changed ... the kids who took language acquisition classes did so specifically because they wanted to work with that population, often they were from that population themselves ... those are the ones who are truly dedicated and now we're faced with a situation where our own state views someone who has taken 45 hours, maybe 60 hours eventually as a highly qualified teacher of ELL students and they're not. I'm not even certain that the ESL or BLE endorsement was enough, but it sure was better than this one class, so I guess I'm of a mixed attitude about this. I'm glad the [pre-service teachers] are getting exposed to this. I'm glad I'm teaching it, rather than someone who's less passionate. On the other hand, I don't have any illusions, so it saddens me in a way that they're not taking away that expertise, but they are taking away at least I hope, is a better understanding of what they will be seeing, so that's why I can't really answer this in a sound bite or one or two words. – (Beth, U)

While district personnel did give voice to those in the margins of school systems, these were usually on the part of teachers rather than language minority students, families or communities. In uncovering the master narratives voiced by instructors/trainers at each of the four institutions, my data strongly shows that university instructors are most likely to honor counter stories while for-profit trainers and community college instructors are less likely to do so. The only trainers that did not overall present strong counter stories were from for-profits. As demonstrated above, many of the instructors from for-profit organizations directly avoided situating SEI within its sociocultural, sociopolitical and ideologically charged genesis.

Trainers' regard for external issues

In answering the sub-question for this portion of the research, – how do trainers, as group members from distinct organizations (universities; community colleges; districts; for-profits), regard sociocultural, socioeconomic, sociolinguistic, sociopolitical issues in SEI training through majoritarian versus counter narrative storytelling? – majoritarian storytelling was characterized by participants from three of the four organizations: for-profits;

districts; community colleges. Regardless of the aspect of SEI training reviewed (Curricular Framework; Language Ideologies; Methodology), for-profit trainers always gave voice to majoritarian storytelling. Three organizations (FP, CC, D) voiced majoritarian storytelling regarding the Curricular Framework and Methods. Only for-profits and community colleges gave voice to majoritarian storytelling regarding Language Ideologies; district participants' responses reflected counterstories.

By extension, in addressing the over-arching research question given this analytic frame – Does SEI training elicit English-only ideology? Given that notions of sociocultural, socioeconomic, sociolinguistic, sociopolitical issues based on English-only ideology align with majoritarian storytelling: Yes – this SEI training policy does elicit English-only ideology *if* it is conducted by for-profits or community colleges. Conversely, No – SEI training does not elicit English-only ideology if it is conducted by universities or districts.

Interpretive policy design

Through the use of Yanow's frame for Interpretive Policy Analysis, I identified four key aspects of SEI training: (1) interpretive communities; (2) symbolic language; (3) symbolic objects and (4) symbolic acts and actors. First, I located certain salient themes in the discourse of trainers/instructors from the distinctive interpretive communities. I also identified important symbolic acts, actors, objects and language that interact and overlap within and around the SEI training mandates, including: overarching Curricular Frameworks, which included symbolic language; required course approval; an ADE oversight, including threats of investigation related to a training survey. Other acts and actors that emerged during data collection and analysis include ELL Task Force meetings (acts) and ELL Task Force members (actors). Each of these reflects other symbols, including member discourse and a 'Draft SEI Models' document (object). The primary discourses of interpretive communities, symbolic language, objects, acts and actors incorporate a version of SEI training that is heavily politicized, and functions on the part of trainers usually as simple compliance, whereas on the part of policymakers as ideologically constructed. It is helpful to view SEI training and trainers from an interpretive policy analysis perspective because their identification represents a key first step in an IPA-based approach – the identification of a group or community sharing a common view of, communication around, and interpretive actions based on, symbolic artifacts. Locating SEI trainers as a community or in-group provides a framing that facilitates unveiling the overarching political and ideological contexts (artifacts) within which trainers/instructors operate and view their work. They are scrutinized by the state and media and charged with a task that is inherently sociopolitical and sociocultural in nature, albeit facilitating SEI training under the guise of objectivity.

SEI training is framed within ideological and political contexts and amidst power structures using Interpretive Policy Analysis through identifying and locating the dominant discourses from interpretive communities (D, CC, U, FP) and identifying points of conflict with ADE symbolic artifacts (L, O, A, Ar). Figure 7.1, illustrates dominant discourses of interpretive communities and related symbolic objects, language, acts and actors.

The dominant discourse of each interpretive community reflects how it frames SEI training because this discourse represents the 'specific meanings being communicated through specific artifacts and their entailments' (Yanow, 2000: 27). Discourses that conflict with that of the ADE are not derived from ADE symbolic artifacts (like the Curricular Framework, Objectives, Course Approval), but rather trainers' and instructors' (as in-group members') joined experiences that are derived beyond these artifacts. These experiences may be in practice with children, families, and other teachers; with theory and research related to aspects of training that are not included in the ADE artifacts, such as sociocultural views of SLA; and/or as advocates working for equity in education for language minority populations. In order to situate research related to SEI training implementation, a first step involved the identification of symbolic dominant artifacts (language, objects, acts) and actors derived from the ADE. These three are the Curricular Frameworks, objects; the Objectives outlined in each of the two Curricular Frameworks, language; and the activity of obtaining course approval from the ADE, jointly representing both acts and actors. To structure data analysis, I identified three dominant discourses from each of the four interpretive communities (organizations) represented among participants. Findings regarding the three dominant discourses from each of the four interpretive communities were then situated within and among the larger context of artifacts and actors as either deriving from dominant symbolic objects, language, acts or actors *or* at odds with them. These symbolic actors or artifacts (language, objects, acts) relate to the SEI training itself, the ADE, the ELL Task Force, and oversight of SEI training mandates. Analysis using the Interpretive Policy Analysis framework indicates that only three discourses from the four interpretive communities (U, FP, CC, D) were in conflict with ADE symbolic acts: viewing SEI through a critical lens (U); a sense of feeling under siege from ADE (D); and the importance of addressing the sociocultural/sociopolitical context (U) of SEI. Only university and district trainers/instructors were at odds with ADE-derived artifacts.

In addressing the over-arching research question given this conceptual framework – Does this SEI training policy elicit English-only ideology?

The answer is yes; this SEI training policy does elicit English-only ideology *if* the ADE continues to sustain and promulgate symbolic artifacts (language, objects and acts; e.g. complaints against the content of training) in oversight and beyond (as with the Discrete Skills Inventory adopted by the ELL Task Force) *and* if SEI training is not conducted by universities and/or, districts.

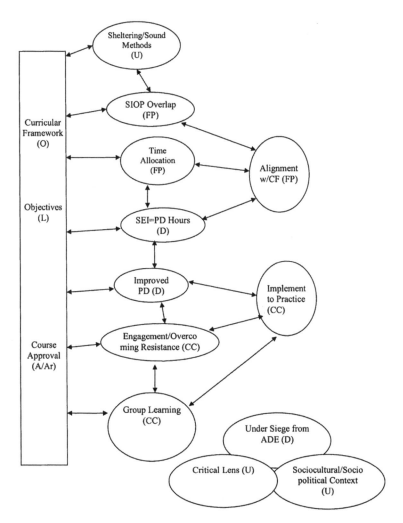

Figure 7.1 ADE symbolic artifacts, U-University; FP-For-Profit; CC-Community College; D-District

Conclusions

Findings from this research illustrate how ADE-mandated SEI training varies across the state depending on the organization offering sessions/courses. Interestingly, both district and university instructors felt strongly about affecting change among SEI training participants through giving voice to silenced, marginalized populations. They were more likely to present counter narratives during sessions/courses, whereas for-profit trainers and community college instructors emphasized methodology over key issues in language minority education, including the sociocultural, sociopolitical and historical–structural context of SEI in society and research in the field. While for-profit trainers did consider themselves advocates for ELLs, they nevertheless usually explicitly stated that politics were outright avoided in an effort to stay on task. Denying the contexts of SEI – especially given current heated debates about immigration reform and immigrant rights in this country – essentially accepts the negative discourses evident in mainstream media related to the language minority population in today's schools. To be certain, when a question is asked and no answer replied, the void does indeed reflect a response – one that echoes neglect for the issue, devaluing it and rendering it unworthy of discussion. When challenges to mainstream media attacking ELs and immigrants are not presented, addressed and critically deconstructed in a professional development scenario intended for educators supporting ELLs, majoritarian narratives that further marginalize ELs, families and communities are further perpetuated. In this way, university instructors tended toward supporting ELLs through providing them with an opportunity for voice and challenging mainstream tendencies, while for-profit trainers tended toward functioning in the polar opposite regard. It is notable that, while some participants may have represented several different organizations, reports indicated a shift in their presentation of training materials and curricula depending on their particular role. For example, while an instructor may take one stance while instructing a university course, one may be deliberately less 'political' while working as a for-profit trainer.

By utilizing Yanow's (2000) framework for interpretive policy analysis, I illustrate the degree to which SEI training requirements abstractly exist among and within the interpretive communities charged with implementation and in the meaning statements communicated through artifacts like symbolic language, acts and objects and actors. The interplay between dominant discourses voiced by actors, trainers and symbolic language, acts and objects is evidence of the ideological and sociopolitical underpinnings of SEI mandates as symptomatic of broader perceptions language minority schooling, educational access, educational efficacy and educational rights. Clearly, the case of SEI training is one scrutinized by the state because of its manifestation in Proposition 203 and the English-only movement.

Given this research and analysis then: Does this SEI training policy elicit English-only ideology? With regard to analysis of data using the concept of storytelling, notions of sociocultural, socioeconomic, sociolinguistic, sociopolitical issues based on English-only ideology align with majoritarian storytelling. Given this relationship evidence from this particular research suggests that, yes, this training may elicit English-only ideology *if* it is conducted by for-profits or community colleges because these are the organizations that, among these participants, voiced majoritarian versions of SEI. Conversely, no, it may not elicit English-only ideology using SEI training *if* it is conducted by universities and/or districts, based on anecdotal findings from these particular participants' responses because these instructors seemed to present counter stories of SEI and language minority schooling. With regard to findings using Interpretive Policy Analysis, SEI training is framed within ideological and political contexts and amidst power structures through identifying and locating the dominant discourses from interpretive communities (D, CC, U, FP) and identifying points of conflict with ADE symbolic artifacts (L, O, At, Ar). In answering the over-arching research question, yes, the SEI training does seem to engender English-only ideology *if* certain decision-making bodies continue to sustain and promulgate symbolic artifacts in oversight and beyond (as with the Discrete Skills Inventory adopted by the ELL Task Force) *and* if SEI training is not conducted by universities and/or districts, based on the analysis conducted from findings that emerged from participants in this particular study.

Implications and Further Research

Based on this small representative study and findings from these particular interviews and observations, the most efficient means for ADE to promote English-only ideology through SEI training may be by using for-profits and community colleges. Districts and universities seem more likely to present versions of 'SEI' in SEI training that do not align with those from the ADE. By mandating 'training', the ADE permits its own oversight of such 'training'. In other words, when newly mandated 'training' is also required as part of pre-service teacher preparation programs, the integrity of university courses may be compromised due to ADE oversight and curriculum derived from the state, rather than from research, theory and scholarly collaboration.

SEI trainers' positionality allows them to act as bottom-up policymakers in conflict with the ADE's top-down SEI training mandate. A necessary next step in research should be aimed at the next level of policy implementation: teachers. Once teachers have completed SEI training and obtained the full SEI Endorsement, how does their teaching change, depending on the organization from which they obtained training? How do they, at this level of policy implementation also act as bottom-up policymakers in their classrooms and schools?

If researchers, policymakers and educators who are truly advocates wish to affect change given the current context of English-only in Arizona, they must work toward revealing the often ideologically and politically charged nature of the debate in this state, particularly given how California and Massachusetts have implemented SEI post-Proposition 227 and Question 2 (more emphasis on program efficacy and practitioner support, less on ideological challenges). Apart from providing a comparative foundation for viewing SEI as it has been written into law, an integral next step is viewing policy from the bottom up, rather than as top-down, from teachers who are working in 'SEI' classrooms. It is vital that we in the field of language minority education take control of the direction in which potential models of SEI emerge. While the Discrete Skills Inventory, which outlines language-based skills training, delivered using a drill-and-skill approach, is now a 'model' of SEI, researchers and practitioners in the field must ensure that in reality, models are derived from educational theory accepted in the field, that they reflect and support practitioner implementation and incorporate language and content learning that promotes academic development for ELs. Advocates for language minority populations must shift the decision-making about *what* SEI is as a *model* toward a better representation of researchers and practitioners.

Findings from this isolated research may provide evidence that the most efficient means for ADE to promote English-only ideology through SEI training may be by using for-profits and community colleges. Districts and universities may be more likely to present versions of 'SEI' in SEI training that do not align with those outlined by the ADE. Important implications of this research are that, by mandating 'training', the ADE may have more opportunity for its own oversight of such 'training'. In other words, when newly mandated 'training' is also required as part of pre-service teacher preparation programs, the integrity of university and community college courses may be compromised due to ADE oversight and curriculum derived from the state – rather than from research, theory, and scholarly collaboration.

Notes

(1) For the purposes of this study, 'for-profit' is defined as those for which trainers receive substantially more economic returns than with the other three organizations and

those for which the cost of attending training sessions was substantially higher than for the other three organizations.

(2) For a teacher counter stories in response to the ELL Task Force Draft SEI Model, see Appendix C.

References

Arizona Revised Statutes, Title 15, Article 3.1, §15-751–17.755 (2000).

Arizona State Legislature (n.d.) Arizona English language learners Task Force. Online document: Accessed 14 January 2008. http://www.azleg.gov/FormatDocument. asp?format=normal&inDoc=/icommittee/Arizona+English+Language+Learners+ Task+Force.doc.htm

Delgado, R. (1989) Storytelling for oppositionists and others: A plea for narrative. *Michigan Law Review* 87, 2411–2441.

Echevarria, J., Vogt, M.E. and Short, D. (2009) *Making Content Comprehensible for Elementary English Learners: The SIOP Model.* Chicago: Pearson.

Gándara, P. and Baca, G. (2008) NCLB and California's English language learners: The perfect storm. *Language Policy* 7, 201–216.

Gándara, P., Maxwell-Jolly, J. and Driscoll, A. (2005) *Listening to Teachers of English Language Learners: A Survey of California Teachers' Challenges, Experiences, and Professional Development Needs.* Santa Cruz, CA: The Center for the Future of Teaching and Learning.

Garcia, O. (2009) *Bilingual Education in the 21st Century: A Global Perspective.* Malden, MA: Wiley-Blackwell.

Ladson-Billings, G. and Tate, W.F., IV (1995) Toward a critical race theory of education. *Teachers College Record* 97, 47–68.

Lightbrown, P. and Spada, N. (2006) *How Languages are Learned* (3rd edn). Oxford: Oxford University Press.

McCarty, T.L. (2002) Between possibility and constraint: Indigenous language education, planning, and policy in the United States. In J. Tollefson (ed.) *Language Policies in Education: Critical Issues* (pp. 285–307). Mahwah, NJ: Lawrence Erlbaum.

Plyler v. Doe 457 U.S. (202) 1982.

Solórzano, D.G. and Yosso, T.J. (2002a) A critical race counterstory of race, racism, and affirmative action. *Equity & Excellence in Education* 35, 155–168.

Solórzano, D.G. and Yosso, T.J. (2002b) Critical race methodology: Counter-storytelling as an analytical framework for educational research. *Qualitative Inquiry* 8, 23–44.

Trueba, H. (1993) *From Failure to Success: The Roles of Cultural Conflict in the Academic Achievement of Chicano Students.* ERIC Clearinghouse, DC.

Valdés, G. (2001) *Learning and not Learning English: Latino Students in American Schools.* New York: Teachers College Press.

Villenas, S. and Deyhle, D. (1999) Critical race theory and ethnographies challenging the stereotypes: Latino families, schooling, resilience, resistance. *Curriculum Inquiry* 29, 413–445.

Yanow, D. (2000) *Conducting Interpretive Policy Analysis.* Thousand Oaks, CA: Sage Publications.

Yosso, T.J. (2006) *Critical Race Counterstories along the Chicana/o Educational Pipeline.* New York: Routledge.

8 Implementing Structured English Immersion in Teacher Preparation in Arizona

Nancy J. Murri, Amy Markos and Alexandria Estrella-Silva

As teacher educators for English Language Learner (ELL) classrooms, we work hard to assure that the curriculum we choose for our students includes competencies known for effective teacher development and opportunities for teachers to practice those competencies. To some extent, teacher preparation programs rely on support and direction from school districts and state and federal policy-makers. Thus, it is of great concern when state policies' determinations about what to teach in teacher preparation curriculum hinder our ability to adequately address competencies needed for teachers of ELLs and minimize opportunities for preservice teachers to practice these competencies while they learn to teach in linguistically diverse classrooms.

In this chapter, we explore how teachers are prepared to teach ELLs, and particularly how preservice teachers view the state-mandated structured English immersion (SEI) course that they are required to pass as part of their initial teacher certification. We begin with a review of research that identifies the knowledge and practices teachers need to work effectively with ELLs. We follow this with a brief discussion of the current situation in Arizona surrounding teacher preparation for working with ELLs through a state-mandated curriculum. Subsequently, we describe our research approach and the findings of our investigation. In the final section of the chapter, we present implications for teacher preparation programs based on our findings.

Research on Preparing Teachers to Work with ELLs

Current research has sought to understand the challenges teachers face in ELL classrooms, their preparation to meet the needs of these students, and perspectives on professional development that would help address teachers' challenges. This body of research presents multiple variables, which influence the preparedness of teachers for effectively educating ELLs (Combs *et al.*, 2005).

Concerns about the growing number of ELLs in schools and an educational field that is fraught with implications from reform efforts, policy and misunderstandings has led to investigating what it takes to prepare teachers for working with ELLs (Gándara *et al.*, 2005; Harper & de Jong, 2004; Lucas *et al.*, 2006). Over the past 25 years, there has been a growing body of research emphasizing the competencies needed for teachers to be effective with ELLs. Commonalities across several studies include: using a student's native language to support English acquisition, using appropriate strategies and materials based on an understanding of language proficiency levels, building on students' prior knowledge (including language, culture and community), using appropriate forms of assessment (both for language and content), and having an understanding of ELLs' families and communities (Gándara & Maxwell-Jolly, 2005; Harper & de Jong, 2004; Milk *et al.*, 1992; Tikunoff, 1983).

In their chapter, 'Critical Issues in the Development of the Teacher Corps for English Learners,' Gándara and Maxwell-Jolly (2005) summarize key competencies of effective instruction for ELLs as:

> a deeper understanding of second language development and the ways in which native language competency can bridge to, and support, English language acquisition, ... understanding how to assess the academic progress of EL students and to discriminate between learning and language problems. (Gándara & Maxwell-Jolly, 2005: 107–108)

They assert that these competencies are seldom, if ever, taught in standard teacher preparation. As part of the research on effective teachers, Tikunoff (1983) reported that effective teachers of ELLs use the student's native language and English to clarify instruction and interactions.

Concerning effective teaching strategies for ELLs, Harper and de Jong (2004) challenge educators to think carefully about the notion that teaching ELLs is tantamount to using 'just good teaching' strategies. They argue that teachers of ELLs need to have an understanding of the language acquisition process in order to choose and implement effective teaching strategies for ELLs. Based on a solid understanding of how students acquire and use language at various stages of acquisition, teachers can implement effective and 'active' teaching behaviors. Some active behaviors include communicating high expectations and maintaining student engagement. Similarly, effective teachers for ELLs communicate clearly when giving directions, specifying tasks and presenting information. They continually monitor student progress and provide specific feedback. In essence, good teaching strategies for ELLs are only 'good' if they are grounded in an understanding of what is appropriate for students at different levels of language proficiency (Freeman *et al.*, 2001; Gándara & Maxwell-Jolly, 2005; Harper & de Jong, 2004; Milk *et al.*, 1992).

Along with a working knowledge of the language acquisition process, teachers need to be prepared for building on students' background knowledge and experiences, and for incorporating students' culture and community into the classroom (Faltis, 1997; Peregoy & Boyle, 2005; Walqui, 2000). Authentic learning stems from students' prior academic and life experiences. Teachers need to be informed on how to access and utilize the knowledge ELLs bring to the classroom (García *et al.*, 2006; González *et al.*, 2005).

Assessment and review can be utilized as trajectory tools for guiding ELL instruction. Research emphasizes quality assessment and authentic assessment to support ELLs' language acquisition and academic success (Echevarria *et al.*, 2004; Short, 1993; Walqui, 2000). Butler and Stevens (2001) consider testing in students' first language, explicit accommodations, and measures of growth in English as alternatives to standardized assessments for content knowledge. However, assessment for ELLs under restrictive language policies has become limiting and at times even confusing. Since most language acquisition assessments are normed based on native English speaker proficiencies and not those of second language learners or bilinguals, Lachat (1999) suggests that assessment tools and methods that effectively survey English skills for language minority students do not exist. Therefore, it is essential that teachers be prepared to discern language acquisition assessment scores. In addition, they must be knowledgeable as to how to effectively assess ELL's language proficiency and content understanding through alternative measures within their own classroom.

The need for teachers to engage in an understanding of families and communities is crucial in creating an optimal learning environment for ELLs. Luis Moll and his colleagues assert that students bring with them to school 'funds of knowledge' referred to the knowledge and skills found within households and community activities (González *et al.*, 2005). They emphasize the importance of teachers and schools tapping into these cultural resources that encompass family, language and culture and use these resources as tools for the foundation of ELLs' learning, and for their educational improvement.

Delgado-Gaitán (2004) reports that unresponsiveness and fear on behalf of schools working with Latino parents creates gaps in communication and lost opportunities for their children to academically advance. She encourages teachers to create a working definition of family involvement in the classroom to help present a clearer understanding of the role families can play in their child's' education. In an effort to connect to families and surrounding communities, schools need to organize opportunities that reach out to open the doors of communication. These opportunities may include parent education training, language translators to assist with communication, information on ways parents can help their child with their homework, and information on activities in the community that connect with students' learning (Epstein, 2001). With this understanding, it is important to encourage research geared toward developing preservice and advanced courses on school, family and community partnerships.

Lucas *et al.* (2006) examined the extent to which prospective teachers participating in teacher preparation programs felt prepared to teach ELLs. They suggest that it is not enough just to inform teachers of the recommended competencies that are beneficial to use with ELLs; teacher educators need to provide *opportunities* for prospective teachers to learn about teaching ELLs within authentic learning environments. Opportunities to practice balancing instructional time in the classroom such as the essential need for more time to teach ELLs due to their academic and language variability. Programs should also make teachers aware of special services for English learners by offering opportunities to access and work with specialists in the field.

A View from Arizona's Teacher Preparation Program

Restrictive language policy and teacher preparation in Arizona

Arizona offers a unique view of what can happen when state policies mandate how teachers are to be prepared for working with ELLs. Restrictive language policies (Arias, this volume) were mandated as part of the teacher preparation curriculum for all teachers. These policies established criteria for the content and time to be allocated for the state approved instructional approach for ELLs: Structured English Immersion (SEI). By limiting course content to only one instructional approach for ELLs, teachers were precluded from gaining a comprehensive understanding of instructional approaches, methods and strategies used with ELLs at different levels of proficiency and age.

Arizona state mandates

As a result of the passage of Proposition 203, Sheltered English Immersion (SEI) became the mandated coursework required for preparing *all* teachers, both preservice and in-service, to work with ELLs in dominant English language mainstream classrooms. As of August 31, 2006, for those working in education or anticipating a position in education (e.g. teachers, principals, supervisors and superintendents) in Arizona, an SEI endorsement is required. In-service teachers who received their teaching credentials before August of 2006 were required to complete a total of 60 hours of SEI training by August of 2009 to obtain their SEI endorsement.

Teachers pursuing a teaching certification on or after August 31, 2006 are required to complete a total of 90 hours of SEI coursework to receive their SEI endorsement. Preservice teachers graduating before August 2009 must complete the first 45 hours of SEI coursework before they graduate. Completion of the SEI 45-hour course is mandatory if preservice teachers want to receive their teaching certification and begin working in schools. In essence, they must obtain their SEI provisional endorsement in order to teach. With state mandates requiring 45 hours of SEI coursework for a teaching certificate, teacher preparation programs are embedding the required 45 hours of SEI into their programs to ensure graduates have the hours mandated to obtain their SEI provisional endorsement. Once preservice teachers receive their provisional endorsement, they have one year to complete the additional 45 hours of SEI coursework to receive their full SEI endorsement (Arizona Department of Education, 2007).

Arizona's SEI curricular framework

The state of Arizona mandates and approves university courses providing a skeletal 45-hour curriculum that all preservice teachers must take to graduate with their SEI provisional endorsement. The state-imposed curricular framework outlines what SEI objectives are to be taught and the minimum amount of hours spent on each objective. Universities, other educational institutions and individual trainers requesting to offer the 45-hour SEI course must submit their syllabus for approval to the Arizona Department of Education. Syllabi must match the minimum hours for each SEI objective as outlined by the state. Yet, the state does not dictate how the content is delivered (e.g. materials, texts, learning experiences), or the timeline for completing the 45 hours of instruction course. Delivery varies throughout the state based on the institution or trainer offering the course. Six SEI objectives covered by the state mandated curricular framework include: (1) ELL standards; (2) data analysis and application; (3) formal and informal assessments; (4) SEI foundations; (5) SEI strategies and (6) parent/home/school scaffolding.

The state-mandated curriculum emphasizes an English-only approach for educating ELLs. In the Arizona State SEI 45-hour curriculum, preservice teachers are only required to learn about Arizona English Language

Development standards, not national standards such as the Teachers of English to Speakers of Other Language (TESOL) Standards. Preservice teacher were required to learn only the Arizona English Language Learner Assessment (AZELLA), as opposed or in addition to other forms of language acquisition assessments. Within the 45-hour state curriculum, only one hour is allocated for learning about second language acquisition and the process students go through as they are acquiring English. With the limited exposure to language acquisition theories and the narrow approach that stems from focusing on Arizona's understanding of assessment and standards, preservice teachers taking the course are restricted to what they learn. When so little time and emphasis is placed on the stages ELLs go through as they acquire English, we find it puzzling that the focus of the course (25 + hours) is on SEI strategies. This lopsidedness of the majority of hours set aside for teaching SEI strategies, with a very limited emphasis on preservice teacher's understandings about the language acquisition theories, seems to promote an illusion among students who take the course that teaching ELLs is 'just good teaching' (de Jong & Harper, 2005).

The Research Study

Purpose of the study

The purpose of our study is to understand how a state-imposed English-Only educational language policy influences teacher preparation in Arizona by examining how preservice teachers viewed how well the required SEI course prepared them to teach English learners. We used a two-step approach to address this purpose. First, we looked at the impact of the dual restrictive language policies on the SEI teacher preparation course. Second, we designed and implemented a survey to gather information from preservice teachers on their self-assessment of: (1) their preparedness to teach ELLs; and (2) the relevance of the content of the SEI coursework on their future teaching. The survey was also administered to a large group sample, but for the purpose of this chapter, we focus only on the data generated from the preservice teachers' self-assessment survey.

Participants

Survey respondents included 71 individuals who participated in the SEI course work at the University during or before the fall of 2007. All of the respondents were preservice teachers in the teacher preparation program at the university enrolled in various teacher education programs ranging from elementary education majors to secondary education majors. All of the pre-service teacher respondents were part of a four-semester teacher preparation program that includes course work and field placements. Most were in their second semester of student teaching, whereas others were in their final semester. We define preservice teachers as those individuals participating in the College of Education Teacher Preparation Program who are in the process of earning a state teaching certificate. The findings section addresses the specific demographic of our preservice teacher participants.

Data collection

Survey methods served as the primary source of data collection. The items on the survey were based on a careful review of the research on teacher preparation for ELLs, and a review of Arizona SEI course syllabi. In addition, survey questions were developed based on previous work conducted on ELL teacher preparation (Cartiera, 2005; Gándara et al., 2005; Lucas et al., 2006). Questions were designed using close-ended with unordered response choices, partially close-ended, and open-ended format. Using varying types of questions and previous studies as a guide, the intent of the survey was to reveal preservice teachers' perspectives concerning their ability to teach ELLs, and the importance of their SEI coursework. We built on questions that had been asked before, and followed a similar design based on Cartiera's (2005) study, which examined perceived levels of preparation and proficiency in beginning teachers of ELLs teaching strategies. Cartiera implemented a beginning teacher survey questionnaire and structured interviews with teacher educators. In the case of our study, we implemented the survey questionnaire composed of one section of the survey asking participants to rate their level of preparation using a 4-point Likert scale. Items in this section addressed topics related to what was taught during the SEI course.

Our goal in administering the SEI survey was to gather perspectives from preservice teachers, and within this population, responses from individuals participating in the SEI course. The survey had five components: (1) background demographics; (2) participants' assessment of the SEI course and program; (3) teacher views of language proficiency and culture of ELLs; (4) knowledge of strategies for teaching ELLs and (5) exposure to and experience with ELLs.

Data analysis

Data were analyzed using hand-tabulation that involved sorting questionnaires into piles, counting answers and calculating results (Salant & Dillman, 1994). Excel spreadsheets served to organize, tally, and analyze responses. Open-ended survey responses were compiled, read, and coded based on words or phrases provided by the respondents. Quantitative data for the survey were analyzed using SPSS software. Analysis included descriptive statistics. The following section presents the survey findings.

Findings

Demographics

In all, 55 of the 71 preservice participants responded to the questions pertaining to demographics. As shown in Table 8.1, a majority of the participants were identified as female, white, and English-speaking, with some participants indicating limited knowledge of a language other than English. Some of the participants identified themselves as Hispanic; a limited number of participants identified themselves as Asian, and African American. A majority of the surveyed preservice sample was under the age of 25. Most of the survey respondents indicated they were speakers only of English and indicated they could not speak a language other than English. In the United States, this demographic profile represents the current state of prospective teachers entering the education profession and teachers in the field (Zumwalt & Craig, 2005).

Experiences with ELLs

The first section on the survey focused on exposure to ELLs through the experiences preservice teachers had in their teacher preparation program. Internships, field placements and opportunities to work with ELLs provide prospective teachers the day-to-day experiences of interacting with students acquiring English. Most survey respondents were in their second field placement while taking their SEI coursework. A few respondents were student

Table 8.1 Participant demographics

Gender		Ethnicity					Age						Speaks a language other than English		
M	F	A	AA	H	NA	W	O	−25	26–30	31–35	36–40	40+	Y	N	Limited
5	50	2	3	7	0	41	2	45	2	4	2	2	8	29	18

A (Asian) AA (African American) H (Hispanic) NA (Native American) W (White) O (Other)
Missing 16 responses for demographics

Table 8.2 Experiences with ELLs

ELLs in current internship		ELLs in previous internship		Amount of teaching time in internships			
Yes	No	Yes	No	None	Low	Moderate	High
54	17	39	32	0	32	30	9

teaching while taking the course and had indicated more experiences with working in diverse settings. As shown in Table 8.2, a majority of the preservice teachers (76%) reported having ELLs in their internship placement during the semester that they were taking the SEI course. Seventeen out of 71 preservice teachers reported they had no ELLs in their internship the semester they were enrolled in the course. More than half of the preservice teachers reported prior experiences with ELLs in their internships, and less than half reported that they had no exposure to working with ELLs. Very few (12%) had a large amount of time to teach in their current placement, less than half (42%) reported a moderate amount of time to teach, and the majority of participants (42%) reported a limited amount of time to teach in their intern placement. Internships varied for numerous reasons. Most of the students taking the course had an opportunity to work with at least one ELL in their placement. However, just because they had ELLs in their internships did not mean they were able to work directly with them.

Just over half (51%) of the preservice teachers believed they would have ELLs in their first teaching placement whereas some (32%) were unsure that they would have ELLs. Only a few (12%) believed that they would not have any ELLs in their first teaching placement. Even if they had exposure, participants experience was limited. This information and previous experience may inform their perceptions of ELLs.

Perceptions of understanding ELLs

The second area addressed preservice teacher perceptions of ELLs and ELL's background. Overall, preservice teachers indicated they felt moderately to highly prepared across all areas concerned with understanding ELLs, as shown in Figure 8.1. Participants felt most prepared in understanding how language proficiency and culture influences learning. They indicated a strong preparedness in their understanding of how students acquire a second language, and their skills for gathering information on a students' cultural and educational background as well as factors that may hinder an ELLs' progress in school. Participants indicated the least amount of preparedness in their understanding of how to use a students' native language in the classroom. A

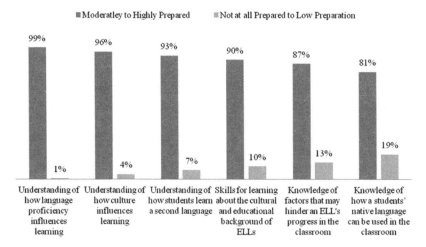

■ Moderatley to Highly Prepared   ■ Not at all Prepared to Low Preparation

Figure 8.1 Perceptions of understanding ELLs

substantial number (92%) of survey respondents completing the SEI course felt that they gained an understanding of how ELLs learn a second language. Eighty-nine percent of survey respondents felt highly prepared and/or proficient in utilizing skills for learning about the cultural and educational background of ELLs.

Knowledge of factors that may hinder an ELL's progress in the classroom is critical to understanding how teachers of ELLs can support and enhance student learning. Survey respondents indicated slight differences in rating their preparation in this area. Preservice teachers reported feeling less adequately prepared or proficient in the areas that hinder ELLs' progress. A slightly higher number indicated that they felt poorly prepared and/or proficient in this area.

Finally, respondents reported most prepared in areas related to how culture and language proficiency influences learning. Survey respondents indicated a majority felt moderately or highly prepared for understanding how culture and language proficiency influence learning. They reported most prepared in understanding how culture or language proficiency influence learning, but less prepared or proficient in the factors that hinder ELL progress and how to use students' native language in the classroom.

Strategies for working with ELLs

The third area addressed the content covered in the SEI course regarding strategies for working with ELLs. Preservice teachers felt the most prepared

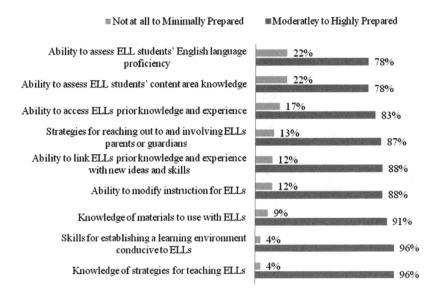

Figure 8.2 Strategies for working with ELLs

to use strategies that fostered a positive learning environment, selecting the types of materials that support ELLs' learning, and utilizing ELL teaching strategies as shown in Figure 8.2. Participant responses indicated strong preparation in modifying their instruction to meet the learning needs of ELLs, knowledge of how to link background knowledge and experience with new learning, and reaching out/involving parents of ELLs. Participants reported least prepared for accessing ELLs' prior knowledge, and assessing both content and English language proficiency. They felt moderately prepared to use strategies to assess ELLs' content knowledge and their language proficiency. Most of the survey respondents reported they were well prepared to utilize building background strategies to access and link students' knowledge and experiences with newly presented ideas and skills. Survey respondents indicated they were prepared with strategies they could use to reach out and involve ELLs' parents and/or guardians.

Assessment of the SEI course

The fourth area addressed participants' assessment of the SEI course benefitting their future teaching. The SEI course is required for all education majors in Arizona, whether or not they had experience with ELLs in their teaching program or plan to teach ELLs in the future. Participants' pre-course ideas about 'the importance of the course and how beneficial they think it will be to their future teaching' was essential to analyzing their ideas about the relevance of the course.

Participants were asked: 'When registering for the 45-hour SEI course, did you think it would be beneficial for your future teaching experiences?' and 'Now that the course is over—do you think that the content of this SEI class will help you in the future with instruction for your ELLs?' The first question addressed participants' assumptions about the content of the course in relation to their projected future teaching needs. The second was asked to determine participant's evaluation, upon completion of the course, of their perspectives relevant to course benefits and how helpful the course will be if they have ELLs in their future classrooms.

Researchers were interested in understanding how, if at all, the views of the participants changed prior to taking the course to completion of the course concerning the benefits of a required course on teaching ELLs. As shown in Figure 8.3, there were substantial changes in participants' views of the course perceived as beneficial prior to taking the course and after taking the course. Specifically, prior to taking the course, the respondents were split concerning their ideas of the benefits of the required SEI course. Fifty-one percent of the survey respondents thought the course would be beneficial. The other half of respondents were unsure if the course would be beneficial to their future teaching needs (41%), and few believed there would be no benefits to taking the course (8%). Upon completion of the course, the majority (85%) of the respondents reported that the course would be helpful in their future teaching experiences. Although university educators would be pleased to see these results as something that would be beneficial to these students' future teaching, research has questioned the impact of stand-alone multicultural education courses on effecting change in the way teachers teach children of color (Sleeter, 2001).

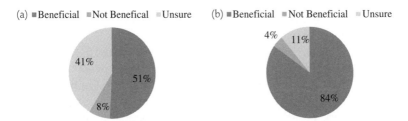

Figure 8.3 Participants' views on how beneficial the course would be to their future teaching: (a) Participants' views prior to taking the course; (b) participants' views after completion of the course

Discussion

This chapter reports on the results of survey data examining preservice teachers' self-assessment of their preparedness to teach ELLs, and the relevance of the content of the SEI coursework on their future teaching. This survey was administered to teachers enrolled at one time at Arizona State University. Results of this study must be interpreted with caution based on the respondent's perception of their preparedness, and the context within this research was gathered. The data presented here raise the questions of whether or not the implementation of an SEI course in the teacher preparation curriculum directly imposes restrictive language policy on higher education practice, and moreover, whether this implementation limits our ability as teacher educators to adequately prepare teachers for ELLs. Findings imply that prospective teachers' participation in these courses may foster unintentional discriminatory practices when teaching ELLs in mainstream English dominant classrooms. This is due to limitations of the SEI course on the lack of questioning *any* policy, and its effect on ELLs.

Intention of SEI coursework

All preservice teachers in Arizona are required to participate in the state-mandated SEI course as part of their teacher education program. The intention of the course is to prepare prospective teachers to teach ELLs in an English-dominant classroom. The course encompasses multiple components including SEI foundations, formal and informal assessments, cultivating ELL parental involvement, and SEI strategies. Preparation includes teaching preservice teachers how to improve student achievement, use instructional approaches for English language development, and selecting appropriate materials to enhance ELLs' learning opportunities within mainstream classrooms. In general, surveyed preservice teachers believed the course positively influenced their preparedness to teach ELLs.

All of the preservice teachers in this study are situated in Arizona where the numbers of ELLs in K–12 classrooms has increased over 90% in the last 10 years (National Clearinghouse for English Language Acquisition, 2008), and responses indicated that many of the preservice teachers were uncertain about the benefits of an SEI course. Several explanations may serve to inform their responses. First, preservice teachers in the SEI course may previously have only completed one teaching internship during the semester prior to taking this SEI course. They may not have had experience with ELLs in their first internship or they may have had very limited interactions with ELLs at that time. Grant and Wong (2003) argue for the need for teacher education programs to provide clinical experiences that scaffold the learning opportunities for preservice teachers that take into account the needs of language minority learners. Second, even if preservice teachers had previous experience in classroom internships with ELLs, they did not foresee themselves taking teaching jobs where they would be required to teach ELLs. Research suggests that many teachers prefer teaching children much like themselves and in environments similar to those they had attended (Goodwin, 2002) and many times teachers entering school settings with ELLs focus on their teaching assignment with the assumption that ELLs receive instruction elsewhere.

Experiences with ELLs

Research indicates the influence of prior experience and direct contact with ELLs as being significant in shaping prospective teachers' work with ELLs. Similar to the findings from Lucas *et al.* (2006) study, teacher educators conducting SEI courses arranged internships whereby preservice teachers participate in authentic environments with ELLs, and work to connect theories and strategies found within the university classroom and apply them to their own intern situation. In spite of preservice teachers' limited experience with ELLs prior to entering their formal teacher education program, participants reported that working directly with ELLs significantly influenced their understandings related to their specific circumstances. Supporting this finding, in their report on building teacher capacity in the education of ELLs, Ballantyne *et al.* (2008) state that central in the preparation of prospective teachers is their actual experience with ELLs in field experiences and clinical practice. Furthermore, they explain how these experiences provide the opportunity to practice pedagogical content knowledge, and interact with students from backgrounds that are unlike their own.

Strategies for teaching ELLs

Experiences in both the SEI course and in their internship placement prepared respondents with strategies to use for teaching ELLs. The preservice teachers reported they were highly prepared in the knowledge of strategies for teaching ELLs including materials to use with and how to modify instruction for ELLs. Teacher educators must acknowledge preservice teachers' limited experience with ELLs may still be a critical factor in their preparedness. In addition, teacher educators must recognize that preservice teachers may lack an informed understanding of the factors that hinder ELLs' progress in mainstream English dominant classrooms. Nevertheless, respondents in our study reported an understanding of the language acquisition process. However, what the survey did not address is whether or not the preservice teachers understood the relation between the two: the process of learning a second language and how that knowledge influences the strategies teachers should use in their classroom.

Research reported by Harper and de Jong (2004) argues that it is not enough for teachers of ELLs to employ teaching strategies, but that teachers must understand the process of language acquisition *to effectively use* strategies for teaching ELLs. Future research should look closely at the relationship between teachers' knowledge of strategies *and their effectiveness* for students of varying levels of language proficiency. To avoid a false sense of preparedness, preservice teachers should understand good teaching strategies for ELLs are only 'good' if they are grounded in an understanding of what is appropriate for students at different levels of language proficiency (Freeman *et al.*, 2001; Gándara & Maxwell-Jolly, 2005; Harper & de Jong, 2004; Milk *et al.*, 1992).

Although preservice teachers reported a preparedness to utilize teaching strategies, they also indicated they were lacking an understanding of how a students' native language can be used within the classroom. Gándara and Maxwell-Jolly (2005) emphasize the importance of teachers of ELLs understanding how to use a student's native language to support the English acquisition process. While students are learning English, their native language can be used as a bridge to new understandings. Respondents in this survey felt prepared to teach ELLs, yet did not understand the role of a student's native language in the classroom. A parallel should be drawn between the delivery of the SEI curriculum in an English-only state and the lack of opportunities for preservice teachers to learn about ways to utilize ELLs' native languages in the classroom.

Conclusion and Implications

This investigation intended to raise awareness of the implications of a state-mandated policy on the preparation of teachers, and further the implications of such policy on ELL students. This study provides evidence that overall, upon completion of the SEI course, preservice teacher felt prepared to teach ELLs. Findings indicate several important issues that pertain to constraints under restrictive language policies that also warrant further attention by teacher educators and policy makers. We surface concerns about the pervasive complacency found both at the state and university level impacting how prospective teachers are prepared, and how this preparation affects the learning experiences of ELLs. Based on what is revealed and not revealed from survey results, we suggest attention be paid to the role of restrictive language policies on preparation programs, and the importance of raising the critical awareness of preservice teachers concerning policy decisions that directly relate to their ability to meet the needs of ELLs.

Redirecting the conversation

As teacher educators, we need to redirect the conversation from specifically teaching English learners to focusing on the relationship between language policy and teacher education for ELLs. Language policies directly affect how preservice teachers are prepared and indirectly affect the daily interactions of prospective teachers and students in classrooms.

Little research has been conducted on language policy in teacher education and within educational contexts (Christ, 1997; Menken & Garcia, 2010). Although not directly connected to teacher preparation, Menken and Garcia (2010) address teacher agency as it relates to navigating policy. Often teacher agency has not been explicitly acknowledged, and many times teachers are left to themselves to do something meaningful that qualifies as navigating policy to better facilitate the teaching and learning situation for their students. Thus, teachers need to recognize their own power, and the implementational space they construct as agents of language policy that may or may not be appropriately interpreted or predictable (Johnson & Freeman, 2010).

Specifically, we suggest the consequences of implementing a state-mandated SEI policy in teacher education must be explored especially for educators preparing teachers to work with ELLs. Ignoring these consequences can be futile to the success and educational experience of both future teachers and their language minority students. Wiley states, 'given the negative legacy of discriminatory language policies in education for language minorities, some focus on the history of educational language policies to the detriment of language minority students should be a part of teacher preparation' (Wiley, 2008: 238). Teacher education programs must be held responsible for explicitly addressing the impact of educational language policy on ELLs. Moreover, preservice teacher education must address the necessary provisions for quality education using strategies, accommodations and cultural connections for ELLs, and acknowledge what is not being taught or addressed, and question why such restrictions are imposed.

Constraints under restrictive language policy

Teacher educators need to raise the critical consciousness of both preservice teachers and mentor teachers (Freire, 1970). Research on the influence of mentor teachers and preservice teachers is well documented (Guyton & McIntyre, 1990; Richardson, 1996). Mentors influence preservice teachers' belief systems, impact their teaching practices, and reinforce compliance to systems in place. With this consideration, it is important to question the influence by mentor teachers' philosophies and views upon less-experienced pre-service teachers. Restrictive language policy plays a crucial role in teacher practices and approaches to teaching, thus it is reasonable to say that restrictive language policies also carry a greater weight in teacher views about language in the classroom. Consequently, teacher educators need to take on dual roles of educating both preservice teachers and their mentor teachers in raising their critical consciousness level, and serving as an explicit bridge between coursework and classroom experience. If these 'ways' do not come to fruition, we will continue to perpetuate acceptance of restrictive language policy and detrimental practices associated with the teaching of ELLs.

Instruction under restrictive language policy is limited and constrained (Wiley, 2004; Wright, 2005). ELLs are expected to comply with and conform to monolingual English-speaking teachers' pedagogical practices as opposed to teachers making accommodations based on students' needs (Adams & Jones, 2006). Educators might consider a 'community of practice' approach (Wenger, 1998) to work against marginalization of ELL students. These practices encompass social spaces, knowledge, values and affinities acquired by such intentional participation. ELLs' success is determined by their level of participation and can be enhanced by implementing conversational and academic language in multiple ways. These are essential components to learning a second language while simultaneously succeeding in school. Under restrictive language policy, it is easy to ignore or not draw attention to the benefits of these practices in the classroom. This study brings attention to the need for teacher education to address the role of sociocultural theory, defined as creating new identities and becoming members of real or imagined communities of practice by apprenticeship (Edelsky et al., 2002; Gee, 2004; Lave & Wenger, 1991; Wenger, 1998). After all, learning a second language is an experience of being apprenticed into a new community. Restrictive language policy fails to bring these considerations into practice.

When teacher educators and district administrators advocate for preservice teachers and in-service teachers to openly discuss what is working and what is not working in terms of their linguistically diverse students, language policies will be held accountable to provide answers. When the answers cannot be found, it is pivotal to not accept policy just because it is policy. Language policies and ELL models need to be held accountable to their stated goals and mission. Further questions arise and need to be considered such as:

(1) Are ELLs becoming proficient enough to succeed in a mainstreamed classroom in less than a year?
(2) Are teachers adequately trained to teach ELLs and provide quality education for these students after one year?

Demand to answer such questions are fundamental to equitable education for all ELLs, especially those under restrictive language policy (Garcia et al., 2008). Academic failure for language minority students can no longer serve as the repercussions to this growing concern, neither can changing assessments or calculations to 're-label' or 'reclassify' under performing to performing school labels.

Reversing the impact of complacency

Teacher education programs and policy makers can no longer afford to ignore the needs of ELLs (Short & Fitzsimmons, 2007). Change is necessary on current restrictive policies that serve as the foundation for the future of many language minority students. If time is not made by instructors in teacher education programs to question or look more deeply into current policy, then it is inevitable that students in teacher education programs will not take the time to do so either. This is evident by the responses of half of the preservice participants in this study that did not view SEI as beneficial to them upon the commencement of the course. All prospective teachers must understand the importance of their role in the education of ELLs that have stemmed from solid foundations in a multilingual and multicultural education perspectives. Prospective teachers need optimal time and scaffolded support in comprehending the linguistic and social marginalization that is occurring in schools under restrictive language policy. As shown in Figure 8.4, college and school-level complacency contributes to the illusion of what compromises good teaching practices for ELLs which in turn implements unintentional discriminatory practices due to limited understandings of linguistic and social elements of language minority students resulting in conformity to one-size fits all curriculum.

Given the demands of English-only environments in states under restrictive language policy, constraints with time to teach, time to question, and time to change are critical factors that will continue to impede the

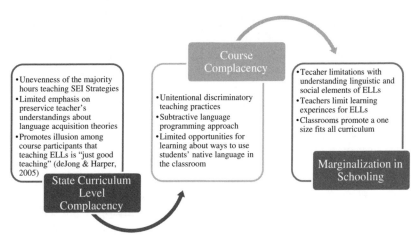

Figure 8.4 Cycle of complacency and marginalization under restrictive language policy

progress of ELLs. Language policies do indeed affect the daily interactions that occur within teacher education colleges, schools and classrooms, and between teachers and students, and schools and families. Changes are necessary in the preparation of educators to teach ELLs and more importantly, under this guidance, that prospective teachers understand the linguistic and social marginalization that occurs in schools under such reform, and can henceforth take action against such inequities. Our hope is that considerations are made to make necessary revisions in order to move beyond a lack of resistance and complacency and toward equitable preparation and instruction for teacher preparation.

References

Adams, M. and Jones, K.M. (2006) Unmasking the myths of structured English immersion. *Radical Teacher* 75, 16–21.

Arizona Department of Education (2007) *Curricular Framework for (SEI) Endorsement Training.* Office of English Language Acquisition Services. Online document, accessed 15 October 2008. http://www.ade.state.az.us/asd/lep/downloads/SBEapprovedSEIcurriculaframewok.pdf

Ballantyne, K.G., Sanderman, A.R. and Levy, J. (2008) *Educating English Language Learners: Building Teacher Capacity.* Washington, DC: National Clearinghouse for English Language Acquisition. Online document, accessed 15 January 2009. http://www.ncela.gwu.edu/practice/mainstream_teachers.htm

Butler, F.A. and Stevens, R. (2001) Standardized assessment of the content knowledge of English language learners K–12: Current trends and old dilemmas. *Language Testing* 18, 409–427.

Cartiera, M.R. (2005) Best practices for teaching English language learners found in teacher preparation programs in Connecticut and beginning teachers' level of preparation and proficiency in these practices. PhD dissertation, Central Connecticut State University, New Britain, CT.

Christ, H. (1997) Language policy in teacher education. In D. Corson (ed.) *Encyclopedia of Language and Education* (Vol. 1, pp. 219–227). Dordrecht: Kluwer.

Combs, M.C., Evans, C., Fletcher, T., Parra, E. and Jiménez, A. (2005) Bilingualism for the children: Implementing a dual-language program in an English-only state. *Educational Policy* 19, 701–728.

De Jong, E. and Harper, C. (2005) Preparing mainstream teachers for English language learners: Is being a good teacher good enough? *Teacher Education Quarterly* 32, 101–124.

Delgado Gaitan, C. (2004) *Involving Latino Families in Schools: Raising Student Achievement through Home-School Partnerships*. Thousand Oaks, CA: Corwin.

Echevarria, J., Vogt, M. and Short, D. (2004) *Making Content Comprehensible for English Language Learners: The SIOP Model* (2nd edn). Boston: Pearson/Allyn & Bacon.

Edelsky, C., Smith, K. and Wolfe, P. (2002) A discourse on academic discourse. *Linguistics & Education* 13, 1–38.

Epstein, J.L. (2001) *School, Family, and Community Partnerships: Preparing Educators and Improving Schools*. Boulder, CO: Westview Press.

Faltis, C.J. (1997) *Joinfostering: Adapting Teaching for The Multilingual Classroom*. Englewood Cliffs, NJ: Prentice-Hall.

Freeman, D., Freeman, Y. and Mercuri, S. (2001) Keys to success for bilingual students with limited formal schooling. *Bilingual Research Journal* 25, 203–213.

Freire, P. (1970) *Pedagogy of the Oppressed*. New York: Continuum.

Gándara, P. and Maxwell-Jolly, J. (2005) Critical issues in the development of the teacher corps for English learners. In H. Waxman, H. Tellez and K. Tellez (eds) *Preparing Quality Teachers for English Language Learners* (pp. 99–120). Mahwah, NJ: Lawrence Erlbaum.

Gándara, P., Maxwell-Jolly, J. and Driscoll, A. (2005) *Listening to Teachers of English Language Learners: A Survey of California Teachers' Challenges, Experiences, and Professional Developmental Needs*. Santa Cruz, CA: The Center for the Future of Teaching and Learning.

García, E., Jensen, B. and Cuéllar, D. (2006) Early academic achievement of Hispanics in the United States: Implications for teacher preparation. *The New Educator* 2, 123–147.

Garcia, O., Kleifgen, J.A. and Falchi, L. (2008) *From English Language Learners to Emergent Bilinguals, Equity Matters: Research Review No. 1*. New York: Teachers College.

Gee, J.P. (2004) *Situated Language and Learning: A Critique of Traditional Schooling*. London: Routledge.

Goodwin, A.L. (2002) Teacher preparation and the education of immigrant children. *Education and Urban Society* 34, 156–172.

González, N., Moll, L. and Amanti, C. (2005) *Funds of Knowledge: Theorizing Practices in Households, Communities, and Classrooms*. New Jersey: Lawrence Erlbaum Associates.

Guyton, E. and McIntyre, D.J. (1990) Student teaching and school experience. In W.R. Houston (ed.) *Handbook of Research on Teacher Education* (pp. 514–534). New York: Macmillan.

Grant, R. and Wong, S. (2003) Barriers to literacy for language minority learners: An argument for change in the literacy education profession. *Journal of Adolescent and Adult Literacy* 46, 386–394.

Harper, C. and de Jong, E. (2004) Misconceptions about English-language learners. *Journal of Adolescent & Adult Literacy* 48, 152–162.

Johnson, D.C. and Freeman, R. (2010) Appropriating language policy on the local level: Working the spaces for bilingual education. In K. Menken and O. García (eds) *Negotiating Language Policies in Schools: Educators as Policy Makers* (pp. 13–31). New York: Routledge.

Lachat, M.A. (1999) *Standards, Equity and Diversity.* Providence, RI: Brown University, Northeast and Islands Regional Educational Laboratory.

Lave, J. and Wenger, E. (1991) *Situated Learning: Legitimate Peripheral Participation.* Cambridge: Cambridge University Press.

Lucas, T., Villegas, A.M. and Reznitskaya, A. (2006) Exploring the preparedness of classroom teachers to teach English language learners. Annual Meeting of the American Educational Research Association, San Francisco.

Menken, K. and Garcia, O. (2010) *Negotiating Language Policies in Schools: Educators as Policy Makers.* New York: Routledge.

Milk, R., Mercado, C. and Sapiens, A. (1992) *Rethinking the Education of Teachers of Language Minority Children: Developing Reflective Teachers for Changing Schools.* Washington, DC: National Clearinghouse for Bilingual Education.

National Clearinghouse for English Language Acquisition (2008) *Arizona LEP Growth 2005–2006.* Washington, DC: Author. Online document, accessed 15 January 2009. http://www.ncela.gwu.edu/policy/states/reports/statedata/2005LEP/Arizona-G-06.pdf.

Peregoy, S.F. and Boyle, O.F. (2005) *Reading, Writing, and Learning in ESL.* Boston: Allyn & Bacon.

Richardson, V. (1996) The role of attitudes and beliefs in learning to teach. In J. Sikula (ed.) *Handbook of Research on Teacher Education* (2nd edn, pp. 102–119). New York: Macmillan.

Salant, P. and Dillman, D.A. (1994) *How to Conduct Your Own Survey.* New York: John Wiley & Sons, Inc.

Short, D.J. (1993) Integrating language and culture in middle school American history classes. In *Educational Practice Report 8.* National Center for Research on Cultural Diversity and Second Language Learning. Online document, accessed 15 March 2009. http://escholarship.org/uc/item/16k3r7bc

Short, D. and Fitzsimmons, S. (2007) *Double the Work: Challenges and Solutions to Acquiring Language and Academic Literacy for Adolescent English Language Learners – A Report to Carnegie Corporation of New York.* Washington, DC: Alliance for Excellent Education.

Sleeter, C.E. (2001) Preparing teachers for culturally diverse schools: Research and the overwhelming presence of whiteness. *Journal of Teacher Education* 52 (2), 94–106.

Tikunoff, W. (1983) *An Emerging Description of Successful Bilingual Instruction: Executive Summary of Part I of the SBIF Study.* San Francisco, CA: Far West Laboratory for Educational Research and Development.

Walqui, A. (2000) *Access and Engagement: Program Design and Instructional Approaches for Immigrant Students in Secondary Schools.* McHenry, IL, and Washington, DC: Delta Systems and Center for Applied Linguistics.

Wenger, E. (1998) *Communities of Practice: Learning, Meaning and Identity.* Cambridge, MA: Cambridge University Press.

Wiley, T.G. (2004) Language policy and English-only. In E. Finegan and J.R. Rickford (eds) *Language in the USA: Perspectives for the Twenty-First Century* (pp. 319–338). Cambridge: Cambridge University Press.

Wiley, T. (2008) Language policy and teacher education. In S. May and N. Hornberger (eds) *Encyclopedia of Language and Education* (2nd edn, Vol. 1, pp. 229–241). Boston: Springer Science & Business Media LLC.

Wright, W.E. (2005) English language learners left behind in Arizona: The nullification of accommodations in the intersection of federal and state policies. *Bilingual Research Journal* 29, 1–30.

Zumwalt, K. and Craig, E. (2005) Teacher's characteristics: Research on the demographic profile. In M. Cochran-Smith and K. Zeichner (eds) *Studying Teacher Education: The Report of the AERA Panel on Research and Teacher Education* (pp. 111–156). New Jersey: Lawrence Erlbaum Associates.

9 The Politics of Preservice Teachers

Kate Olson

Schools and classrooms across the nation have become ever more diverse while concerns about immigration, immigrants and their language acquisition and use, and their effects on our social, educational and economic system loom in the media and are debated in the government. Twenty-four states have mandated English as the official language policy of their government (Crawford, 2008), and states with increasing numbers of immigrants, such as Arizona, have mandates that legislate English-only instruction in schools. In Arizona the law that limits students' language use in schools is Proposition 203. This education policy eliminated bilingual education as a choice of instruction for English learners (ELs) with the goal to improve their social and academic skills in English measured by a high-stakes standardized test. To improve instruction for linguistically and culturally diverse students, Arizona has taken other steps to increase preservice teachers' knowledge and skills in instructing ELs by mandating structured English immersion (SEI) endorsement courses that focus on English language, learning and instructional needs of EL student populations.

While some preliminary research documents that endorsement courses do have a positive impact on changing preservice teachers' attitudes about and confidence in teaching ELs (Olson & Jimenez-Silva, 2008), this work does not examine whether these new beliefs translate into improved instruction for this population of students. In fact, research on the effects of the SEI endorsement on practicing teachers' instruction indicates that it has not changed classroom practices for ELs (Wright & Choi, 2005). I contend that the reason for the failure of the mandate to improve instruction for ELs is that SEI endorsement curriculum does not address the socio-political and educational inequalities that our present educational system perpetuates for these diverse learners. Because the SEI mandate focuses its training on 'best' instructional practices in English, teachers never have to think critically about the underlying reasons that students of diverse linguistic and cultural backgrounds underachieve in school. In other words, preservice teachers are not required to examine their beliefs and their fundamental assumptions about ELs. They never have to make explicit their own ideological positions about larger societal issues and their ramifications for ELs.

There is a growing need for an examination of preservice teachers' beliefs about ELs, especially since the majority of students who choose to enter the teaching profession are white, middle class, European-American women who are monolingual and have little or no experience with diverse student populations (Zeichner, 2003). This reality speaks to the need to examine preservice teachers' ideologies toward ELs and their education in Arizona, especially in this time of increased alarm about immigrants and the impact they have on the educational system. For this reason, the goal of this chapter is to examine preservice teachers' underlying beliefs about ELs at the time they begin their teacher education courses, in order to document what they believe about the education of diverse student populations in the highly politicized environment in which they live in Arizona. Because an important step in improving teaching and learning for ELs is to change teachers' attitudes and beliefs (Gándara et al., 2005), this work has important implications for how to organize teacher education courses to best serve both preservice students' and EL students' needs.

This chapter contends that to improve instruction for ELs, teacher education programs in Arizona cannot solely offer endorsement courses that focus the majority of the curriculum on new strategies and methods of instruction for diverse learners. Rather, to influence the educational practices for ELs, the preservice curriculum needs to first address the underlying ideological beliefs and assumptions that preservice teachers have about ELs, by providing them with both social and academic experiences with ELs to make connections with students on deeper, more personal level. These experiences will enable the preservice teachers to better empathize and recognize ELs' repertoires of practice (Gutierrez & Rogoff, 2003) that are important parts of each child's knowledge base (Moll, 2000, 2001). At the same time, teacher educators need to bring to light and expose the larger macro-ideologies (Voloshinov, 1973) about ELs that are offered in the media and played out in our schools every day that dehumanize diverse language learners by perpetuating a deficit view of them, their capabilities, and their families and communities (Gutierrez & Orellana, 2006; Valencia, 1997). In other words, teacher educators need to organize their courses so that preservice students engage in praxis to reflect upon the state of the world and then to act upon it (Freire, 1970). By doing this, teacher education programs will have a better chance of providing a truly liberating pedagogy (Freire, 1998) that allows preservice teachers to take a conscious, reflective and critical stance on the mandated programs, policies and curriculum in their instructional practices to provide ELs expanded opportunities to learn.

Ideologies and Preservice Teacher Education

I use the theoretical construct of ideology grounded in Bourdieu and Passeron's (1977) notion that teaching is an act of ideological reproduction. Beliefs and ideologies are co-constructed by people through their participation in cultural activities and practices that are historical in origin and social in nature (Anderson-Levitt, 2002; Cole, 1996; Freire, 1970). The ways in which people participate and interact, their everyday behaviors, in sociocultural activities form their 'habitus' (Bourdieu, 1990). This habitus helps us make sense of our surroundings and actions by involving our beliefs and assumptions about society (Bourdieu, 1990), and enables us to qualify what is considered acceptable and normal and what is not (Foucault, 2003). These distinctions, however, are manifested historically and perpetuated socially through the use of particular rhetoric, policies and accepted norms of behavior, and social and cultural capital in order to maintain the status quo (Bourdieu & Passeron, 1977). Preservice teachers, therefore, are socialized *through* language and interaction in cultural practices in and out of schools throughout their lives. These socialization experiences are imbued with pressure *to use* the same ideological language and interaction in the cultural practices in which they participate in schools (Ochs & Scheiffelin, 1984). Because these cultural practices are part and parcel of the larger, established macro-ideologies of society (Voloshinov, 1973), they are thereby mechanisms that maintain social order (Bartolome, 2004). I argue that these macro-ideologies shape preservice teachers' underlying beliefs and assumptions about diverse language learners and ultimately influence how they enact curriculum and organize instruction in their future classrooms.

Research indicates that the most effective teachers of students who differ from teachers along ethnic, cultural and linguistic dimensions are teachers who are caring, knowledgeable educators who desire to help all children learn by implementing a culturally relevant pedagogy for social justice (Ladson-Billings, 2000; Nieto, 2000a, b, 2005). While the research on the influence of this type of multicultural curriculum on preservice students' beliefs and practices is limited in terms of changing their notions of ELs (Sleeter, 2001), the teacher education programs that have been most effective in preparing preservice teachers are those that help preservice teachers understand the importance of validating ELs' cultures and identities by providing the teachers real-life experiences in urban schools (Haberman, 1991; Howard, 2000; Nieto, 2000a, b; Zeichner, 1996). This type of training is important in improving teachers' empathy toward diverse student populations. However, I argue that teacher education programs that do not directly address the socio-political and economic realities with which diverse students contend every day in and out of schools may not affect preservice teachers' beliefs about ELs enough to challenge the status quo in educational programs and practices.

There are particular ideologies about ELs that are built into the educational policies and programs that districts and schools implement in schools in Arizona. These macro-ideologies both shape the legislation of policy and influence how people directionalize and operationalize the mandated policies in schools and classrooms (Johnson, 2005a, b; Olson, 2007; Pachler *et al.*, 2008). In particular, there are districts and schools that have implemented Proposition 203 by requiring submersion for ELs into English instruction by prohibiting any primary language support for ELs' comprehension of instruction or content (Gutiérrez *et al.*, 2002). While a meta-analysis of the research on effective practices for ELs shows that bilingual education is more successful in improving the achievement of ELs in Arizona (Rolstad *et al.*, 2005), the media has portrayed the debate about bilingual education as a war against unfortunate EL victims on whom pro-bilingual educators are perpetrating a crime (Johnson, 2005a, b). By doing this, the social institutions of the media, state departments of education, districts and schools reinforce the macro-ideology that ELs are less qualified and less knowledgeable, and, for that reason, they need to be remediated and immersed in the English language exclusively in order to receive equitable educational opportunities.

These subtractive images in the media, in conjunction with mandated regulations on language use and standardized testing in English in schools, help to reproduce students' and teachers' beliefs about ELs, their capabilities and their communities in Arizona, as they highlight ELs' deficits rather than promote their capabilities (Gutierrez & Orellana, 2006; Stritikus, 2006). Districts, schools and teachers are thereby complicit in propagating negative assumptions and beliefs about ELs that perpetuate English-only ideologies of instruction. This ideological reproduction (Bourdieu & Passeron, 1977) demonstrates that teachers' autobiographies and experiences in schools influence how they perceive students, ELs in particular, and how they make sense of and justify their instructional practices within the larger socio-political context of reform (Anderson-Levitt, 2002; Olson, 2009). Therefore, these beliefs are the underlying ideological assumptions that teacher education programs need to influence in order to have a more positive effect on the type of instruction and interactions that will be organized for diverse student populations in Arizona.

In the section that follows, I share the results of a survey I conducted of 177 preservice teachers' underlying beliefs and ideologies about ELs, education and the instructional methods and programs that they believe are best for linguistically diverse student populations at the beginning of their teacher education program in Arizona. The examination of these ideologies is important because these beliefs are the foundation upon which teachers support their understanding of the methods and theories offered in their SEI endorsement courses. I found in my analysis that the undergraduate, preservice teachers' beliefs mapped onto larger ideological notions about the practice and purpose of education for students, and ELs in particular, that are reflected in the state's educational policies and institutions. In this chapter, I describe the preservice teachers' beliefs, and discuss how a pedagogy of praxis (Freire, 1970) might enlighten and empower preservice education students. Praxis would involve critical *reflection* about the underlying ideologies that are pervasive in Arizona that shape how programs and practices are implemented for ELs, and *action* in classrooms that would allow the preservice teachers to build empathy, understanding and liberating views toward ELs as people and students.

The Study

This investigation focused its analysis on preservice teachers' ideological beliefs about ELs, their education and the best instructional programs and practices in a post-Proposition 203, high-stakes context in Arizona to answer the following research questions:

(1) What are preservice teachers' beliefs about teaching, the education of ELs and the programs needed to educate them before they enter teacher education?
(2) How do preservice teachers perceive their future instruction for ELs as a result of the highly politicized environment in which they live in Arizona?

To answer these research questions, I conducted a survey that measured the preservice teachers' ideological beliefs toward the education of ELs during the first week of instruction in the largest teacher education program in Arizona.

To collect the data on preservice teachers' beliefs, the survey was administered in eight different sections of the first mandated SEI endorsement course that every student is required to take in the first semester of the teacher education program. To administer the survey, I gave each instructor a set of surveys and asked them to invite the students to complete the survey at the end of the class session during the first week of the course. Each instructor was advised to tell his or her class that the survey was voluntary, completely anonymous, and that it had no effect on their grade in the course. In addition, the professors informed each class that the purpose of the survey was to see what they believed about ELs and education to help us better understand what they thought about these issues. This way, I hoped that the students would feel free to answer the survey questions honestly and without undue pressure to answer the questions in a way that would please the instructor or researcher. As a result, I collected 177 completed surveys with a response rate of 98%.

After I collected the completed surveys, I entered the data into SPSS. For my quantitative analyses, I ran descriptive statistics on the student demographic information to profile our preservice teacher population in terms of the gender, age and ethnicity. In addition, frequency tables were then used to determine the mean scores on the yes/no questions that describe the preservice teachers' language ability, experience abroad and desire to instruct ELs in their future classrooms.

To describe the students' ideological beliefs about ELs, education and the instructional methods and programs that they believe best for linguistically diverse student populations, my data analysis centered on four questions in the survey that asked the preservice teachers to write about their beliefs about education, its purpose and the instructional programs and practices that they believe best for ELs. Specifically, two questions asked the preservice teachers to reflect on why they want to be teachers and what the goal of education is. These questions allowed me to see what their overarching ideologies of education were. The next two questions asked the preservice teachers to write what they believe is the best way to educate ELs and to write the reasons why they either wanted to or did not want to teach ELs in their future classrooms.

To analyze the written responses for each question, I coded and categorized the data according to each belief statement within each response following rigorous qualitative methodology using grounded theory (Huberman & Miles, 2002; Strauss & Corbin, 1990). Each statement was coded according to the preservice teachers' beliefs. These codes were then analyzed according to patterns in the belief statement and then clustered with similar responses to determine their frequency in the data. Once the patterns were established, representative samples of written data were used to illustrate the influence of particular beliefs about ELs and education to explain how the preservice students perceive ELs ideologically.

Findings

The findings of this study are presented in two sections. First I describe the demographic information on our preservice teacher population who began the teacher education program in a large, public university located in a metropolitan area in Arizona ($n = 177$) and their responses to the yes/no questions indicating their knowledge of a second language and their experience and knowledge of other cultures and countries. Next, I present the themes that arose out of the students' written statements regarding their beliefs about education, ELs and best instructional practices.

Preservice teacher population and experience

The preservice student population in the teacher education program is representative of most teachers that enter the profession: they are female (81.4%), white (69%) and under 30 years of age (70%). The fact that Arizona's population is growing and diversifying more each day makes the implications of these demographics a serious one. It is important that teacher education programs are designed to enhance preservice teachers' understanding of the socio-political issues that affect ELs in the state and country, inhibiting them from achieving in schools. This is especially important in preservice education, since the majority of teachers has no real experience living abroad (77%) and has no proficiency in a second language (71.3%). The preservice teacher population, therefore, has little knowledge of or experiences with people of different cultural and linguistic backgrounds, which may limit their empathy toward and understanding of ELs and the challenge of learning a second language and living in a foreign country. This confines the extent to which the preservice teachers understand the socio-political and educational realities that immigrant and minority students experience in schools that hinder their social and academic opportunities to learn.

Preservice teacher beliefs about education

To uncover the preservice teachers' beliefs about education and teaching in general, the survey asked them to report why they want to be teachers and what they believe is the goal of education. This information helps us understand better their ideological positions on the purpose and value of education, personally and professionally. Table 9.1 shows the number of occurrences of each type of statement.

Table 9.1 Code index of preservice teachers' reasons to teach

Code	Sub-code	Frequency
To impact others		
	Children	120
	Society	32
To continue to learn		5
Because of past teachers		27
Other		10
		N = 194

Ideologies of teaching

For the first question, I analyzed 194 belief statements out of the 167 responses received about why the preservice teachers want to be teachers. The most prevalent theme related to the teachers' beliefs that education is a tool to make a difference in children's lives and to positively impact society (78.4%). Most responses indicated that the preservice teachers wanted to make a difference for children, to help them achieve their learning potential, as the following representative quote illustrates: 'I want to be a teacher so I can impact the lives of children and their education.' While this goal is an encouraging demonstration that our preservice teachers are caring and dedicated to the profession (Nieto, 2005), it does not have an ideological clarity (Bartolome, 2004) or reflect understanding of what it means to truly 'make a difference in a child's life', especially with a child who is not of the mainstream culture or who does not speak the dominant language. Without knowledge of the socio-political and economic realities that many ELs face, the preservice teachers may not have the skills to recognize the reasons why many of these children underachieve in school, thereby perpetuating the myth that minority students are unintelligent and less qualified (Bartolome, 2004).

The reasons given for entering the teaching profession, however, were also based in the preservice students' beliefs that as teachers they would be able to positively impact society through their profession (16.5%), 'I believe that the success of our future depends on the education of our children. I would like to be a part of that success by guiding children down the right path.' While these beliefs are based in the preservice teachers' good intentions, you can see them laden with macro-ideologies that education is a socializing tool and teachers are the agents maintaining what society deems 'the right path'. This is not to say that preservice teachers do not want all children to succeed, as I believe they do. Rather, these education students do not realize that they have been socialized to believe that the children need to learn and behave like the majority and to accumulate majority approved social and cultural capital in order to succeed in society (Bourdieu & Passeron, 1977). They do not question the hegemonic discourse and practices that predominate our social institutions, and legitimate and empower the cultural and linguistic knowledge of particular groups of students over others when they state that they want to 'inspire students to reach their full potential and help give them the necessary skills to be productive in society.'

Ideologies of education

For the second question, there were 174 belief statements that constituted the data set. After coding and quantifying the responses, I found that the great majority of preservice teachers believed that the goal of education was to prepare students to become productive citizens in society (91.4%). The ideology that school and education are the mechanisms to create citizens who productively contribute to society were important underlying assumptions that the preservice teachers had about the purpose and practice of school, as the following quote shows. 'Education is to equip students with the necessary tools to create effective members of society.' This ideological stance that underlies the belief that schools need 'to prepare students for the real world' indicates that the teachers suppose that a significant part of their job is to socialize their students into the established social order. Only a small percentage of students mentioned the idea of social justice (8.6%); that the goal of education was to 'recognize the problems/challenges of society and create an educational environment that allows positive change for future generations.' However, even these notions of social justice were unarticulated in terms of understanding the injustices that exist in society that prevent access to particular groups of people.

Thus, the students overwhelmingly believed that the goal of education is neither to validate the students' skills and knowledge, nor to overcome the existing inequalities that exist for diverse student populations. Rather, the preservice teachers' ideologies overwhelmingly supported the conservative notion that the purpose of education is to 'teach children to become model citizens', demonstrating their lack of any ideological understanding of the social, political or economic inequalities that exist for particular disadvantaged students.

Preservice teachers' beliefs about the education of ELs

To document the preservice teachers' beliefs about the education of ELs, the survey asked the students to describe their beliefs about the best way to educate ELs. This information helps us understand better what knowledge they have of the educational programs and practices that they believe to be best for ELs, and whether their beliefs are representative of the larger sociopolitical ideologies of education that are portrayed in the media and enacted in districts and schools in Arizona.

Ideologies of education for ELs

For this question, there were a total of 171 belief statements coded within the 163 total responses. As Table 9.2 shows, I found that there were two types of answers that the preservice teachers provided. A majority of the preservice teachers reported that the best way to teach EL students was through English-only instruction (58.5%). This category was further broken down into students who believed solely in what they called 'immersion' (41.5%); students who believed that ELs should receive assistance in English through instructional strategies (9.4%), and students who believed that ELs should receive specialized and separate instruction in English language development (7.6%). These statements showed that the preservice teachers' beliefs about the education of ELs were in alignment with the state's mandate of English-only instruction.

The second most prevalent theme was the students' belief that ELs should receive primary language instruction (28.8%). This theme was not broken down as the students either believed in using ELs' native language in instruction or not. Table 9.2 shows the number of occurrences of each type of statement.

Table 9.2 Code index of preservice teachers' beliefs about the education of English learners

	Code	Sub-code	Frequency
Ideologies of instruction	English-only instruction		
		Immersion	71
		Instructional strategies to learn English	16
		English language development instruction	13
	Primary language instruction		48
	Don't know		23
			$n = 171$

The data showed that the preservice students' responses substantiated the state educational policy for ELs, as the majority of preservice teachers believed that immersion was the best method of instruction to educate ELs, 'it is best to immerse them more in English throughout the day.' In fact, it was evident that the students adopted the language of the English-only mandated Proposition 203; that 'they should be in an English speaking classroom and given support to help them grasp the language.' Thus, the larger argument portrayed in the media that ELs should only receive English instruction to achieve in schools is clearly reflected in the students' statements of how best to educate ELs. This mindset dehumanizes this student population in its simplicity, as it does not reflect any empathy for or understanding of ELs, language acquisition, culture or community and the importance of these factors in the social and academic development for students of diverse linguistic backgrounds.

Along with English-only instruction, some preservice teachers articulated that they believed that ELs should be provided with additional instructional strategies, such as, 'pair them with an English-speaking buddy', or 'put with an ELL teacher for part of the day to practice English until they can be mainstreamed'. While it was clear that some students understood that ELs needed assistance in English to acquire language and learn content, they did not indicate that they understood why services and modifications in instruction were necessary to assist ELs' learning and development. If the students believe that the answer to ELs problems is to 'provide them with strategies' without thinking of all the larger social and academic issues that arise by submersing the students in English or only using a particular 'method' to help make the content comprehensible, then the preservice teachers will continue to place blame on the students for their underachievement if the 'acceptable' intervention does not work. These beliefs have the potential to be detrimental to ELs' social and academic achievement if they are never examined critically in teacher education programs or acted upon in ways that help them change their understanding of diverse learners (Freire, 1970).

Likewise, 28.8% of the responses indicated that primary language instruction was the best way to educate ELs. These preservice teachers' answers showed that they believed that it was important that ELs understand the content and feel comfortable in the classroom, as the following quote illustrates, 'it's best to teach them the curriculum in their own language and over time they can gain progress in learning English.' The preservice teachers' statements showed an understanding that it would be difficult to learn content if the EL student did not have any English language ability because, 'the most important part of education is making sure that they [ELs] can master concepts no matter what language it is in.' While this set of responses demonstrates a greater sense of sympathy and understanding toward ELs' social and academic needs in schools, it does not show any evidence of questioning the status quo or critical awareness of the reasons why primary language support is important for learning and development.

Preservice beliefs about teaching ELs in the future

To describe the students' beliefs about teaching ELs, the survey asked the students to answer whether they would like to teach ELs. The first part of the question invited the students to respond either yes or no to whether they wanted to teach ELs. From these data I learned that 57.7% of the preservice students did <u>not</u> want to teach ELs, 32.8% wanted to teach ELs, and 9.6% had no answer. These findings are significant in that the majority of preservice teachers who are entering the profession in Arizona already have negative feelings about teaching a particular student population. Since districts and schools are becoming increasingly diverse, there is little chance that our teacher graduates will not have to teach any EL students. For this reason, if teachers do not look forward to, and feel optimistic or efficacious about teaching this group of students, the quality of instruction for ELs will suffer (Gándara et al., 2005). This lack of enthusiasm to teach ELs has larger implications for issues of equity in and access to learning opportunities for EL students that may be detrimental to their success in school.

The second part of the question asked the students to explain why they either wanted to teach or did not want to teach ELs. Their responses clearly indicated their ideologies and beliefs about themselves and their abilities, in addition to showing that their ideologies about ELs and about teaching influence their feelings about whether they wanted to teach ELs or not. Table 9.3 shows the number of occurrences for each type of statement.

I do not want to teach ELs

As Table 9.3 shows, the statement that occurred most frequently in the data was the preservice teachers' insecurities about their own skills and capacity to teach ELs. If the students did not feel efficacious in their own second language abilities, then they reported that they did not want to teach ELs, as the following representative quotes illustrate, 'I grew up only having English so I don't think I'd be equipped to teach those who only speak another language.' Likewise, the preservice students who believed that they did not have the skills or training to teach ELs reported that they did not want to teach them, 'Because I think it will require work and I don't feel able to help them acquire the skills they need.' They believed that they did not have the 'patience' or ability to 'communicate effectively'. The responses indicate that the students who did not want to teach ELs believed that the

Table 9.3 Code index of preservice teachers' beliefs about teaching English learners

	Code	Sub-code	Frequency
I do NOT want to teach ELs			
	Beliefs about themselves		
		Beliefs about language skills	26
		Beliefs about capabilities	23
	No reason		12
			$N = 61$
I DO want to teach ELs			
	Beliefs about themselves		
		Skills and capabilities	76
	Beliefs about teaching ELs		
		To learn and grow as a professional	32
			$N = 108$

work would be too difficult and challenging for them; that they were 'not qualified ... or educated enough to teach ELs.'

I do want to teach ELs

The students who reported that they did want to teach ELs believed in their own skills and qualities as teachers. These students believed that they were 'patient, open and sensitive to all family and student needs' and they believed that they had the language skills and knowledge to teach ELs. They envisioned the experience as an opportunity to learn, 'I believe it would be a great challenge for me to learn and grow as an educator.' This group of teachers had the confidence and attitude that they could work with diverse language learners and that they have the capacity to learn from their experiences with the children to become better educators, as the following quote shows, 'Although I am not fluent in language such as Spanish, I think working with ELs would be a rewarding experience for both the learner and the teacher.' Thus, the preservice teachers' ideological beliefs about their own skills and capabilities will either enable or inhibit the students' willingness and desire to teach diverse student populations in their future classrooms.

The most salient themes that arose out of the analysis of the preservice teachers' written responses were: (1) preservice teachers' ideological beliefs are representative of larger conservative macro-ideologies regarding the purpose and practice of education; that teaching is the act of instilling knowledge to create productive citizens. These ideologies do not question the status quo and in fact perpetuate ideals that manifest themselves in particular social and economic inequalities; (2) preservice teachers overwhelmingly believed that English-only instruction was the means by which ELs should be educated in Arizona. This ideology is marked by larger discussions of the education of ELs in the media and the programs and practices mandated by the state and the Arizona Department of Education; and (3) confidence and efficacy for teaching ELs are significant factors in whether teachers want to teach diverse student populations. These themes speak to the importance of creating teacher education programs and coursework that allow students to explore their knowledge and assumptions about education, about ELs and of larger ideologies that guide what society deems normal and abnormal (Foucault, 2003) in order to think critically about the practice and purpose of education to either reproduce or emancipate stereotypical assumptions of particular student populations.

Discussion

As a scholar dedicated to training preservice teachers, the results of this study are important. In fact, understanding the stance that our undergraduate students in education have about teaching and, especially, the education of ELs is important if we are to educate all children well in a state that is becoming increasingly diverse. The challenges that preservice teachers have to face in their future classrooms exceed what undergraduate curriculum is able to offer in terms of understanding the larger implications of educational policies and programs and their effects on real students in real communities. Furthermore, we cannot make up for the fact that our preservice teachers are predominately white females with little or no experience with diverse cultures or peoples and do not speak a second language. This inexperience can greatly inhibit their ability to relate to EL students with diverse language and learning needs (Taylor & Sobel, 2001). The question remains, then, how do we make the pedagogy and curriculum in teacher education truly liberating? How do we enlighten our preservice teachers about their underlying ideologies in a way that is productive so that they build not only empathy and compassion for ELs, but also take a critical stance in mandated programs and practices to provide all students with increased opportunities to learn? To answer these questions, I will review what we learned about preservice teachers' ideologies in Arizona and then discuss a program of practice-based Freirian views of pedagogy of liberation that I believe would enlighten teachers and practitioners in education.

First, the findings clearly indicated that preservice teachers have good intentions about to why they want to teach. They want to make a difference in order to improve the society in which we live. While this goal is inspiring, it is also unclear. It lacks any critical consciousness of society and of the social and cultural capital that particular groups of people and students have that facilitate their social and academic achievement in and out of school (Bourdieu & Passeron, 1977). In fact, I found in the teachers' responses that their beliefs mapped directly onto larger ideological notions of the purpose and practice of education for ELs. This finding demonstrates that preservice teachers have been socialized to particular notions of diverse language learners that are promoted and propagated by Arizona's social and educational institutions, as the language of 'immersion' was clearly in their lexicon as the program and practice of choice. This ideological reproduction makes sense because Proposition 203 has been in effect in Arizona since 2000. The undergraduate students in education have grown up with this policy in place in schools and with the media disseminating news in favor of English-only instruction, informing the public that all ELs need to achieve in school is one year of intense English immersion (Johnson, 2005a, b). This underlying ideology of ELs and language acquisition lays the foundation for preservice teachers' habitus about teaching and learning for ELs. What is problematic about this ideology is that it devalues ELs as people and learners by equating them solely by their language character (Gutierrez & Orellana, 2006). This, in turn, places the blame directly on ELs for their own underachievement in school.

Furthermore, the findings clearly showed that the confidence and efficacy that preservice teachers have in their knowledge is an important and valuable objective to meet in order to begin the process of affecting their decision-making processes and behaviors with students with diverse learning skills and needs (Gándara et al., 2005). But efficacy is just the first step in improving instruction for ELs. Of course, our preservice teachers will feel more confident in their skills and qualities after they have taken the SEI endorsement courses because these classes provide them with a toolkit of strategies to use in their future classrooms (Olson & Jimenez-Silva, 2008). This alone will increase their confidence when they see that these strategies are manageable and reasonable, as well as similar to those advocated in their methods courses. However, teaching strategies and lesson plans are but mere window-dressing on the real issue. This ready-made focus on packaged solutions allows teachers to think that simple methods and procedures will fix ELs' 'problems', rather than examining the fact that the 'problem' exists in the policies, programs and mandated curriculum that fail to recognize ELs' cultural repertoire of skills and knowledge (Gutierrez & Rogoff, 2003). In order to make a difference for all students in Arizona, research shows that the most successful curriculum in changing teachers' beliefs is one that provides preservice teachers with real-life opportunities in urban schools to build empathy, compassion and understanding of EL students both socially and academically (Haberman, 1991; Zeichner, 1996). In addition, well-organized, deliberate and enriching activities that allow preservice teachers to truly 'get to know' an EL student, his/her skills, history and cultural practices in and out of school will be the most successful at changing teachers' notions of ELs' funds of knowledge (Moll, 2001). This way, preservice teachers have a way to reflect upon what these new experiences with ELs with the hope of laying the groundwork for an additive understanding about the skills and needs of diverse student populations (Stritikus, 2006). This foundation will have the best chance of allowing our preservice teachers to become more self-aware and cognizant of their stance in education, their own beliefs of ELs, and the educational practices that are mandated in Arizona that perpetuate education inequalities for children. With this type of liberating praxis that makes the relationship between ideology and practice transparent (Freire, 1970), preservice teachers in Arizona may be able to take a more critical stance in the instruction and curriculum that they choose to organize for children that will build upon the students' culture and knowledge in ways that expand their opportunities to be achieved both in and out of school (Orellana & Gutiérrez, 2006).

References

Anderson-Levitt, K.M. (2002) *Teaching Cultures: Knowledge for Teaching First Grade in France and the United States*. Cresskill, NJ: Hampton Press.

Arizona Department of Education (2009) Curricular framework for full structured English immersion (SEI) Endorsement Training. Online document, accessed 2 February 2008. http://www.ade.az.gov/oelas/

Bartolome, L. (2004) Critical pedagogy and teacher education: Radicalizing prospective teachers. *Teacher Education Quarterly* 41, 97–122.

Bourdieu, P. (1990) *The Logic of Practice*. Cambridge: Polity.

Bourdieu, P. and Passeron, J-C. (1977) *La Reproduction: Elements pour une Theorie du Systeme d'Enseignement*. Paris: Minuit.

Cole, M. (1996) *Cultural Psychology: A Once and Future Discipline*. Cambridge, MA: Harvard University Press.

Crawford, J. (2008) Language legislation in the USA. Online document, accessed 15 April 2007. http://www.languagepolicy.net/archives/langleg.htm

Gándara, P., Maxwell-Jolly, J. and Driscoll, A. (2005) *Listening to Teachers of English Language Learners: A Survey of California Teachers' Challenges, Experiences, and Professional Development Needs*. Santa Cruz, CA: The Center for the Future of Teaching and Learning.

Gutierrez, K.D. and Rogoff, B. (2003) Cultural ways of learning: Individual traits or repertoires of practice. *Educational Researcher* 32, 19–25.

Gutierrez, K.D. and Orellana, M.F. (2006) The problem of English learners: Constructing genres of difference. *Research in the Teaching of English* 40, 502–507.

Gutiérrez, K.D., Asato, J., Pacheco, M., Moll, L.C., Olson, K., Horng, E., Ruiz, R., García, E. and McCarty, T.L. (2002) 'Sounding American': The consequences of new reforms on English language learners. *Reading Research Quarterly* 37, 328–343.

Foucault, M. (2003) *Abnormal*. New York: Picador.

Freire, P. (1970) *Pedagogy of the Oppressed*. New York: Seabury.

Freire, P. (1998) *Pedagogy of Freedom: Ethics, Democracy, and Civic Courage*. Landham, MD: Rowman & Littlefield.

Haberman, M. (1991) Can culture awareness be taught in teacher education programs? *Teacher Education* 4, 25–31.

Howard, G.R. (2000) *We Can't Teach What We Don't Know: White Teachers, Multiracial Schools*. New York: Teachers College Press.

Huberman, A.B. and Miles, M.B. (2002) *The Qualitative Researcher's Companion*. Thousand Oaks, CA: Sage Publications.

Johnson, E. (2005a) Proposition 203: A critical metaphor analysis. *Bilingual Research Journal* 29, 69–84.

Johnson, E. (2005b) WAR in the media: Metaphors, ideology and the formation of language policy. *Bilingual Research Journal* 29, 621–640.

Ladson-Billings, G. (2000) Fighting for our lives: Preparing teachers to teach African-American students. *Journal of Teacher Education* 51, 206–214.

Moll, L. (2000) Inspired by Vygotsky: Ethnographic experiments in education. In C. Lee and P. Smagorinsky (eds) *Vygotskian Perspectives on Literacy Research: Constructing Meaning through Collaborative Inquiry* (pp. 256–268). New York: Cambridge University Press.

Moll, L. (2001) The diversity of schooling: A cultural–historical approach. In M. de la Luz Reyes and J. Halcon (eds) *The Best for our Children: Critical Perspectives on Literacy for Latino Students* (pp. 13–28). New York: Teachers College Press.

Nieto, S. (2000a) Placing equity front and center: Some thoughts on transforming teacher education for a new century. *Journal of Teacher Education* 51, 180–187.

Nieto, S. (2000b) Bringing bilingual education out of the basement, and other imperatives for teacher education. In Z.F. Beykont (ed.) *Lifting Every Voice: Pedagogy and Politics of Bilingualism* (pp. 187–207). Cambridge, MA: Harvard Education Publishing Group.

Nieto, S. (2005) *Why We Teach*. New York: Teachers College Press.

Ochs, E. and Scheiffelin, B.B. (1984) Language acquisition and socialization: Three developmental stories. In R. Shweder and R. LeVine (eds) *Culture Theory: Essays on the Mind, Self, and Emotion* (pp. 276–320). Cambridge: Cambridge University Press.

Olson, K. (2007) Lost opportunities to learn: The effects of education policy on primary language instruction for English learners. *Linguistics and Education* 18, 121–141.

Olson, K. (2009) Systemic reform and superficial compliance: Teacher loyalty to lived experience. *International Multilingual Research Journal* 3, 72–89.

Olson, K. and Jimenez-Silva, M. (2008) The campfire effect: A preliminary analysis of preservice teachers' beliefs about teaching English language learners after state-mandated endorsement courses. *Journal of Research in Childhood Education* 22, 19–33.

Orellana, M.F. and Gutierrez, K.D. (2006) At last what's the problem?: Constructing different genres for the study of English learners. *Research in the Teaching of English* 41, 118–123.

Pachler, N., Makoe, P., Burns, M. and Blommaert, J. (2008) The things (we think) we (ought to) do: Ideological processes and practices in teaching. *Teaching and Teacher Education* 24, 437–450.

Rolstad, K., Mahoney, K.S. and Glass, G.V. (2005) Weighing the evidence: A meta-analysis of bilingual education in Arizona. *Bilingual Research Journal* 29, 43–67.

Sleeter, C. (2001) Preparing teachers for culturally diverse schools: Research and the overwhelming presence of whiteness. *Journal of Teacher Education* 52, 94–10.

Strauss, A. and Corbin, J. (1990) *Basics of Qualitative Research: Grounded Theory Procedures and Techniques*. Newbury Park, CA: Sage.

Stritikus, T. (2006) Making meaning matter: A look at instructional practice in additive and subtractive contexts. *Bilingual Research Journal* 30, 219–227.

Taylor, S.V. and Sobel, D.M. (2001) Addressing the discontinuity of students' and teachers' diversity: A preliminary study of preservice teachers' beliefs and perceived skills. *Teaching and Teacher Education* 17, 487–503.

Valencia, R. (1997) *The Evolution of Deficit Thinking: Educational Thought and Practice*. London: Flamer Press.

Voloshinov, V. (1973) *Marxism and the Philosophy of Language*. Cambridge MA: Harvard University Press.

Wright, W. and Choi, D. (2005) *Voices from the Classroom: A Statewide Survey of Experienced Third-grade English Language Learner Teachers on the Impact of Language and High Stakes Testing Policies in Arizona*. Tempe, AZ: Language Policy Research Unit, Educational Policy Studies Laboratory, Arizona State University. Online document, accessed 15 April 2007. www.asu.edu/educ/epsl/EPRU/documents/EPSL-0501-101-LPRU.pdf

Zeichner, K.M. (1996) Educating teachers for cultural diversity. In K. Zeichner, S. Melnick and M.L. Gomez (eds) *Currents of Reform in Preservice Teacher Education* (pp. 133–175). New York: Teachers College Press.

Zeichner, K.M. (2003) The adequacies and inadequacies of three current strategies to recruit, prepare, and retain the best teachers for all students. *Teachers College Record* 105, 490–519.